6 Steps to
Better Marriage Communication

Copyright © 2024 by Altared Spaces, LLC

All rights reserved.

Names: Rebecca S. Mullen, author
Title: 6 Steps to Better Marriage Communication by Rebecca S. Mullen
ISBN 978-1-7332572-2-0

Cover art by Rebecca Mullen
Cover design by Katie Elliott

6 Steps
to
Better Marriage Communication

by Rebecca S. Mullen

Altared Spaces
PUBLISHING

For David, who helped me learn to communicate better.
And for our children, Logan and Kaitlin, who showed me I succeeded.

The 6 Steps

STEP 1	STEP 2	STEP 3

Overcome Fear	Get Clear	Ask Cleanly

STEP 4	STEP 5	STEP 6
		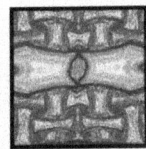
Beware Conditions	Affirm Lovingly	Build Boundaries

Contents

STEP ONE
Overcome Fear   19
When you give into fear, your world gets smaller and smaller.
1. **Learn How Fear Hides:** Discover the disguises fear wears
2. **Naming is Taming:** Give your fear a name
3. **Befriend to Mend:** Get curiouser about the worst-case scenario
4. **Protect to Connect:** Nurture the part of you that is afraid
5. **Fly into Fear:** Make yourself competent to face danger

STEP TWO
Get Clear   49
Confusion creates fear; clarity builds trust.
1. **The Black Hole of Confusion:** How confusion keeps you lost and far from intimacy
2. **Your Personal Gravity:** How staying in your own business anchors you to your desire
3. **Dive Deep into Your Desire:** How to claim—or reclaim—your personal power and know what you want
4. **(Re)Map Your Universe:** Because you may be navigating from an obsolete map
5. **You Won't Always Agree:** How to value love more than being right

STEP THREE
Ask Cleanly   87
Because a clean ask inspires a clean response.
1. **The Clean Ask Formula:** Feeling + Desire = A Clean Ask
2. **Avoid the Dirty Ask:** Because a dirty ask inspires alienation and distance
3. **Design a Clean Ask:** How to stay in your own business and stop arguing with reality
4. **Sprouting Love:** Own your fear. Own your desire. Own your agency
5. **Stay Clean Even When Your Sweetheart Asks Dirty:** Because one clean asker can change the dynamic in a relationship

STEP FOUR
Beware Conditions   **135**
We impose conditions because we think the rules of love will keep us safe.
1. **How to Recognize Conditions:** An example of conditional love from my marriage
2. **Recognize Your Worthiness:** How compassion, curiosity, and transparency will help you avoid condition on love
3. **Listen to Your Body:** Get familiar with the signals your body senses
4. **Cherish Yourself:** Unconditional love for others begins with unconditional love for yourself
5. **Untangle Conditions that Hide:** Worksheets to help you untangle what feels so messy inside
6. **Turn Conditions into Agreements:** Overcome fear. Get clear. Ask cleanly. Then cherish.
7. **Agree to Disagree:** Because you won't always agree, learn to disagree without conditional love

STEP FIVE
Affirm Lovingly   **165**
Intentionally offer a counterweight to your negativity bias.
1. **Make the Invisible Visible:** The power of hello, goodbye, and thank you
2. **Turn Yes-But into Yes-And:** Why saying "yes-but" kills connection and how to switch to "yes-and"
3. **Apologize Well:** Counteract the vulnerability and doubt that arise after conflict
4. **Cherish Yourself:** Unconditional love for others begins with unconditional love for yourself
5. **Demonstrate Belief:** Show your sweetheart you think they're great

STEP SIX
Build Boundaries   **199**
Conditions withhold love. Boundaries magnify love.
1. **Invitation to Build a Boundary:** A story about a fence, a dog, and a neighbor who doesn't take responsibility
2. **Avoid Takesies Backsies:** How to avoid sending mixed signals as you create a boundary
3. **The Full Stop:** How to shut your mouth and let your boundary do the talking
4. **Receiving The Full Stop:** When you don't like the boundary your sweetheart has drawn
5. **Identities and Payoffs:** Why boundaries are difficult to form and enforce

6. **Wishing, Willing, and Worthiness:** Why it's worth it to stay the course, even when it's really hard
7. **Pick Your Battles:** Because a boundary takes energy and tests your relationship
8. **Beyond Identity:** Invite the truest love you each want to give and receive

EPILOGUE
Marriage Meeting 247
How to include your sweetheart in all that you've learned.
1. **Create an Invitation:** 3 scripts
2. **Create an Emotional Container:** A safe spot for emotions until they can be fully expressed
3. **Tend Your Own Emotions:** Because emotions need expression
4. **The DUC Formula:** One option for organizing your Marriage Meeting
5. **Plan*Do*Review:** Another option for organizing your Marriage Meeting
6. **Topics for Your Marriage Meeting:** Because it helps to know you're not the only one who needs to discuss details
7. **My Dream for Your Marriage:** The reason I wrote this book

Appendix 279
- List of Try This Tools
- Resources List
- Acknowledgements

Begin with the End in Mind

Let's get the biggest picture first.

Communication has two parts: speaking and hearing. *Giving* and *receiving*.

In the first part of this book, we'll talk about how to speak so your partner can hear you. How can you give generously without excess baggage or pollution?

In the second part, we'll discuss how to hear what your partner is saying. How can you truly receive the love and communication your partner is giving to you?

Our focus in both parts of the book, however, will be on you. How *you* can speak clearly so your partner hears you most effectively, and how *you* can listen most effectively to what your partner is saying, then respond accordingly.

If you stay in your *own* business—both talking and listening—you'll have the greatest chance of effective communication. This is more difficult than it sounds, but it is one of the essential practices of intimacy.

This sounds backwards, right? Isn't intimacy about getting so close to a person that you blend? I'll challenge this thought and propose that, actually, the deepest intimacy is available only when you and your sweetheart stay true to yourselves first. Then you enter the relationship as whole individuals, ready to create a unique union together.

Part 1 of this book—Overcome Fear, Get Clear, and Ask Cleanly—will help you see how your internal dialogue contributes to what your sweetheart hears. When you let past demons, assumptions, or confusion flavor your words, you speak through a veil and you block the deep intimacy you crave.

We'll discuss how to erase that veil so you can connect deeply with your partner.

Part 2—Beware Conditions, Affirm Lovingly, and Build Boundaries—helps you to preserve your personal integrity. Romantic love—the kind filled with the orgasmic pleasure of blending bodies—erases the boundaries between you and your partner. This is lovely and filled with bliss until it totally sucks.

We'll discuss how to increase the bliss and mitigate the suck as you blend your lives and grow more autonomous simultaneously.

In short, until you **overcome fear**, your communication will be flavored with the Amygdala Hijack behavior of fight, flight, or freeze. None of these foster intimacy.

But once you can remove the fear response, your relationship is flavored with peaceful power that warms your relationship with a contented glow.

Fear is one of the chief reasons for a lack of clarity. Without clarity, you remain confused about what you want. When you're confused, you send mixed signals to your sweetheart.

There can be no deep intimacy when you start out confused. But once you **get clear**, you're able to **ask cleanly**—both verbally and non-verbally—for exactly what you want. These clean asks cultivate a powerful connection between you and your sweetheart.

A clean ask is respectful and kind. It fosters gentle connection between you and your sweetheart.

Without the clean ask, your relationship will be polluted with sloppy side-door requests that undermine your relationship's intimacy.

Once you've learned the practices to Overcome Fear, Get Clear, and Ask Cleanly, our discussion will shift to study how to listen effectively so you can Beware Conditions, Affirm Lovingly, and Build Boundaries.

We all love conditionally. But one of the most beautiful transformations that happens inside a committed relationship is the ability, over time, to reduce the conditions on love.

We do this by actively changing assumptions and conditions on love into spoken agreements. Conditions are undercover requests. We will expose those **conditions** so you and your sweetheart can talk about them openly, then agree—or respectfully disagree—about how to treat each other.

This transformation in love from conditions to agreements allows you to **affirm** your sweetheart for exactly who they are. You'll rediscover the invisible moments in life that add to your daily pleasure.

Unconditional love doesn't mean you become a doormat for your sweetheart to treat you any way they want. So, in our final chapter, we'll discuss how to **build boundaries** that say to your sweetheart: *I'm worth loving as I am. I won't tolerate disrespectful behavior from you.*

These six steps take a lifetime to master. I offer no quick fixes. But this I can promise: the moment you begin to cultivate these six practices, you will respect yourself more. When you respect yourself, you become braver in your relationship. Your confidence grows. This confidence will open the door wide so you can deepen the intimacy between you and your sweetheart.

Why am I qualified to write this book?

This book was born from me-search and research.

As a life coach, my clients come to my office for a variety of reasons:
- Clutter is overwhelming me.
- My life feels boring. I've lost my mojo.
- I've got this new job, and I really want it, but my skills are lacking.

But the reason that brought them in the door was never the most transformational work we did together.

Everyone wanted help communicating with the person they love most.

I began to notice a pattern with my clients: We'd talk about the reason they came in for about 4-6 sessions, then my client would begin to talk about their relationship.

- A manager who could easily run a 20-person meeting couldn't talk to her husband.

- A husband who thought his marriage was over because every day was filled with a mean argument: "What's for dinner?"
- A couple who still loved each other, but it had been more than a year since they had sex.

Every client was embarrassed to talk about their relationship, and every client thought they were the only one who struggled this way.

This hidden shame in my clients' lives matched my biggest interest: *What makes relationships work?* I've asked this question since I was five years old when my parents divorced.

Even as a very little girl I asked everyone about their relationship. As a 12-year old I didn't hesitate to ask people what they argued about, and as a 20-year old I was brazen enough to ask people two or three times my age about their sex life.

And you know what happened? People were grateful I asked. They talked to me and they were glad to find out they weren't alone in their struggle.

I want to talk with you in this book like you've walked into my office and we're just chatting. A coaching session with me has a informal vibe and lots of laughter. (Tears are common too.)

Toward that end, my conversational tone is casual. You'll hear me say, "gonna" and "wanna." I'm doing this on purpose because I want us to have a friendly, cherished conversation.

As for my own marriage, my husband and I met in junior high school. Our marriage has died twice, but each time we managed to resurrect a new marriage, more beautiful than the one before. We learned things during those marriage-deaths, and we've both worked hard to build communication strategies that help us connect.

The strategies I've learned in my own marriage worked for my clients. My clients experimented, then, deep in conversation with those clients we refined those strategies. I hope you'll consider this book an open invitation to tell me about your arguments, your sex life, and your hopes and dreams for your marriage.

While being married to my husband, David, has been filled with personal challenges, our marriage has transformed me. I know how to receive love now, and I didn't before. I think the love I offer now is much more unconditional.

These two shifts—giving a purer love and receiving the same—occurred because I learned to communicate better. One tiny habit at a time.

My intention is that the love you give and receive will also expand. I want you to know what it feels like to truly share your life and home with the person you love. Communication is foundational to that connection.

I'm glad you're here. Let's get started.

Part I
Giving

Fear
Clarity
and the ability to
Ask Cleanly

In this first part of the book, we'll examine how to overcome fear so you can get clear and then ask cleanly.

The strategy of the clean ask will improve your marriage communication exponentially, but until you can get past your **fear**, and then know **clearly** what you want, you aren't capable of the **clean ask**.

In order to understand the three components—fear, clarity and the clean ask—I've broken it up into three chapters: Overcome Fear, Get Clear, and Ask Cleanly. But life isn't as tidy as a book.

When you're falling in love, this gorgeous thing happens and you get tunnel vision. You only see the person you adore. You feel the boundaries between yourself and "the other" slip away and you are seduced into revealing things about yourself.

This is called falling in love. Literally, your everyday protections *fall away* and maybe you realize you want to bust out singing because you love musicals and singing brings you joy. You have no hesitations.

So you open your mouth to let out a song when suddenly you are haunted by a voice, *Are you crazy?* Shut up! *If you start singing this wonderful person will think you're nuts and disappear.*

Instead of a song popping out of your mouth, you cough.

You swallow a few times.

Finally, that impulse to sing is buried safely inside.

Except. Except for the next time you hear the words to *Climb Every Mountain* roll around in your head and you just want to feel the freedom Maria had on the top of that hill.

This is how fear and love work. There's a tug-of-war constantly happening between them. The love shows up and wants to bubble over and be free, and the fear tries to swallow it and keep it inside.

You get confused. You say crazy things that have almost nothing to do with what you truly meant, and suddenly that lovely falling-in-love feeling has turned into a maze of horror and disappointment.

You felt love—*I want to sing with you!*—then you felt fear—*Are you kidding?! That's nuts*—then you get confused about what you really want.

The song doesn't get to be sung, then you resent your sweetheart because they stopped you from singing, and suddenly love is tarnished.

In this first half of the book, we'll tease apart these three components —fear, clarity and asking—so you can sing more and fight less. (Of course, if you're not a singer we'll also free you up to do whatever it is that love inspires in you.)

We'll take the trio one by one—first fear—but they unfold in your daily life as a trio, so be thinking about how they show up in your life all overlapping and tangled together.

STEP ONE

Overcome Fear

When you give into fear, your world gets smaller and smaller.

When fear is allowed to rule your words and days, your life gets smaller and smaller.
- When you don't know what to expect, it's frightening, so you don't do anything new.
- Adventures are scary, so you don't explore.
- People you haven't met might do you harm, so you don't make friends.

Fear leaves you lonely, bored, and boring.

But fear itself isn't bad. Indeed, your fear is trying to protect you. I love the acronym Anne Lamott uses, "FEAR: Fear Expressed Allows Relief."

When you feel fear, your amygdala wakes up to sound the alarm. Seth Godin calls this ancient part of your brain your Inner Lizard. This alarm kept your cave-dwelling ancestors safe by alerting them to a nearby saber-toothed tiger.

Fear warned your ancestors to flee, to fight, or to freeze. All these were attempts to stay safe from that fearful tiger.

The problem is that your fear-alerting-amygdala doesn't always know the difference between a saber-toothed tiger and a new kitten at your friend's house who unexpectedly leaps into your lap. It treats all fear the same: with a smoke-detector-loud, terrifying alarm.

Your Inner Lizard Alarm won't stop hollering at you until you understand exactly what's frightening.

Consequently, the biggest job when it comes to overcoming fear is to listen carefully to you fear says, so you know whether you're dealing with a tiger or with a kitty.

In this chapter...

You'll learn that actions are the antidote to fear.

- **Learn how fear hides** and discover the disguises fear wears
- **Naming is Taming** so when you give your fear a name, that name calms your Amygdala Hijack
- **Befriend to Mend** because fear is there to protect you, so listen carefully to the message fear brings
- **Protect to Connect** because fear responds better to laughter and compassion than concealment or judgement
- **Fly into fear** and make yourself competent to face the impending danger

---

Until you have mastery over your fear, your fear will command all that you do.

Until you can control your fear, your fear will control you.

Until you can overcome fear, fear will overcome you. Your life will get smaller and smaller. Fear will alienate you from your sweetheart and fear will leave you lonely.

On the other hand, when you can overcome fear, your communication with your sweetheart is set free.

Once you can overcome your fear, you'll feel liberated to communicate all the desires of your heart.

When you get clear, you understand yourself and your sweetheart more and more. That clarity will open opportunity after opportunity to know each other more completely and deepen your intimacy.

Intimacy doesn't stand a chance of growing in a fearful environment, so the very first step to improve your marriage communication is to overcome your fears.

First, I'll tell you a story to illustrate the subtle way fear pollutes your communication. Then, in Strategy 1, we'll identify your fear so you can recognize it instead of blundering forward, letting fear drive your communication.

In Strategies 2, 3, & 4 you'll get concrete help too you can overcome your fear. Finally, in Strategy 5, you'll even find that fear can be a fabulous guide to reveal your biggest life full of meaning.

* * *

My story to show you how fear hides is about River and Phoenix, a couple who've been living together for three years. River wants to take the relationship to the next level and buy a house, but, in addition to that desire (or maybe because of it), River is afraid Phoenix won't want to make that big commitment.

In this story you'll notice three phases of fear:
- Your Inner Lizard Alarm sounds!!!
- Your Animal Body sends signals
- You suffer from an Amygdala Hijack Blindness

We think we're communicating, but fear takes hold of our words and disguises them. Consequently, your sweetheart may hear something very different than what you say.

Remember our basic premise about communication? Communication has two parts: giving (speaking) and receiving (hearing).

When fear disguises your true intentions, your nonverbal cues send a very different message than your words. Even when you think your words are crystal clear, they don't get received the way you gave them. This is how fear pollutes our communication.

In this story, your task is to listen for all the ways that fear is hiding and gumming up the communication between River and Phoenix. I'll be there to draw your attention to it.

When you can clearly pinpoint the fear to be overcome, you can then employ the ladder of strategies I offer later in the chapter to help you overcome those fears.

Here's the story. See if you can spot fear in all its hiding places.

Your Inner Lizard Alarm protects you from danger

River has a dream. The dream is to send out holiday cards that signal *I belong with Phoenix*. The dream is to have return address labels in the lefthand corner of those cards imply:

River & Phoenix

123 Our Home

Together Forever

When River grew up, there were no holiday-card-matched names. Holidays were especially lonely because of divorce and division in River's family.

All those childhood years, when River was shuffled between houses, there was an empty feeling. River wants to fill the empty feeling with a promise of love and security. Two names. In the left-hand corner of the envelope. That's the fix for what always felt wrong in River's life.

As you can imagine, River cares deeply about Phoenix saying yes to buying a house together. But the stakes are high and River is afraid.

River's deep desire creates an equally deep fear: *What if Phoenix says no to buying a house? Does that mean we'll break up? And I'll only have my name in the lefthand corner of my holiday cards? Forever and ever?*

So, instead of laying all the cards on the table and asking Phoenix, "Do you feel ready to buy a house together?" River's Inner Lizard Alarm steps in to disguise the desire because that Inner Lizard is charged with protecting River.

River's Inner Lizard thinks it's best to ask more enigmatically and say, "Wow. Housing prices are really dropping around here."

If we could invent some way for fearful words to come out of your mouth in a cartoon-like bubble wearing a warning label of blue smoke, Phoenix would instantly know River is afraid and it's important to pay attention.

But fear wears no blue smoke.

Instead, fear attacks. Fear runs away. Fear ignores. Fear doesn't know how to say "I'm afraid," because even speaking those words is vulnerable and ignites more fear.

Now it's Phoenix's turn to hear (receive) what River is saying (giving). Phoenix can hear, "Housing prices are dropping around here," many ways: Is River reporting the news? Or sounding an alarm about potential economic disaster?

Phoenix doesn't know about River's envelope and the names in the left-hand corner.

But we communicate with more than just our words. Humans are animals, and like other animals, our bodies have instincts. These instincts told us a saber-toothed tiger was nearby even if we couldn't see it or hear it.

We could sense that tiger.

Your Animal Body communicates non-verbally

You have an Animal Body. It reacts instinctively without your permission. When your Animal Body senses danger, it will react. Unconsciously. In order to protect you.

Remember our ancestors whose lives depended on sensing that saber-toothed-tiger? Your Animal Body has a keen sense of awareness and ignores words in favor of pheromones.

Phoenix's Animal Body senses danger.

But River is being purposefully casual with the comment, "Housing prices are dropping around here," so Phoenix doesn't recognize that the fear resides inside of River.

Phoenix just *feels* the fear River is sending out into the relationship.

Phoenix's Inner Lizard Alarm instantly and invisibly references thousands of scenarios that might explain why this comment—housing prices are dropping—should ignite fear, and finds one.

When Phoenix was eight years old, an economic downturn combined with a parent's job loss and the family suddenly had to move. Phoenix had no friends at the new school. It was lonely.

Bingo! Phoenix "understands" River's fear.

Because Phoenix doesn't want River to feel this terrible loneliness, Phoenix becomes reassuring, "Your job is super secure, River. There's nothing to worry about."

Now we have two people who are both afraid. River thinks Phoenix heard and understood what River said, but Phoenix has completely misunderstood River's intention.

River knows nothing about the job loss and the family move. Phoenix doesn't know about the names in the left-hand corner of the envelope.

The blinding terror of the Amygdala Hijack

Fear isn't subtle. Fear is blinding. Fear identifies things as black or white: safe/not safe.

When our ancestors' Inner Lizard Alarm went off—Danger! Tiger nearby!—all attention was devoted to finding the tiger until there was certainty life was again safe.

The same thing happens to you and to me. These days psychologists call this an amygdala hijack. This means your brain is blind to anything except solving the question: Where is the danger located?

River won't stop feeling fear (and reacting to fear) until the envelope is guaranteed. Phoenix won't stop feeling fear (and reacting to fear) until there's a safety net to make up for the job loss, the move, and the lonely new school.

River wants to hear Phoenix say, "I'd love to own a house with you! Then we could send out holiday cards with both our names in the return address label." This is the only response that will truly put River's fears at ease and remove River's Amygdala Hijack Blindness.

Can you see how difficult fear makes communication?

If there was no Amygdala Hijack Blindness, River could say, "I wasn't worried about my job, Phoenix. I was asking you to buy a house with me." But River is blind to every response except the one that will calm River's fear.

River's fear is so disguised as to be invisible to River as well as Phoenix. Not even River realizes that until Phoenix mentions the envelope—or at least says something that makes River believe Phoenix intends to be together forever—nothing will remove that fear.

When Phoenix says, "There's nothing to worry about," River hears, "I don't want to buy a house with you."

River instantly feels the burn of tears threaten to fall, so turns quickly and leaves the room. Phoenix, who has no idea what just happened, tosses their hands in the air and says, "What? What did I do?"

Isn't it ironic that River's intention—to avoid rejection—inspires a coy approach. But it's that same coy vagueness that causes Phoenix to become afraid of something completely different and miss the moment of connection with River.

Both people feel rejected because River didn't ask cleanly.

Fear is the first reason you don't know how to cleanly ask for what you want.

Naïve misunderstandings like this one happen all the time in marriage. The problem is that unclarified misunderstandings like this one turn into wounds: *You don't want to invest in a future with me.* Walls go up: *I say the simplest thing and you're mad.*

Backs get turned. Rejection gets anchored. And love fades.

We all feel the need to protect ourselves, but, ironically, protection can drive the intimacy we crave further away than ever.

This is why it's imperative to fully understand the warning signs your fearful Inner Lizard is sending.

STRATEGY 1

Learn How Fear Hides
Discover the disguises fear wears

Fear wears many disguises.

The words Phoenix offered, "Your job is secure," were meant to reassure River. But Phoenix didn't understand River's fear. River didn't even understand River's fear.

River didn't understand their fear because they used avoidance to disguise that fear. Disguises to hide fear work so well that we often can't identify our own fears.

What River really wants is a future with Phoenix. River wants to share a front door and a toilet with Phoenix. The front door to welcome people into their shared home over and over, and the toilet to symbolize the support they'll give each other during the shitty times in life.

River could have used a number of other disguises to hide fear:

- Anger
- Suspicion
- Control

Would you have known it was fear that made River say, "Housing prices are dropping around here" if I hadn't told you? Does that statement truly and clearly signal River's true wish of the holiday envelope?

Probably not. Fear thinks it's being helpful when it wears disguises. Fear thinks it's protecting River by hiding. It's not. Not helpful at all. It's confusing. It's maddening. It's frustrating.

In order to get your fear to come out of hiding, let's first look at all the ways that fear hides. First, we'll look at avoidance—the disguise River used here—then we'll change it up a little to look at the other disguises fear could wear.

Fear disguised as avoidance haunts your relationship

Avoidance is what River used above to hide from fear: "Housing prices are dropping around here."

Avoidance works well for people who want to run away from the potential conflict of a situation. Avoidance is sort of like that hot potato game you played as a child: Hot! Hot! Hot! Drop it! Don't touch it! Avoidance works well for people who want to drop hold of their fear.

Oh. Except that then fear is just lingering about; haunting the entire room by causing complete confusion.

If you use avoidance to disguise your fear, you make intimacy difficult because there's no you there with whom to connect. You've disappeared.

If your fear hides as avoidance, you might notice the following sensations in your body:

- An airy, spacey, ungrounded feeling in your limbs.
- A feeling of confusion. Dizziness.
- There are no words. None. You open your mouth to speak, and there's...nothing.

- Your eyes dart about, looking for a handle to hold, or a place to land, but, again, there's nothing. Just air. And space. And more nothingness.

An ungrounded or hollow feeling is an identifier if your strategy to disguise fear is avoidance.

If you tend to disguise fear as avoidance, you will be a cave of emptiness with nothing to offer your sweetheart. Real attractive, right?

Fear disguised as suspicion undermines your relationship

Suspicion is sort of the opposite of avoidance. With suspicion, instead of backing away from conflict, River would assume conflict is inevitable and so go looking for it.

Instead of saying, "Housing prices are dropping around here," River would see evidence for all sorts of reasons Phoenix doesn't want to buy the house. The two of them are at the hardware store and Phoenix doesn't want to buy mouse traps: "Aha!" Thinks River, "Phoenix doesn't care if our home gets over-run with rodents because Phoenix has no plans to stay with me long term."

Suspicion shows up in people who have great imaginations and are prone to make assumptions. Suspicious people build a case and gather evidence to prove their case.

Oh. Except now they treat the world the way they were treated, so they actually create the world they fear. The problem is their case is based on a wounded way of seeing the world. They were hurt, so they expect the world to hurt them.

If you use suspicion to disguise your fear, you make intimacy difficult because you can only see your past—and the ways you were wounded—in your sweetheart's eyes, rather than embracing the way your sweetheart wants to help you heal.

If your fear hides behind suspicion, you might notice the following sensations in your body:

- Darting eyes to see things that go "on the list" of evidence.
- Chewing and stewing over details ad nauseam.
- A tight or churning stomach or tight throat.
- A recurrent inner voice that says, "I knew it!" then fills in the blank with the imagined scenario.

"Aha! I knew it!" is a key identifier for suspicion.

If you tend to disguise fear as suspicion, you'll have lists of reasons your sweetheart fails you.

Fear disguised as anger blows up your relationship

Anger can be seen as suspicion that escapes in an explosion. Our fears—until they are overcome—are the lens through which we see the world. River is afraid: *Phoenix doesn't want to make a commitment.*

When fear becomes the lens for viewing the world, River has microscopic vision for every time Phoenix demonstrates a lack of commitment. This is suspicion, right? Then River gets angry about those pieces of "evidence."

Instead of "Housing prices are dropping around here," when River uses anger to disguise fear, River accuses Phoenix, "You never do anything around this house." Or "Phoenix, I'm so sick of your lack of commitment to this house. The sink gets clogged and I have to drain it. It snows and I have to shovel. Have you ever—ever once—cleaned a bathroom since we moved in here?"

The anger/accusation model is used by people who tend to blame or find fault. There's a lot of tension that gets stored in your body when you're afraid, and a burst of anger is a great release.

Oh. Except that it destroys relationships.

When you use anger to disguise fear, you make intimacy difficult because you blow up moments of intimacy and cause fear in the heart of your sweetheart.

If your fear hides as anger, you might notice the following sensations in your body:

- A hot burning feeling under your skin.
- A feeling of pressure that might manifest as headaches.
- A quick temper about tiny, unrelated things.
- Bursts: burst of language, energy, or eating. Energy that comes in waves.

Outbursts are key identifiers if your strategy to avoid fear is anger.

If you tend to disguise fear as anger, you will often find fault with your sweetheart.

Fear disguised as control strangles your relationship

Instead of "Housing prices are dropping around here," River could say, "We have an appointment with a realtor on Saturday at 11:00am."

The control model to keep fear at bay works well because you go through the world fixing what everyone else got wrong. It doesn't even feel scary because you can fix everything.

People resort to this disguise for a combination of reasons: avoiding conflict, or a secret pride that their way of seeing the world is superior. Control is certainly one way to avoid anger for those who don't like explosions.

Oh. Until the illness, the earthquake, or the job loss comes along that is sadly out of your control.

If you use control to disguise fear, you make intimacy difficult because you erase your sweetheart's individuality. There's no room for variety, an alternative way, or frankly, your sweetheart.

If your fear hides behind control, you might notice the following sensations in your body:
- You know the universal truth for how the world works: The fork tines go down in the dishwasher, why doesn't everyone realize this?
- Tightness. In your hands, your core, your voice.
- You fix the world: if the forks are aimed tine-up, you turn them the right way, and point them down.

"My way or the highway" is the key identifier for control.

If you tend to disguise fear as control, you'll be constantly trying to change your sweetheart into someone else.

Summing up

These are some of the ways people disguise fear, but it's not an exhaustive list. The key thing to remember is that these disguises are fear's way of trying to protect you.

Protection is a worthy intention. When you can approach yourself and/or your sweetheart with this gentle and kind assumption that fear is an attempt at protection, you can cultivate compassion and understanding which open the door wide to cultivate intimacy.

Now you know how to recognize fear. Let's look at strategies to overcome fear.

Try This Tool: Identify Your Fear's Disguise(s)

How does your fear tend to hide? Which of the above disguises do you most relate to? (Avoidance, suspicion, anger, or control?)

Write your most common strategy here:
_____
_____

Can you think of a time you disguised fear?
Write that memory here:
_____
_____

It will help you later in the chapter to use a very specific memory.

We'll look at four more strategies:
- Naming is Taming
- Befriend to Mend
- Protection Before Connection
- Fly into Fear

STRATEGY 2
Naming is Taming
Give your fear a name

The second strategy for overcoming fear—Naming is Taming—gives you a clear understanding of your fear. Your Inner Lizard is afraid, and fear doesn't speak in dulcet, clear tones. Fear is alarmist, urgent, and emotional. So, it confuses you and anyone else around.

To overcome fear, name what's frightening you. It's amazing how powerful this is! It's also incredibly difficult.

If River could have Named to Tame, it would sound like this: *Phoenix, I'm afraid you won't want what I want. I want to send out holiday cards with our names in the corner for years and decades to come. I'm afraid you won't want this.*

I'm afraid you won't want this because my parents didn't know how to do this, and, as a result, I don't really know how to do it. When I don't know how to do something, it's so big and confusing and overwhelming that I get afraid. And that's when I imagine you leaving me or not wanting to buy a house with me.

That's very clear, right? That's how you overcome fear: naming the fear tames the fear. It doesn't sound so big and hairy and scary like that, right?

Here's the problem: it's tough at first to hear your Lizard fears, even when you truly try to listen to your Inner Lizard. You probably just catch phrases from your Lizard like, "Get out!" or "hide!" Be patient and tenacious about listening to your fear.

"Hide!" is all that River could hear, and that's why "Housing prices are dropping around here" was so enigmatic.

Name your inner fear

Many of my clients name their inner fear, and I recommend you name your fear too. I mean actually personify your fear and give it a name. I learned this from my teacher, Martha Beck, in her great book *Finding Your Own North Star*.

When you name your fear, you can see your fear as separate from yourself. This small distance is amazing at helping you deal with your fear rather than being ruled by your fear.

It's fun to hear the variety of personalities people's fear take on. I've seen fear manifest as Terry, the enormous and terrifying T-Rex who has such tiny arms they're completely helpless (fear that tends to wear the disguise of control, then can't effect much change). I've also seen fear manifest as Flounder, a fish who tragically disappears in the water the instant someone reaches out (fear that tends to wear the disguise of suspicion, but can never get close or intimate).

I wonder what form your fear takes. I also wonder how your fear behaves. How does you fear try to protect you?

Is your fear great at the giant roar (fight)? Or is your fear better at the disappearing act (freeze)? Some people run away the instant they're afraid (flight), while others become niceness-embodied as a way to fix a fearful situation (fawn).

My inner fear's name is Lance. Sometimes Lance is a lassoing lizard. My biggest fears involve people leaving me. Lance thinks he's my hero and chases people down, first lassoing them, then, running round and round and round them, so they're tied close to me and can't escape.

The people close to me will hear Lance say: "Where are you going? Why do you have to go? What time will you be home? What do you want for dinner? Do you want asparagus or salad? What kind of dressing do you want on the salad? Where did you say you were going again? What time will you be home?"

Yes. The people I love get put in a prison of questions. Isn't that thoughtful of Lance?

Other times Lance is a long spear. Lance is able to pierce the people who cause me fear long before they get anywhere close to me: "Get away! Let me do it. You're always doing it wrong."

Lance has made it tough for me to foster sweet, tender intimacy. Lance's job is to either SECURE relationships or FEND THEM OFF before they get dangerously close.

But now that I can see Lance so clearly, I can both laugh at Lance and have compassion for Lance. The best part about naming Lance is that I notice Lance isn't me. Lance is my fear, and I don't have to be identified by my fear.

When you can find even a tiny bit of distance from your fear—realizing your fear isn't who you are, but rather a feeling you're having that will pass—you can tame your fear much more easily.

After you've named your fear and you have an idea of its character, buy a stuffed animal or some other tchotchke so you can see your fear.

This tiny symbol allows you to see your fear on the outside of your body and will help you deal better with your fear. You get less attached to your fear. Your fear isn't YOU. You can see your fear as separate.

Try This Tool: Imagine Your Fear Embodied

What does your fear look like?

_____

_____

How does your fear behave when it wants to keep you safe?

_____

_____

Give your fear a name:

_____

_____

This allows you to listen to your fear with a small—and as you practice, a large—amount of detachment. You can notice you're afraid, but you have a visible place to locate that fear and deal with it appropriately.

This external representation of your fear allows you to listen to your fear more easily. The more carefully you listen, the better you'll get at hearing precisely what it is you're afraid of.

Now that your fear is on the outside of your body and you've named it, it's easier to hear everything your fear is saying rather than your fear taking control of your arms, legs, mouth and eyes.

In the next couple strategies, I'll offer a roadmap for how to interact with that fear that now has a name.

STRATEGY 3

Befriend to Mend
Get curiouser about the worst-case scenario

Once you've named your fear, listen to it. Listen like a really good friend.

Have you ever been terrified of a dream? You wake up, and you tell a friend your dream, and, even as you're telling the dream, the dream loses its potency?

Fear is tamed with friendship. Fear doesn't like to be alone. If you can befriend your fear, you'll mend the damage fear wreaks.

It helps to practice with an old fear. Picture an old fear that is now ancient history. Remember how it felt when you were afraid. Imagine the smell of the room where your fear was most intense. (Smell helps to recall emotion.)

Then ask yourself what feels most frightening. Write it down, or tell a friend. It helps to completely articulate the fear (written or spoken aloud). You may discover there is another layer to your fear than you realized. You may discover reasons for your fear that help to explain why the feeling was so intense.

It's easier to practice taking dictation from a fear that is no longer as threatening because your Inner Lizard knows a safe outcome is now guaranteed. Your Inner Lizard is more forthcoming when it's not terrified.

Your Inner Lizard wants to be taken seriously, however, and when you listen fully enough to take dictation (or to recount your fear to a friend), your Inner Lizard begins to trust the process of revelation.

Using the box below, practice taking dictation from your fearful Inner Lizard.

This practice is nearly impossible in the beginning because fear is so powerful. I recommend you begin with an old fear that's lost its juiciness. As you practice, your fear will be more willing to reveal itself.

You'll get better at noticing what scares you. You'll see patterns to your fears. You'll get better at picking up cues from your Inner Lizard.

Remember that your Inner Lizard is trying to protect you. When you are grateful to your Inner Lizard for this protective impulse and you're willing to listen to the whole story you Lizard wants to tell you, your relationship communication won't be sabotaged by your fears.

Try This Tool: Befriend to Mend

Take dictation from your fear. Write down precisely what your fear says.

_____
_____

Ex: Hide! Get outta here!
Ex: Phoenix will never want to buy a house with you, you dufus.

Write down the disguise you're tempted to use (avoidance, control, suspicion, or anger).

_____
_____

Ex: (avoidance) "Housing prices are dropping around here."

Notice how your sweetheart misunderstands you as a result of this disguise.

_____
_____

You'll be able to manage fear rather than letting your fear poison your relationship communication.

Get curiouser about the worst-case scenario

Have you ever had a friend that wanted to know everything about you? And you felt safe to reveal even your ugliest secrets? This is the type of friend your fear needs in order to recover from the way fear hijacks your amygdala.

River wanted to avoid rejection so tried to back away from a full request by saying, "Housing prices are dropping around here." But as we saw, that backfired.

It helps to get wildly curious about your fears, even to the point of asking your Inner Lizard over and over, "What's the absolute worst that could happen?" And then what? And then what? Keep this train of curiosity running until you're sure you've heard the entire worst-case scenario.

This is the irony of fear: fear is afraid, so it wants to stay hidden. But the only escape from fear is exposure.

Try This Tool: Explore the Worst-Case-Scenario

Escape fear by exposing it. Tell yourself the entire story of the worst-case-scenario here:

_____
_____
_____

Continue to explore by asking, "What's the worst part about that?"

_____
_____

Once more ask, "And what is the worst part about that?"

_____
_____

When you get curious about the absolute worst-case scenario that's causing your Inner Lizard to be fearful, you get the WHOLE STORY onto the table where it can be seen and where plans for adaptation can be made.

When River gets curious about the worst-case scenario, this is what comes out: "I'm afraid Phoenix won't want to buy a house with me."

And what's the worst part about that? "I'll be lonely," says River's fear.

So, if Phoenix never wants to buy a home with you, and Phoenix knows that now, is it better for you to not know that? And to go on living with Phoenix?

"Hmmmm," says River's fear, contemplating. That possibility hadn't registered.

This is typical of how fear works. It is only the imminent danger that registers with your Inner Lizard. The Inner Lizard doesn't think about long term consequences.

It helps to ask those worst-case-scenario questions like:

- What's the absolute worst thing if _____ (state fear) happens?
- And why is _____ (that outcome) so horrible?
- What will you do if _____ (that outcome) happens?

River can think about the worst thing that could happen if Phoenix didn't want to buy a house together. "Well, I'll be terribly, horribly sad," says River. "But, actually, if Phoenix is NEVER gonna buy a house with me, I guess I'd rather learn that now instead of after I've invested ten years in our relationship."

This is typical of how your Inner Lizard works. It can only see what's on the horizon, threatening you today.

Your Inner Lizard has no long-term context. That's not your Inner Lizard's job. Your Lizard is there to protect you from imminent attack.

When you draw out the long-term consequence for your Inner Lizard, often you will see that, while the short-term fear is real, it's worth facing because of the long-term consequence.

Many, many relationships I've coached only needed to see the long-term payoff after the short-term fear in order to dissolve the power of that terrible, horrible, paralyzing fear.

When you befriend your fear, listening to the whole story—even the very worst-case scenario—that wild part of fear that wants to flee, freeze, fight, or fawn, settles down. Your fear has a friend, and we all know anything can be mended with a friend.

Strategy #3 to overcome fear is Befriend to Mend. Listen to your fear like a friend. Listen to everything. Even the worst-case scenario.

Strategy #3 works best if you have employed strategies #1 and #2. You've identified how your fear hides, and you've given your fear a name. You've externalized your fear and it isn't living inside you, tied to and tangled up with your identity.

Now let's look at Strategy #4, where you'll learn how to nurture the part of yourself that's afraid so you can enlist your resilience.

STRATEGY 4
Protect to Connect
Nurture the part of you that is afraid

Once River was able to see the worst-case-scenario, River realized pain now would be better than pain in 10 years. But River is still incredibly nervous to broach the subject with Phoenix because the risk of losing the love they have causes a deep ache in River's stomach.

In order to get brave enough, River needs to talk kindly to that Inner Lizard, to be a strong and nurturing adult to the vulnerable and fearful Lizard inside River's heart.

River learns to say, "You know what, Lizard? This might really suck for a while." There is a long pause with a deep sigh here. Then River continues, "But I'm attractive and smart. I'm a good catch. I'd rather know that Phoenix and I have different ideas for the future rather than wasting time on the assumption we'll live happily ever after."

Because fear is often disguised, talking to your Inner Lizard like this is hard at first. But avoidance doesn't make fear go away. When you can be honest and speak the truth your fear sees, you can begin to make friends with your fear.

River realized that if Phoenix never wanted to buy a house, Phoenix probably isn't interested in a long-term commitment. This was a sad thing to imagine (and remember, it's just a fear, not a fact). But leaning into the fear allowed River to assure that Inner Lizard they—River and River's Inner Lizard—would be OK.

Something magical happens every time I watch someone learn to comfort their Inner Lizard. They suddenly have a courage they never imagined was available to them.

This is because you avoid things that terrify you. But the truth is you're much more resourceful than your Lizard would give you credit for. When you can SEE the whole problem, you almost instantly discover tools for DEALING with the whole problem.

River suddenly feels attractive. Confident. Desirable, even.

River had been looking through the blinding eyes of fear and hadn't seen that attractive, confident, desirable face staring back.

Not only does River now realize it would be better to know about the future with Phoenix, but River also realizes how dumb Phoenix would be to miss out on a life together with their names on a holiday card envelope each year.

Nurture the part of you that is afraid

Seeing past the fear allows River to realize how much love is available. Loving someone for a lifetime doesn't die just because River's Inner Lizard worries that Phoenix may not want it.

You can comfort your Inner Lizard by channeling your favorite nurturer:

- Avoid "there, there" euphemisms that essentially send the message, "Your fear isn't so bad."
- Instead, lean into the fear, and play out what will happen if that fear becomes reality.
- When you do this, you realize you're more resilient than your Inner Lizard would have you believe.

Now, instead of fostering your inner fear, you're focused on your inner resiliency.

You've protected the fear by building a plan for your own resilience. You feel courageous.

When your Inner Lizard feels the protection of a plan, it feels safe. All that wildness of fear softens and you're able to welcome connection wholeheartedly. You've accepted responsibility that, if the worst-case scenario happens, you will be OK.

This is protection before connection.

This imagined resiliency not only tames the fear; it builds your confidence. It offers hope—the antidote to fear—that you will survive the fearful circumstance. When you have hope, you're willing to take more action. You're willing to be vulnerable. You know you'll survive, so you reach for the bigger life.

Remember, some fears are real, but most are imagined. Spoiler alert: Phoenix has always imagined forever with River. Phoenix would be shocked to hear River wondering about it.

But because Phoenix doesn't wonder if they'll be together forever, Phoenix doesn't need to talk about it. River needed to overcome fear and see that life would be OK—although tremendously sad—if Phoenix didn't want to buy the house.

The pain inside of River was never about Phoenix. It was about River. Once River realized "I guess I'll be OK either way, and I really want to buy a house," River could move past fear to clarity: I want to buy a house.

Try This Tool: Nurture Your Fear

Channel your favorite nurturer.

Who is most comforting to you when you're afraid?
_____

What would this nurturer say to you and to your fear?
_____
_____

How are you up to the task of facing your fear? What resiliencies do you possess?
_____
_____

The bulk of fears will respond to this pattern of four strategies. You'll realize that even though you're afraid, you're also capable of facing and overcoming fear. When you realize this—and especially when you practice this—you grow confident.

When you welcome your fear—as a friend with a protective message, rather than an enemy to be avoided—you tame it.

There will be the occasional fear, however, that still terrifies you. For that, we'll use Strategy #5, which will help you embrace fears and use their energy to live a bigger life.

STRATEGY 5

Fly into Fear
Make yourself competent to face the danger

Remember when I said that fear is your Inner Lizard trying to protect you? And that until you have mastery over your fear, your fear will steer your life? The first four tools concentrate on trying to tame fear.

Sometimes you can't tame fear, though. Sometimes you are right to be afraid because what you want to do is beyond your current abilities, and for that reason, it's scary.

This strategy takes a totally different approach and uses fear as an engine of energy to help you fly into a bigger and bigger life. You'll learn to harness the energy of fear to help you grow. This is how you expand your comfort zone: you need to find a way to do uncomfortable—or terrifying—things.

When you can fly through the window of invitation that your fear presents, your skill, wisdom, and confidence will grow.

I first understood this Flying into Fear strategy when I taught skiing.

I'm not a great skier, but my boss at the ski area, Kate, said she can teach anyone to ski and teach them to teach skiing. "I can't, however, teach people to be kind," she said.

I am kind, so I got the job.

The job came with an hour of ski instruction every morning with Stephanie Reynolds, one of the great ski instructors in Colorado.

Stephanie taught me that skiing moguls expertly is about learning to leap into your fear rather than run from or resist fear. Moguls are big bumps on the ski hill. The goal is to weave your way down the mountain, bouncing off one mogul and into the next. They terrified me, so I avoided them.

Backing away from the bumps is called skiing in the backseat and it's a guaranteed way to fall down when you ski.

If you ski in the backseat, you feel off balance. As you lean back on skis, the front of the ski slides out from under you. Your arms flail around and you look like a pinwheel in a tornado.

"In order to ski moguls well," Stephanie told me, "you need to fly through the window at the top of the bump."

The top of the bump is the scariest place to be. Lemme tell ya, flying into that terror was hard. My body didn't want to do it. But Stephanie broke it down. "Bend your knees as you're coming up to the bump. Then push the ground away at the top, that way you can really explode through the window."

She followed me down the hill, and each time I got to that scariest part of the bump she encouraged me to fly into the window of fear instead of backing away.

Stephanie skied right behind me and called out moment by moment directions. "Bend. Push. Bend. Push." She was so encouraging and had such belief in me. "Fly, Rebecca. Leap now. Leap now."

The bigger my leap, the more easily my skis negotiated the bump. I began to find a rhythm: up, top, TERROR! Leap! Up, top, TERROR, leap.

After several times down the mountain, the TERROR became merely terror and the rhythm changed: up, top, terror, leap.

After a few more runs down the mountain, the terror shrunk to a baby fear. And after a few more, it shrunk until my rhythm became up, top, fly! Up, top, fly!

I was skiing! And not only was I skiing, by leaning into my fear instead of away, my body found the buoyancy of flight.

Confidence replaced my fear.

Many things you encounter with your Inner Lizard are going to be more terrifying than skiing moguls. When you bump into them, though, picture it as bumping into a mogul. When you imagine this, you can feel your body physically pushing into the fear to leap through that window of opportunity. In this way, fear can become an invitation, rather than only serving as a protection device.

Fear vs Competency

Fear makes your life smaller and smaller as your dreams—one by one—are stolen from you.

Competence grows your ability—which grows your dreams—making your life bigger and bigger.

When you fly into fear, you become the best version of yourself

The invitation into intimacy is possibly the hardest one to accept. Intimacy leaves us vulnerable to all sorts of hurt. You might get rejected. You might not be valued. You might get taken advantage of. You might actually—TERROR ALERT!—be seen for exactly who you are. And then… what if you're actually LOVED for exactly who you are?!

All this is why your Inner Lizard tries to protect you from intimacy.

But the invitation into intimacy is the greatest one to accept. Only by flying into our fear and accepting that intimacy can we be truly loved. Truly seen. Truly valued.

A visceral example of this comes from astronaut Jerry Linenger's TED Talk. Nominally, it's a story about his experiences in space. But on a deeper level, it's a story about fear's invitation to become competent, about how fear prepares our hearts for intimacy.

Linenger was stationed on The Mir Space Station when a fire broke out. Fire in space is more dangerous than on earth because of the confined space and the unique way that gravity works—or doesn't work, actually—in space.

One minute Linenger is asking, "What's wrong?" And the next minute he can't see his hand in front of his face, so thick is the smoke. Linenger is facing terrible danger. But he has made himself competent. He has worked through this worst-case scenario and knew how to respond.

He instinctively reaches for the oxygen suit, slips it over his head, turns it on and…nothing. It doesn't work. He reaches for a second suit as his lungs are heaving and polluted with smoke. He slips it over his head and takes one, two, three deep breaths.

This astronaut has prepared for this exact scenario. He's competent.

He knows the risks inherent in this danger and he suddenly begins to see the end of the scenario unfold: This is his moment. This is the end.

He speaks his son's name aloud, "John." And in this moment of gravest danger, the refiner's fire does its work, separating the purest metal from its impurities. Captain Jerry Linenger makes the distinction: more than he is afraid of dying in this fire, he regrets what he didn't say to his son back on earth.

"I didn't leave him a note. A simple note that said, 'Dear John, I love you.'"

His fear at that moment—when he was quite certain his skin and bones would catch fire and destroy his physical body—wasn't about burning and turning to ash. His fear became refined into regret at the love and intimacy he didn't leave behind.

Fear invited him to have a new perspective. He survived the fire in space and returned to Earth, to his family. When you hear him speak, you know for certain that each day he looks at the people he loves—his wife and children—and speaks their name and tells them about the certainty of the love he feels for them.

Deep love comes packaged in terrifying vulnerability. Like Linenger, though, we can push through that fear, be refined by it, and learn to lean into the intimacy that makes our lives wonderful.

How can you learn to tame your vulnerability so that you feel ready to fly into the invitation that love offers?

Fear invites you to do hard things.

But you are unique. You have a unique way of loving in this world.

If you accept fear's invitation and you become competent in the dangerous face of vulnerable love, what impurities will burn away? What qualities will you strengthen?

Try This Tool: Fear's Invitation

What competencies will you need to acquire to better face this fear?
_____
_____

How will your life get bigger if you lean into this fear?
_____
_____

What will you miss out on if you let this fear determine your future?
_____
_____

Chapter Review

- **Fear's Disguises.** Which disguise are you most likely to wear when you're afraid? What disguise is your sweetheart most likely to wear?
- **Naming is Taming.** Name your fear to tame its power to pollute your relationship. What is your fear's name? How about the name of your sweetheart's fear?
- **Befriend to Mend.** Listen to everything your fear has to say, even the very worst-case scenario. When your fear has a friend, it's not likely to damage your relationship.
- **Protect to Connect.** Offer your fear a cloak of resilience. Review all the ways you're up to fear's task.
- **Fly into Fear.** Accept fear's invitation to live a bigger life. Fear makes you aware of the competencies you need to gain in order to live that bigger life.

Overcome Fear: Putting it All Together

First: Identify the disguise
As you notice communication tension with your sweetheart, ask yourself, *how might this be fear in disguise?*

Remind yourself of your typical go-to fear disguise (suspicion, avoidance, anger, or control). How is this moment similar to your pattern?

_____

Second: Name to Tame
Ask yourself, *what am I afraid of?* Or ask yourself, *if I reframed this frustration (or anger, or loneliness, etc) as a fear, what would that fear be?* Write that fear here:

_____

Third: Befriend to Mend
Get super curious about the worst-case-scenario. Exposing a fear sucks out all that fear's juice.

Take this space and write the whole story of your worst-case-scenario.

_____

_____

Fourth: Protect to Connect
When you are separate from your fear, you're able to comfort the fear in advance. When you see your resilience, you have hope which inspires confidence.

Use this space to comfort your fear by noting how you're up to the task.

_____

_____

Fifth: Fly into Fear
What competency to you need to practice in order to have the skills to fly into this fear?

_____

_____

You've just taken in a lot of information.

To make real changes, you need time to synthesize.

What will help you turn what you just read into a habit you can practice?

STEP TWO

Get Clear

Confusion creates fear; clarity builds trust.

Remember when you met your sweetheart and you had that giddy excitement that inspired you to share the depths of who you are with this lovely new person?

Maybe it was talking all night. Maybe it was fishing companionably all day.

Or maybe you wanted to burst out in song because you felt so fabulous with this lovely person, but your fear steps in and says, *Are you crazy? People don't just start singing! Shut up.*

Fear is the part of you that tells you to shut up.

Clarity is the part of you that knows you want to burst into song.

Clarity gives you courage and inspires action. Action to become more of who you are. When you feed the fire of your desire, you create an irresistible warmth that draws your sweetheart closer to you.

In this chapter, you'll get the tools to become *clear yourself*. You need to be clear yourself before you try *communicating*.

You'll **get clear** about what you want: *I want to sing. I want a singing lifestyle.*

You'll **get clear** about your fear, so you can overcome it: *I'm afraid my singing will push people away.*

You'll **overcome your fears** of vulnerability: *I'm afraid my singing will push people away. But I want to sing with my sweetheart because I only want to live in a house where it's embraced that I sing.*

Which lets you live a lifestyle of the **clean ask** (which we'll discuss more in the next chapter): *I'm afraid you won't like me if I sing, but I really, truly want my life and relationship filled with songs. So, will you sing with me?*

Without clarity, your relationship is haunted by confusion. Confusion sucks the life out of you and your relationship. It paralyzes you with fear of the unknown.

In an effort to escape the desert of loneliness that confusion creates, you blame or shame your sweetheart, or, like a turtle, you hide inside your shell because you have no idea how to connect.

Instead of fear that causes us to attack or pull away, we need desire that tempts us to lean in, investigate, and jump into the pool of togetherness.

Clarity is how you charge the battery of your desire.

Desire is a driver of intimacy. Desire drives your enthusiasm, your curiosity, and your ambition. Then desire drives you to connect and share who you are with your lover.

Without desire, your life will feel flat and boring. Loneliness is an outgrowth of that sort of boredom. Then feelings of alienation arise because you don't feel connected to your sweetheart.

This chapter will give you specific strategies to awaken or reawaken your desire. Then you will learn how to include your sweetheart in the magical dance of intimacy that comes from two people sharing their desires.

Clarity creates spaciousness—both inside you and inside your relationship. Space to be freely yourself, and to welcome abundant love.

The opposite of that spaciousness is what I call the Black Hole of Confusion. Confusion sucks you into a vortex where you can't see choices. You're stuck.

In this chapter I help you see that the more you hone your own desire, the more you'll be able to see that your desire is also wrapped up in your sweetheart's desire.

In this chapter...

You'll understand why clarity is key to vulnerability and intimacy.

- **The Black Hole of Confusion** and the romance of blending are two elements that alienate you from your sweetheart
- **Own your personal gravity** and learn why it's so important to stay in your own business and question the stories you tell yourself
- **Dive deep into your desire** so you can know precisely, exactly, specifically what you want
- **Map your universe** because you may act as if you and your sweetheart live in completely different worlds
- **You won't always agree** so how do you value love more than you value being right?

Knowing what you want is more challenging than it seems, because often you want mutually exclusive things. Especially in your most intimate relationship.

You want togetherness, but you also want independence. You want intimacy, but you also want autonomy. You want a safe place to feel vulnerable, but you also want to be seen as heroic and strong by your sweetheart.

These juxtaposed desires can be confusing. In this chapter, as with the rest of this book, let's focus on you. On your desire and on your clarity. When you can get clear about what *you* want, it makes relating to your sweetheart much easier.

A lack of clarity can *cause* fear, and being afraid can make it difficult to see clearly. You got some strategies about how to **overcome your fear** in the previous chapter.

Getting clear and overcoming fear are linked in a cycle. The more you can overcome fear, the more clarity you're able to get. The more clarity you can get, the less you fear.

Remember that **overcoming fear** and **getting clear** prepare you to make a **clean ask** in your relationship. When you can ask cleanly for what you want in your relationship, you set yourself up for deep intimacy that lasts. We'll talk about clean asks in the next chapter.

STRATEGY 1

The Black Hole of Confusion

How confusion keeps you lost and far from intimacy

A black hole is a place in space where the gravity is so strong that even light can't escape. Light! Who knew that light was affected by gravity? You may experience a black hole feeling in your relationship at one time or another, or certain subjects or topics of conversation may feel like a black hole that allows no communication.

If you plan to spend your life with your sweetheart, there will be a few things that stump you in the clarity department. I attribute these blind spots to our life lessons. They have the power to cause turmoil in your relationship, so much turmoil that you feel lost in the vacuum of a black hole with no light.

Would you believe that one of the black holes of my marriage was about making our bed? It sounds inane, but this tiny, microscopic thing seemed to represent the macro-relationship I wanted.

I was typically up and out of bed before my husband. Each day, after he woke up, he'd stumble out to the kitchen to make coffee, leaving the sheets tangled and the blankets bunched up.

Later in the day, when I went back into our bedroom, I got frustrated by the mountain of sheets and blankets. I saw that big ball of mess and felt my jaw tighten. A feeling of hopelessness haunted my gut.

I felt abandoned and neglected.

Isn't that interesting that I took the messy bed so personally? But we all do it, right? You give attention to the tiny spaces in your life because you are a physical creature and a meaning maker.

Many times, I walked into my bedroom and realized that *I cared more about our marriage than my husband did.* I mean, come on, if he loved me, he'd make the bed we shared.

The minute I asked Dave to make the bed, he'd start making it, but that only confirmed in my head that he didn't *think* about our marriage until I reminded him.

How was I going to stay married to a man who didn't care about me and about our relationship unless I *reminded* him to care?

Can you hear how lost I was in a Black Hole of Confusion? I had absolutely no clarity about what a teeny, tiny problem our unmade bed was.

If my make-the-bed conundrum resonates with you, read on to find out how you can discover the tools that helped me to distinguish between tiny things that feel so important—like an unmade bed—and the huge things—like living happily ever after.

Why the romance of blending causes confusion

Communication is that magical summation when speaking and hearing are united. We all strive for communication where there's no difference between what is spoken and what is heard.

This is simple to articulate, but not easy to achieve.

I thought I was clearly communicating that I wanted David to make the bed. Why wasn't he hearing me?

My answer is romantic. The gorgeous thing about romantic love is that blending feeling. Sex is the epitome of this blending. That orgasmic moment when the boundaries that define you and the boundaries that define your sweetheart disappear and you are ONE.

This ONEness erases the existential angst we all live with. Those lovely sex hormones erase that feeling of separateness and make you feel like you and your sweetheart are one person.

Now watch the Black Hole of Confusion that gets built inside of me because of this feeling of ONEness:

- David and I are one person.
- We want the same things.
- I want a made bed.
- So, David must want a made bed.

OK. I've already got you giggling at the ridiculousness of this line of thinking, right? But what can I say, those hormones are powerful.

But wait. It gets worse.

It does NOT occur to me to question this made-bed-truism because, after all, we are the same person and I want a made bed because a made bed is what happily married people have and I want to see that we are happily married each time I walk into our bedroom.

And then—shock of the century—I walk into the bedroom and there it is: a rumpled pile of sheets and blankets.

Now I get afraid. (But my fear disguises itself as anger.)

Isn't that funny that seeing an unmade bed is freaking me out? But again, come on, people like you have come into my office and whispered to me stories just like this one.

And I hear their fear too.

So, I know I'm not alone in this wacky way of seeing the world.

Your hormone-filled brain desperately wants to believe the premise that you and your sweetheart are the same person, too. It's terrifying to question that. So, instead of questioning that you're the same person, you question your sweetheart's intention about the tiny thing, like the unmade bed.

I decide David's message to me is I don't care all that much about maintaining our love. I'll leave that to you, Rebecca. I'm sure you'll take care of our love life the way you make our bed each day.

I arrive at this fear:

- Because of my parent's divorce, I'm sure David and I will be divorcing any moment. Finally, I've found the moment: the unmade bed will be the death of our marriage.
- So, I leap to the far-flung conclusion that IF David loved me, THEN he would care about a made bed.

Armed with this (false) *awareness*, each time I see those sheets and blankets piled up, I practice this message in my head: *David doesn't care about our marriage.*

Of course, this is my fear talking. It's not even remotely rational, but rarely is your Inner Lizard rational.

Because the template in my head was that marriage doesn't work, I was pre-programmed to see evidence for the impending divorce I knew was coming.

David didn't have the fear that we would divorce. So, no matter what happened in our relationship, he never saw evidence for divorce.

However, David did fear that marriage would usurp his independence. So, he saw every tangle we had as a threat to his independence.

He didn't like rules like: *Make the bed when you get out of it.* That made him feel beholden. Subconsciously, maybe he didn't make the bed to prove to himself he was independent. No one could tell him what to do.

Lack of clarity causes confusion. And confusion leads us to fear. We each had a fear. Fear was messing with the way we saw things.

Can you see the power of this Black Hole? Can you see where we were each lost in our fears?

The tools in the remainder of the chapter, as well as the remainder of the book, will help you work with those Black Holes, pulling you out of the darkness and toward the light that guides you.

Try This Tool: Identify Your Black Holes

You can't look for a black hole. By definition it's impossible to spot. But you can go looking for the symptoms of a black hole.

Identify those conversations or situations where you feel the following emotions: conflict, emotional sink holes, loneliness, alienation, despair, resistance, or confusion.

Use this space to write down one of these wretched-feeling spots in your life:

_____

_____

Your task for now is simply to identify these spots. It's enough simply to name it.

When you name your troubled spaces, it allows you to glimpse why you and your sweetheart might see the same situation and come to very different conclusions about what is true.

STRATEGY 2

Your Personal Gravity

How staying in your own business anchors you to your desire

Stay in your own business.

The Most Important Tool I can recommend:

Stay. In. Your. Own. Business.

All those years that David forgot to make the bed, I took it personally. I imagined he was neglecting the bed on purpose *to send me a message.*

It never once occurred to me that David just doesn't really care about making a bed.

It was never about me. It wasn't really even about David. David's not a morning person and each day, when he got out of bed, he was groggy and in search of coffee.

Byron Katie—in her excellent book entitled *Loving What Is*—talks about three kinds of business: yours, mine, and God's. Your business is the things you can control. My business is the things I can control. God's or The Universe's business is the things beyond human control.

Here's a quick overview of how these three businesses intertwine:

- It rains. **That's God's business.** I can't control the rain, and you can't control the rain.
- I want to run outside and feel all that rain on my skin, so I do. **That's my business.**
- You don't like the feeling of how rain makes your clothes stick to your skin, so you stay inside. **That's your business.**

But what if I say, "You should come outside with me! We'll get caught in the rain together and then drink pina coladas." Now I'm in your business, telling you what you should want and what you should do.

The Most Important Tool when it comes to finding clarity in your relationship is: Stay in Your Own Business.

All those years I came into our bedroom and saw that unmade bed, I got right into David's business:

- He's not making the bed on purpose to send me a message that I can't control him.

- Each time he "forgets" to make the bed, he's "forgetting" me.

Can you see that I am in David's business? I'm imagining his motivation. I'm making meaning of his actions.

But how can I know what David is thinking? That's his business.

Yet, we do this. All. The. Time.

This singular tool—Stay in Your Own Business—will help you get clear right away. When you hear yourself say, *My sweetheart should stop leaving crumbs on the counter*, you're in your sweetheart's business.

I hear you! But it's so rude to leave crumbs on the counter! I know. Maybe your sweetheart is rude.

But there are so many other options. Maybe your sweetheart is so hungry they can't be bothered to sweep away crumbs before they get eating that sandwich. Maybe your sweetheart doesn't mind crumbs. Maybe your sweetheart is more of a clean-the-kitchen-once-a-day sort of person, and will catch those crumbs in that cleanup.

None of these reasons matter. Because it's your sweetheart's business.

Anytime you're attributing meaning to your sweetheart's actions, you're in their business. Anytime you're telling your sweetheart what to do (even if it's only in your head), you're in their business.

Being in your sweetheart's business will sour your relationship quickly. Why? Because you have no power there. Every minute you ponder life from a position where you have no power, you will get frustrated/angry/sad/despondent and a host of other emotions.

Stay in your own business where you are powerful and you have agency and you can change things. When you stay in your own business, you anchor your feet on the terra firma that is your singular life.

This is the first step to clarity: in this moment, are you—mind, body, and spirit—seated directly in your locus of power? When you are, you will feel clear, because you have the agency to change things.

However, when you don't stay in your own business, the world gets confusing quickly because you make meaning of all the reasons your sweetheart does things. And your Inner Lizard, who we all know has a negativity bias and is always looking for the worst-case scenario in order to provide protection, will make up a story that is scary.

The truth of the unmade bed saga is that my husband doesn't value a made bed. At night, he's totally fine to crawl into a bed full of rumpled covers.

Yep. I wasted two decades of my life trying everything in my power to get that man to make our bed. I imagined horrid scenarios, rehearsing pain every day. Then I find out the simple reason he didn't make our bed is that he wasn't interested in a made bed.

The magic question that will help you discover that you are in someone else's business is to ask yourself, "Is that true?"

Is that true?

For years I chewed on the thought, *David should make the bed because I want him to make the bed*. But then I asked, *Is that true?*

Let's tackle this in two parts: "David should make the bed," and "David should do what I want him to do." Can you hear these two parts of how I'm in David's business? First, I'm telling him what to do: make the bed. Second, I'm telling him why he should do it: because I want it.

"David should make the bed." Is that true?

…Hmmm…well, I guess I can't be absolutely positive this is true. And, if it's not true, why *might* it not be true?

Will you believe me when I tell you the very first time I asked this question, *Why might it not be true that David should make the bed?* I immediately knew my husband didn't value walking into a room to see a made bed.

Suddenly, I was free. After 19 years.

David hadn't been sending me passive-aggressive messages all these years. He just didn't think about making the bed. Because it wasn't important *to him*.

Is that true? is the fundamental focus-changing-question that will help you get clear. Because it shifts your focus. What has felt absolutely certain is

Two Key Questions
Is that true?

Whose business am i in?

These are the two fundamental questions that will allow you to get out of The Black Hole of Confusion and find your way to clarity.

brought into question. When you ask yourself this question—*Is that true?*—your brain instantly explores things from a different point of view.

It allows you, in one small leap, to get past your biological imperative: your negativity bias, and that Amygdala Hijack. Instead of focusing on what's wrong, you're able to focus on all the other possibilities.

Exploration like this allows you to get clear.

When you ask, *Is it true?* you give yourself permission. Fabulous permission. Expansive permission. *Is it true?* allows your brain to think about things differently. You cultivate flexibility.

Flexibility is crucial to getting clear. This is because confusion breeds in places of your being where you are stuck.

Is it true? and other questions that challenge your Inner Lizard and relieve your Amygdala Hijack get you unstuck.

The more tools you collect that give you flexibility and get you unstuck, the more clear you will be able to get.

Now let's tackle the other half of my thought about the unmade bed, "David should do what I want him to do." This is a popular thought in my coaching practice. My clients aren't concerned about *my husband* doing what they want, but they always have a person. And they want that person to do what *they want* just because they want it.

"David should do what I want him to do." *Is that true?* It would be nice if it were true. It would be easier if it were true. It would cause less conflict if it were true.

So, I ask myself what would happen if it were always true, if David would ALWAYS do what I want him to do.

You know what happens? I'm instantly bored. I realize that an enormous part of what attracts me to David is that, although he cares about me and wants to make me happy, he will never, ever do something *just* to make me happy. Especially if that thing doesn't make *him* happy.

I am a people pleaser by nature. (I've trained myself out of most of this tendency because it isn't healthy for me.) I've spent a good portion of my life doing mental gymnastics with my desire so that I can accommodate other people's wishes.

David doesn't have that tendency and it has allowed me great freedom (once I learned to stop being a people pleaser myself).

Here's the freedom for me: If David is going on a hike with me, it's because *he wants to*. If David is talking to me, it's because *he wants to*. If David is cleaning the kitchen, it's because *he wants to*.

David doesn't do anything he doesn't want to do.

The magic of this quality is that I never—never ever—feel like I'm one of David's obligations. If he's with me, I feel wanted. Being wanted is one of the fundamental qualities to your happily ever after. (I talk about this a lot on my podcast, *Habits for Your Happily Ever After*. I hope you'll listen.)

It took me some time to see this quality as a freedom.

Gretchen Rubin's book *The Four Tendencies* helped me to put a name on this freedom. She describes four tendencies when it comes to how people relate to expectations like making the bed.

Rubin divides expectations into inner expectations—you want to write a book—and outer expectations—your family is hungry and wants you to cook them dinner. If you respond best to outer expectations and you're more likely to keep promises to other people, Rubin categorizes you as an Obliger.

I'm an Obliger. And believe me, I have felt obliged to do things in my life. How about you?

If you're a person who doesn't want anyone to have expectations of you—including yourself—Rubin categorizes you as a Rebel. Guess who is a Rebel in my home?

(The other two categories are Upholders—people who respond to both sorts of expectations—and Questioners—people who question all expectations and, essentially, turn all expectations into inner expectations. If you're interested in these distinctions, I encourage you to take her free quiz that will tell you if you're an Upholder, an Obliger, a Rebel, or a Questioner.)

It's really frustrating living with a Rebel especially when you see that pile of rumpled blankets. It's really frustrating to live with a Rebel except when you want to feel wanted.

No one makes me feel as wanted as my rebel husband.

The reason I feel so wanted is that he never ever does things he doesn't want to do. If he kisses me, it's because he wants to. If he texts me in the middle of the day to say, "Hey, I had fun with you last night," it's because he wants to.

And if he makes the bed, it will ONLY be because he wants to.

I'm not gonna lie to you. His rebel-I-do-what-I-want-quality frustrates me. One of the most frustrating moments is when I want him to make the bed, and he doesn't do it because he doesn't want to.

But when I ask the question, *Is it true that David should do what I want him to do?* on balance I can say, no.

No, Dave *shouldn't* just do what I want him to do.

Again, I get freedom when it comes to all those stories I told myself about the importance of making the bed or not making the bed. If I have to choose, I'll take the guy who *wants what he wants*. Especially exciting because he wants *me*.

Try This Tool: Stay in Your Own Business

Take a look at one or two of the mouse-sized details that you tend to fixate on and leap to the world-view that, without fixing this detail, your relationship is doomed.

Here's a list to get you thinking, but there's an infinite number of options:
- My sweetheart never kisses me hello.
- My sweetheart never invites me to go out for dinner.
- My sweetheart always finds fault with the clothes I wear.
- My sweetheart doesn't like to take vacations.
- My sweetheart doesn't like winter.
- My sweetheart only eats meat and potatoes and I want to have salads.
- My sweetheart doesn't want to get a dog, even though I want one so badly.
- My sweetheart won't attend our kids' ballgames.
- My sweetheart has too much stuff in our garage.

Put your complaint here:
_____

Put your next complaint here:
_____

Put your next complaint here:
_____

You can add as many blanks as you need.

This tool is continued on the next page.

Try This Tool: Stay in Your Business (continued)

Now consider, what is the story you tell yourself? Why is your relationship doomed because of this complaint? Write that story here:

_____
_____
_____
_____

Now ask yourself, *whose business am I in?* Mine? Yours? God's/the Universe's?

_____
_____

Next, ask yourself, is it true? (I encourage you to go global. Is it ALWAYS true?)

Yes?_____ Or no? Not ALWAYS?_____

Then ask yourself how **might** that **not** be true?

_____
_____

Finally, how can you stay in your *own* business?

_____
_____

Let's try one of the above examples:
- *My sweetheart never kisses me hello.*

What is the story you tell yourself when your sweetheart never kisses you hello?
- *My sweetheart isn't glad to see me.*

Whose business are you in?

- *My sweetheart's.*

Now, ask the question, **is it true?**

- *It feels true.* Take a breath here. Allow yourself to feel what you feel, noticing where that feeling lives inside your body.

Then ask, how **might** that **not** be true? This allows you to find a different story.

- *Maybe my sweetheart doesn't want to interrupt me.*
- *Maybe my sweetheart needs a few minutes to decompress and needs to be alone before connecting.*
- *Maybe my sweetheart never saw kissing hello modeled and didn't know that was a thing.*

Now, how can you stay in your own business?

- *I could ask myself if I want to kiss my sweetheart hello.*
- *I could kiss my sweetheart hello.*

This tool come straight from the work of Byron Katie. If you'd like to see more examples of this tool, go to www.TheWork.com.

What happens when you consider things from a different point of view?

Clarity comes more frequently and easily when we're able to be flexible about the viewpoint we have. The more you practice (and wow! This is a skill that takes some practice), the more clarity you will have in your relationship.

We all get stuck in Black Holes of Confusion because we don't question our point of view. We make a decision (or even an assumption) that our way is the only way to view the world.

Would you say that the mouse and the eagle live in different worlds? Or simply that they have different perspectives on the same world?

What would happen if you changed your perspective? Especially on those areas where you and your sweetheart have the biggest tangles?

OK. We've talked about how confusion traps you in a gravity-sucking Black Hole. You have two great ways to change your perspective so you can escape that confusion:

- Ask yourself, *Whose business am I in?*
- Ask the question, *Is it true?*

But what if you're not confused? What if you simply can't figure out what you want?

STRATEGY 3

Dive Deep into Your Desire

How to claim—or reclaim—your personal power and know what you want

How can you know precisely, exactly, specifically what you want?

Remember River and Phoenix? River was caught in a Black Hole of Confusion by thinking only about the possible rejection from Phoenix if Phoenix didn't want to buy a house together.

Inside that Black Hole, there was no light and River was stuck. River couldn't see the situation in any other way than *Phoenix either buys a house with me, or I will be forever lonely.*

Can you see how River is basing happiness on external circumstances? If Phoenix doesn't buy a house with River, then loneliness is the only other option.

Whose business is River in? Phoenix's business. All the power to bring River a happy life lies in Phoenix's hands.

You will never taste unfettered happiness if your happiness always resides outside your control. This is why it's so critical to *Stay in Your Own Business.*

But it's not enough for River to get out of Phoenix's business, River needs to get precisely, exactly, specifically clear about *River's* desire.

Desire is a driver of action. Wake up your desire for precisely, exactly, specifically what you want, and you will have courage to face your fears, and energy to take action.

Clarifying questions: *How do I feel? What do I want? What is it I don't want?*

Clarity comes when you understand your feelings. But feelings alone can be fickle. Feelings shift and change because you didn't sleep enough last night. Or because you downed a half gallon of ice cream two hours ago and now you're in sugar-withdrawal-rebound.

Feelings get clarified when you know what you want. Sometimes it's hard to know what you *do* want, so you investigate what you *don't* want.

When you answer these three questions—*How do I feel? What do I want? What is it I don't want?*—you will hone your desire. Your feelings won't drive the bus of your life. Instead, your feelings will become just one of many pieces of informational input to reveal your desire.

When you become a detective of your desires, those desires ignite intimacy in your life. You **get clear.**

Let's revisit the example of River who was confused and backed away from a **clean ask**. We'll examine: *What did River feel? What did River want? What was it that River didn't want?*

The first thing River feels is afraid. Except that isn't how River phrases it. River says, "I AM afraid." Rather than, "I FEEL afraid"

In order to overcome fear you need to stop *identifying* as afraid. You feel fear, yes. But you are not identified by your fear.

Remember the entire chapter you read called **Overcome Fear?** Here is that fear showing up first in the list of emotions River feels. And it's not enough to just add fear to the list and then move on to wants and don't wants.

Fear needs time. So, let's take that time and do a quick review. Until you overcome your fear, fear will keep you stuck in that Black Hole of Confusion..

Overcome Fear Review

Fear will run rampant until you harness your power to overcome it.

River felt afraid. Instead of simply naming to tame the feeling of fear, River's identity became *I AM afraid*. River then let the feeling of fear drive a ton of other thoughts:

- What if Phoenix thinks it's a BAD TIME to buy a house?
- What if Phoenix doesn't want to buy a house WITH ME?
- What if Phoenix only intends to live with me UNTIL a better offer comes along?

See how fear quickly gets out of control? If you let fear run wild, you will quickly end up in a Black Hole of Confusion the way I did with the unmade bed.

This review is continued on the next page.

Overcome Fear Review (continued)

Naming is Taming: When you name your fear, the emotion feels less overwhelming.
- River needs to ask, "How do I feel?" because naming a feeling tames a feeling.
- By naming the feeling—fear—River changes from I *am* scared to I *feel* scared.

Naming is Taming, so now that River has named this fear, it gets a little more manageable.

Befriend to Mend: When you treat the feeling like a friend, you don't resist fear. You welcome the feeling so it can inform you.

River says, "Hey, Friend Lizard, I appreciate your concern. Thanks for the warning. It's true, buying a house is scary."

When you befriend your fear, you stop resisting. The stress of fear is mostly our resistance. Notice how you feel when you welcome fear and its message rather than resisting.

Protect to Connect: You protect your fear by connecting with all the ways you're up to the task of handling that fear.

This is where River is gonna have a conversation with their Inner Lizard to point out their resilience and competencies.
- "It's true that buying a house is scary, but I've saved up some money, and I want to investigate all the options."
- "I'm flexible. When one idea doesn't work, I'm OK moving on to explore the next."

Now that River has overcome their fear, River is able to look at all their other feelings, as well as their wants and don't wants.

Let's return to the I feel…I want…I don't want tool.

River asks, "In addition to fear, how else do I feel?"
- I feel hopeful.
- I feel excited.
- I feel my dream coming true.

When River names fear as just one of *many* feelings, there's a chance to for all those other feelings to balance out the fear. Once you've named your feelings, proceed to asking what you want.

River asks, "What do I want?"
- I want to invest in my happily ever after with Phoenix.
- I want the adventure of buying a house with Phoenix because I've never done that, and Phoenix makes everything more fun.
- I want the feeling of connection that comes with shared work so Phoenix and I are teammates.

Now it's time to list the don't wants. The *I don't wants* will help River get super clear before asking Phoenix about buying the house.

When you explore what you *don't want*, what you *want*, and the *feelings* that arise, the trio of these questions help you gain clarity about the big picture of your own desire.

River asks, "What is it I don't want?"
- I don't want to wait any longer to invest in real estate.
- I don't want a partner who isn't IN THIS with me.

Going back and forth—between feelings, wants, and don't wants—allows River to gain clarity. Where previously all River could feel was the vulnerability that Phoenix wouldn't want to share a life together, now River sees another option that might be worse.

River asks, "What do I want AND don't want?"
- I do want to share my life and house with Phoenix.
- But if Phoenix isn't going to fully participate, I don't want the burden of an uncommitted partner.
- I'd rather buy the house on my own than have a partner who's only half committed.

Suddenly River feels a lot of clarity.

Putting it all together: River's list of I feel... I want... I don't want...

- I feel excited and hopeful at the idea of Phoenix and me taking this step together of buying a house.
- But if Phoenix doesn't want that commitment, I want to move on.
- I want to buy a house.
- I don't want to wait to secure my own future.
- I want to buy a house now.

River doesn't get to dictate how Phoenix will handle the house buying decision. But River can clearly state both fear and desire: "Phoenix, I'm afraid you're not ready for a deeper commitment. I don't want to lose what we have together. And I'm also clear that I want to buy a house. Do you want to buy a house with me?"

This is a **clean ask**.

We'll talk more about the difference between a clean and a dirty ask in the next chapter. For now, notice River's fears and desires both articulated aloud.

River was able to get to this clear articulation after spending time examining *I feel..., I want..., I don't want....* You will gain clarity as well when you unearth your desires with this tool.

But what if you're not confused, and you are wholly in touch with your desire but, still, you can't **get clear** about what you want?

Maybe you're asking the wrong question. Read on to discover how changing the question you ask impacts the clarity you feel.

Try This Tool: I feel...I want...I don't want...

Think of a situation that's bothering you (agitation, conflict, aimlessness), and describe that situation here:

_____
_____

As you consider this situation, what do you feel? Write all your various feelings here:

_____
_____

If you feel afraid, take your fear-feeling through the Overcome Fear Review above.

As you consider this situation, what do you most want? List your wants here:

_____
_____

As you consider this situation, what is it you **don't** want? List your **don't** wants here:

_____
_____

Now that you can see what you feel, what you want, and what you **don't** want, how do you see the situation differently? Write that here:

_____
_____

Note: Sometimes it's easier to identify what you don't want first. Feel free to start there.

STRATEGY 4

(Re)Map Your Universe
Because you may be navigating from an obsolete map

A cartographer is a person whose job it is to make maps. Cartographers collect and analyze data, then they take that data and present it in a way that conveys how "here" and "there" relate to each other.

What a cartographer sees, and thus the map they create, depends upon the question they ask. When the world was believed to be flat, a cartographer may have asked, "What lives at the edge, where the world comes to an end?"

A cartographer who asks this question will be looking for evidence of monsters at the edge of the world, or a waterfall where all the water from the oceans pour off. You and I both know, however, this cartographer will never find anything at the edge of the world because the earth is round.

There is no edge. The question itself is flawed.

Some of the questions you unwittingly ask in your relationship are equally flawed.

The wrong question

When you stay up late and then oversleep, it's tempting to stumble out into the kitchen and say, "Why didn't you wake me up? Now I'm late for work." We all want to be the child who has no agency, and is lifted from the pile of temptation, then plopped somewhere safe, a kiss planted on our head.

Actions have consequences. We don't like the consequences, and we try to get out of them. Blaming your sweetheart is one of the best ways to avoid the clarity of owning what's yours. And it's easy to do if you ask the right question (which is the wrong question if what you really want is relationship intimacy).

"Why didn't you wake me up?" is a great question if your underlying assumption is *my sweetheart should make the world perfect for me.*

But just as the world isn't flat, your sweetheart isn't in charge of making the world perfect for you.

When you believe the assumption, *my sweetheart should make the world perfect for me*, you treat your sweetheart lousy because now you can outsource all the responsibilities to your sweetheart. Then you can blame someone else, and you don't have to take responsibility, and that is a huge relief.

But I've gotta warn you: If you choose this sort of pass-the-buck approach to your relationship, you will miss out. You will never feel the confidence that comes from standing in your own power. You won't be able to look your sweetheart in the eye and see their respect reflected back at you.

If you want to taste clear, clean love, you need to accept the world as it is, including the unpleasant consequences. You can stay out late partying. No problem. But that choice comes with a twin: you feel pretty lousy the next day.

Your task, as a relationship-cartographer, is to update the map of your relationship universe regularly so you don't fall prey to the temptation to imagine a world that's more convenient, more lovely, or more tolerant of all your foibles.

When you accept reality, you might stumble out to the kitchen and apologize for the multiple times the alarm clock went off and you kept hitting snooze. You recognize how your behavior impacts your sweetheart and you take responsibility, "I hope I didn't keep you awake."

Try This Tool: Update Your Map

Look at the assumptions under the questions you're asking.

Think of a question you asked your sweetheart that caused conflict. Write that question here:
_____
_____

What are the assumptions you make when you ask that question? Write those assumptions here:
_____
_____

Example
The question: Why didn't you wake me up?
Assumption: My sweetheart is in charge of how long I sleep.

Mapping your universe means you constantly act like a cartographer, collecting data, then analyzing that data to get a clear vision of the world in which you live. This allows you to see the "here" and "there" of your actions and their consequences.

As you increase your relationship-cartography skills, you can avoid the Black Holes of Confusion. You will also increase your center of gravity, because when you see the world as it is—rather than a world of your invention—you can hone your desire about what you want and what you don't want.

You can use your map to guide you where you want to go.

In the previous strategy you learned to turn your desire into a driver of intimacy. Let's look at how your desire might clash with a desire your sweetheart has. You can navigate effectively only when you learn the details of your relationship topography.

You want toast with your morning coffee, you just don't want to be bothered with the resulting crumbs, so you make your toast and leave those crumbs sprinkled on the countertop. Cleaning crumbs can happen later.

When you make your morning toast and coffee, therefore, you walk away before wiping up the crumbs.

Then your sweetheart comes into the kitchen to make a morning smoothie. As your sweetheart opens the fridge and gets out the spinach, the wet spinach picks up your toast crumbs and your sweetheart is grossed out.

"Ew!" shouts your sweetheart, "You left crumbs all over this counter!" Your sweetheart wants a tidy kitchen. Your sweetheart doesn't want to clean up your crumbs.

Sometimes what you want or don't want is at odds with what your sweetheart wants and doesn't want. These are the moments we're tempted to lie to ourselves about the world we live in. We don't want to detour from our desires to make room for our sweetheart, so we invent a universe that's more to our liking.

Your invented universe in this moment might be: *My sweetheart is so demanding!* or, *My sweetheart is so persnickety.*

You can see why a universe where you think of your sweetheart as demanding or persnickety is preferable to the world where you should clean up your own crumbs, right? I'm mean, come on, cleaning crumbs is a hassle.

I know you think I'm being silly, but we all make up stories about our universe so we are the hero or heroine. The alternative is that we need to do things we don't want to do. Ick!

It is this intersection—where what you want (or don't want) bumps up against what your sweetheart wants (or doesn't want)—that becomes the breeding ground for a Black Hole of Confusion.

You don't want to let go of your wants (or your don't wants), but neither does your sweetheart.

A great fix for this roadblock is to ask a question that connects you and your sweetheart, rather than pitting you against each other.

In this crummy situation, your underlying assumption about the world in which you live sounds like this: "Why can't we just wipe up crumbs once a day when we clean the kitchen?"

It's true. This assumption fits your universe of wanting your toast and coffee and not wanting to clean crumbs. This is a great map of your universal desire.

Until.

Until you also realize you have another want: You want to live happily with your sweetheart.

Then you get tempted to do the same thing I did with my husband and our unmade bed: you simply say, "Well David should just want what I want."

And there it is: the cartographer's conundrum. Because while you are thinking, "My sweetheart should wipe up crumbs once a day," your sweetheart is thinking, "That crumb-leaver should wipe up their crumbs." You have a collision of universes.

You have a collision of universes because you're both working with maps that don't tell the truth. You're both afraid of giving up what you want.

That ancient map where the world was flat changed only after exploration and discovery of new facts changed the perception. The bigger the view of the world, the more accurate the map became.

The task of relationship clarity is no different. You need to explore a bigger picture and make discoveries about your shared lives so that each time you're individually mapping your universe, you have room to include all the hills and valleys in your sweetheart's life as well as your own.

To get a bigger picture and be willing to explore more options requires that you overcome your fear that warns you about *getting less than* or about *sacrificing*. These fears are your Inner Lizard's negativity bias trying to protect you.

When you see a fear like that, Name it to Tame it. Then Befriend to Mend and get curious.

Your assumption about the universe when you can only see *your* wants and don'ts wants is, "Why can't we just wipe up crumbs once a day when we clean the kitchen?" Instead, try changing the question to, "How can we both use the kitchen and be mindful of each other?"

This question doesn't automatically assume you have to clean wipe up your crumbs after your toast, but it does recognize the "here" and "there" of your shared kitchen.

When you map out the kitchen as a shared space, and your actions in that space impact your sweetheart too, you realize it's important to have agreements. You could propose the agreement, "I'm happy to wipe all the counters in the evening after dinner, but it's hard for me to remember to do that all day long."

In this world your shared assumption is, "We want to live harmoniously in the kitchen."

The key is to notice *what is your underlying assumption?* And is that assumption based on solid cartography of the relationship?

The Cartographer's Question

When there's conflict, blame, or shame, examine the question you're pondering and take a look at the underlying assumptions.

Then change the question to reflect the world as it is rather than the world you assumed existed.

Here are some common assumptions and a corresponding reframe of the question.

When it comes to the universe of a shared bed:
- **Conflict:** Why didn't you wake me up?
- **Underlying assumption:** You are in charge of my sleeping and waking.
- **Cartographer's Question:** How can I get myself up on time?

You want what you want and you don't want what you don't want. Isn't that obvious? While it's fun to impersonate Peter Pan and have no responsibility, your relationship won't last if you don't accept responsibility for your own actions.

When it comes to the universe of a shared kitchen:
- **Conflict:** Why are there crumbs on the counter?
- **Underlying assumption:** We clean the kitchen once a day.
- **Cartographer's question:** How can we live harmoniously in one kitchen?

You want to treat the kitchen the way you did when you were single. It's a hassle that your sweetheart needs things to be spotless every second. Instead of assuming your way is best, make an agreement to navigate your differences in temperament and taste.

When it comes to the universe of extended family:
- **Conflict:** Each year there's tension when it comes to how/when/where to spend the holidays.
- **Underlying assumption:** We can talk about that tomorrow.
- **Cartographer's question:** What do we need to talk about today so that our holidays are pleasant "tomorrow"?

You want an intimate relationship; you just want every conversation to be easy. Consequently, you avoid the discussion about calendars because you know you'll be asked to sacrifice some vacation days to visit your sweetheart's family. When you don't have the difficult conversations, the delightful ones become more scarce.

When it comes to the universe of your work environment(s):
- **Conflict:** Why do I have to make every sacrifice to accommodate your work schedule?
- **Underlying assumption:** My job is more important than yours.
- **Cartographer's question:** How can we both feel like our work is valued?

You make more money. Isn't it obvious your job should take priority? Not if you want an intimate relationship. Think about all the ways your sweetheart is making it easy for you to have both: a job you love and a relationship you desire. How can you be appreciative of your sweetheart's sacrifices? Or prioritize your sweetheart's work schedule?

When it comes to raising kids:
- **Conflict:** I'm the only one who drives him to baseball. Why can't you ever help?
- **Underlying assumption:** Children need to participate in club-level-sports.
- **Cartographer's question:** What kind of opportunities do we want to give our kids and how can we make that happen?

When you decided to have kids, you didn't discuss every detail of what that would entail. Now you find you're more bus driver than anything else. It's amazing how much it helps to clarify your shared values when it comes to raising children. When you feel burdened by the work of parenting, remind yourself why the choices you're making are (or are not) in line with those values.

Try This Tool: The Cartographer's Question

Try reframing your map using The Cartographer's Question.

Think of a repeated **conflict** in your relationship. Write that here:
_____
_____

What is the **underlying assumption** in this conflict? Write it here:
_____
_____

If you feel afraid, take your fear-feeling through the Overcome Fear Review above.

Ask a question that reflects the world as it is in a way that seeks the best solution for both you and your sweetheart. Write your **Cartographer's Question** here:
_____
_____

A healthy relationship means you get clear about the burdens and joys of sharing a life together. Then you get clear about how to *share* those burdens and joys. You take time to collect all the data that makes up your shared life.

When you study that data, a universe of circumstances unique to you and your sweetheart will emerge. As you navigate that shared world, you find the questions that allow your basic assumptions to be, *Since this is our shared world, how do we get from "here" to "there"* **together?**

You may not always agree about the route to take, but it's amazing how much you'll reduce conflict and foster intimacy when, at least, you're talking about the same universe of circumstances.

STRATEGY 5

You Won't Always Agree
How to value love more than being right

Many couples come to coach with me to discover "the truth." Here's the truth: there will be times in your shared lives that you and your sweetheart are each crystal clear about "the truth." And, yet, you disagree about the details of that "truth."

Clarity is crucial to good communication with your sweetheart.

And, kindness is more important than clarity.

The way you handle conflict matters more than if you share lifestyle choices like the same topping on pizza, or attending church, or having children. The way you handle conflict will be a large contributor to the character of your marriage. Perhaps it is *the biggest* contributor.

Why am I putting this section in the **Get Clear** chapter? Because you will both feel crystal clear about some things. You'll believe, deep in your soul, that you are right and your sweetheart is wrong.

Then, an interesting thing happens: Over time, you change your mind. You see things differently. You might even get clear that you were wrong in the past; or at the very least, you'll see that your sweetheart wasn't wrong.

The purpose of this section is to give you a tool for when you and your sweetheart both feel clear, but you can't *agree*, and it's causing serious conflict. This tool has three parts: The Pressure Relief Valve, The Emergency Response Plan, and The Reconnection Plan.

Here's a hopeful message: The things you're fighting about today will matter far less in twenty years, if at all.

Here's a warning: The way you fight—and by that I mean silent treatments vs open-hearted conversation, or any other dysfunctional conflict pattern—the way you fight will determine the character of your relationship in twenty years.

It feels like the crumbs on the counter are the most important thing in the world right now. I know. Believe me, *I know*. But I've talked to many people whose spouse has died and they'd give anything to see those crumbs again. Because the crumbs mean their sweetheart was eating toast near them.

When time passes, the details matter less.

Right now, you might be struggling to get clear. But clarity is built on understanding. There are things unfolding in your life now that won't make sense to you until years have passed. I understood my husband (and myself) differently after twenty years. That different understanding enabled me to have a different sort of conversation about the unmade bed.

When I was capable of a different sort of conversation, I regretted that I hadn't been more kind in the past. I don't want you to have this regret. Hence the trifecta tool in this strategy.

While you gain understanding through the years of your marriage, each fight you have with your sweetheart is creating a template for the way you treat each other. *How* you resolve something matters more than the *specific solution* you find.

You'll find things about which you cannot agree. How you handle the tension of this disagreement creates the template of your relationship.

Some people get nervous with too much conflict, while others get nervous pausing a conflict. So, make sure to envision all three elements of this *Kindness is More Important than Being Right* tool: The Pressure Relief Valve, The Emergency Response Plan, and the Reconnection Plan.

The Pressure Relief Valve

Your water heater has a pressure relief valve. Typically, water enters the tank and gets heated up so that, when you turn on your faucet, you get hot water. There's only a limited amount of water that can enter the tank, though, because when water is heated, it expands.

If too much water accidentally gets into your tank, the pressure relief valve is designed to let off excess steam. Otherwise, your water heater tank would blow up from too much pressure.

Your marriage needs a pressure relief valve so that, when excess pressure is building, you don't blow up your relationship.

Start by creating your own, unique, pressure relief valve. The pressure relief valve on your water heater wasn't made when your water heater was about to explode. No. Someone put thought into that valve during a moment of calm so that safety was anticipated.

Give your marriage the same gift. Create a pressure relief valve to use when a conflict is threatening to explode your marriage.

Try This Tool: The Pressure Relief Valve

Kindness is more important than being right, so learn to request a pause before tempers explode.

During a moment of calm, decide upon a phrase or a gesture that can be your signal. Agree that when either of you use this phrase or gesture—your Pressure Relief Valve—the conflict gets paused.

Write down the word or gesture that will be your Pressure Relief Valve here:

_____

_____

ex: put your hands together in a T to make the time-out symbol.

For some of you, it is exceedingly difficult to pause a conflict before it is resolved.

You feel nervous stopping a conflict before you've reached a resolution. But simply the discipline to be able to pause is helpful. The pause tells your sweetheart—as well as that panicked part of yourself—that your relationship is bigger than this singular conflict. You're going to care for the big relationship by pausing this small conflict.

The Emergency Response Plan

During the same calm sit-down when you plan your Pressure Relief Valve, create an Emergency Response Plan too.

If there is a horrible catastrophe in our city—like a fire or an earthquake—there are dedicated help centers where people can go to regroup.

We have a community center near our home that is dedicated to this purpose. I have met with local Red Cross officials to check that the showers, potable water, and supplies there are in order just to make sure we're prepared in the event of a disaster. The Red Cross coordinator had a lovely checklist that made it easy to be sure we were prepared.

You need a similar checklist for your relationship.

You've called for a break with your Pressure Relief Valve. Now, identify those crucial things you need to deal with the catastrophe. The catastrophe you're dealing with is not an earthquake, but an Amygdala Hijack.

Identify things that calm your system, and relax the parts of your physical body that are in fight/flight/freeze mode. Adrenaline rushing through your system is not going to help you resolve your conflict peacefully.

Does it help you to take a walk? Or is it more helpful to you to take a shower? Maybe doing something with your hands like cleaning the dishes or knitting will help you to regroup.

The purpose of your Emergency Response Plan is to locate things that soothe you before you *need* soothing. Find that something, whatever it is for you, that will calm the amygdala part of your brain that just got triggered by your conflict.

I recommend something sensual, something that your body can feel. When you increase your heart-rate with exercise you literally blow off steam by breathing harder. You can feel the adrenaline of that Amygdala Hijack get discharged from your body.

Water can help with that too. When you feel water against your skin you are more awake to your senses. Your body has time to notice there's no impending danger.

Another choice is to give yourself a total change of scenery. When you change your environment, you stop the pattern of escalation and you literally see things from a different point of view.

For those of you who get overwhelmed by conflict, this Emergency Response Plan helps you to regroup. You can calm the frightened part of you that lost control. You get your breath regulated. You flush the adrenaline out of your body.

Try This Tool: Emergency Response Plan

Kindness is more important than being right. Create a checklist of things that calm you (so you can be kind). List three things that help calm your nervous system here:

1._____
2._____
3._____

Example:
1. Shoot baskets in the driveway
2. Do a big scrub of the bathroom
3. Go run an errand

For those of you who get nervous taking a pause before conflict is resolved, focus on giving your frightened sweetheart space.

When you give your sweetheart space, you're creating a relationship template that's focused on meeting each person's needs before solutions are explored. This approach magnifies the tenderness you offer to each person and diminishes the penchant to find a "correct" solution. The template, then, is about kindness over being right.

As you take your break—but after you've calmed your own body—try imagining the conflict from your sweetheart's point of view. See if you can articulate your sweetheart's position.

Some of you need a break during a conflict. For others, that break is terrifying. When you know when you'll talk again, it's easier to pause. That is why the Reconnection Plan is crucial and needs to be decided *before* the break begins. Let's look at that next.

Create a Reconnection Plan

Some people get panicked when there is a break—even a planned break—in a relationship. I'm afraid of divorce, so any break makes me very nervous.

A Reconnection Plan calms that fear. Yes, you'll take a break. But there will also be a time to regather. And you get to know how and when that will happen before the break begins. This is the safety net that will hold your relationship together even as you take a break.

At the same meeting when you establish your Pressure Relief Valve and your Emergency Response Plan, develop your Reconnection Plan.

There are a few elements that I believe make a Reconnection Plan effective:

- Pause long enough to lose yourself in another activity. This resets your amygdala.
- Don't pause so long as to cause perseveration, because fear will return.
- Create an agreed meeting place.
- Touch. Studies show that touch softens conflict and speeds resolution.
- Purposefully begin the conversation differently, each person demonstrating they've considered their sweetheart's point of view.

Try This Tool: The Reconnection Plan

Kindness is more important than being right.

In the same way you've agreed to pause and then to part ways for a bit, agree to come back together. Having a reliable Reconnection Plan helps ease tension for people who are nervous to pause a conflict before it resolves.

How long is your pause? (I recommend at least an hour, but I don't recommend pausing for days.)

_____
_____

Where will you meet at the agreed time?

_____
_____

Try This Tool: The Reconnection Plan (continued)

Touch helps. What is a reliable way you can touch each other to create calm, but not smother someone who might still need some space?

_____
_____

Agree to seek understanding rather than proving you're right. What helps you with this intention? Write that here:

_____
_____

Example:
We will break for two hours; then we'll meet on the turquoise couch, hold hands, and try to articulate the other person's point of view.

We all want to avoid conflict if we can. Since some measure of conflict is inevitable when you live together, it's kind and tender to your relationship to have a plan in place for how to deal effectively with conflict.

My hope for you is that, as you handle conflict tenderly and with kindness, the trust in your relationship will be fostered and a deep intimacy will grow.

You will not always have clarity, or you and your sweetheart will be clear that you differ. This trio of tools allow you to be kind and loving even when you don't understand why something is hurting.

Chapter Review

- **The Black Hole of Confusion.** You get lost in a Black Hole of Confusion when you don't know what what you want or when your sweetheart can't seem to hear your requests. On the other hand, you also get lost when the romance of blending creates the illusion that your sweetheart experiences the world exactly as you do.
- **Own Your Personal Gravity.** Two questions allow you to find clarity in a new way: *Whose business am I in?* and *Is that true?*
- **Dive Deep into Your Desire.** Three questions—*What do I feel? What do I want? What is it I don't want?*—help you get precisely, exactly, specifically clear about what you want.
- **Map Your Universe.** When you pair your wants (and don't wants) with your sweetheart's wants (and don't wants), life can get complex. Question your assumptions to regularly update the map with which you navigate your shared lives.
- **You Won't Always Agree.** Three rescue principles—The Pressure Relief Valve, The Emergency Response Plan, and The Reconnection Plan—help you surf your conflict with more gentleness and create a template of kindness in your marriage.

You've just taken in a lot of information.

To make real changes, you need time to synthesize.

What will help you turn what you just read into a habit you can practice?

STEP THREE

Ask Cleanly
Because a clean ask inspires a clean response.

You think you're asking cleanly. You're not.

It's a lot of work to **overcome your fear** and **get clear**. It's so much easier to opt out of the work and expect your sweetheart to do the work for you.

We treat communication like it's a game of tag. *Tag! I got you. Your turn.*

Remember River who wants to buy a house? River's afraid Phoenix doesn't want to invest in a future together. This fear dirties River's ask and it sounds like this: "Housing prices are dropping around here."

Phoenix can't even find an ask in there—dirty or clean. It's a statement, right? River hasn't *given* a **clean ask** because River is held hostage by fear.

River is playing tag rather than communicating. Speaking words so Phoenix will say the words River longs to hear.

River wants Phoenix to respond, "What makes you say that, River? Why are you concerned with housing prices?" But see how this makes Phoenix responsible for *giving curiosity* to River?

Communication is giving and receiving.

Instead of harnessing fear, River tagged Phoenix with a bunch of words strung together and essentially said, "You're responsible for figuring out what I want and driving this conversation forward."

There's a big payoff for this strategy of tag: when your sweetheart responds poorly, you get to feel like your sweetheart is the incompetent one.

You got to avoid the tough work of overcoming fear and getting clear and you get a convenient place to blame, shame, scold or offer the ever-friendly *cold shoulder*.

You communicated.

Except you didn't. You simply dumped a word-salad in your sweetheart's lap.

It's understandable why you don't want to do the work to make a clean ask. We all want to avoid that work. It takes time, self-reflection, responsibility. It's so much easier to opt out.

The bummer is, the alternative is worse: confusion, frustration, loneliness, and alienation.

When you play word-tag and handoff your *confusion* – instead of your *communication* – to your sweetheart, your sweetheart will *think* they heard you, and will respond.

But then you run a big risk.

What if your sweetheart's response has nothing—not a single thing—to do with your request/announcement/newsflash?

Then you're off to the races: spinning a tale of misunderstanding by tagging each other. You holler or hush up. You get hurt, so you hurt back. You feel lonely and abandoned, so you leave or you build a wall of protection.

When you learn to employ the **clean ask**, you'll build trust with your sweetheart, and avoid the drama that results when you blame, shame, scold, or freeze out your sweetheart. And Bonus! You're much more likely to get what you want.

In Chapters 1 and 2, improving your communication was an internal job: You are the only one who has the power to **overcome your fears**. You are the only one who has the power to **get clear** about your desires.

You've done the challenging internal work. Now it's time to reach toward your sweetheart and speak your truth. No drama. No baggage. Just a **clean ask**.

A clean ask takes responsibility for the communication so you can give your request to your sweetheart and let them take full control so they can respond to your request.

This is true whether you're asking something simple like, "Would you cook dinner Thursday?" or something complex like, "If I make this job change, will you be able to take up the slack around our home, because I won't have energy for both?"

Here are the tools you'll learn in this chapter to help you create a clean ask over and over:

In this chapter...

You'll learn the transformational power of The Clean Ask.

- **The Clean Ask Formula** has three elements. You'll learn each of the elements so you know when you are (or are not) asking cleanly
- **What does a dirty ask sound like?** We all ask dirty sometimes. You'll learn to identify your Dirty Ask Strategy so you can be watchful when it shows up
- **How to design your clean ask.** You'll learn how to stay in your own business as you ask cleanly as well as learn to phrase your ask such that it has a "yes" or "no" implied answer
- **How to sprout love.** Cultivate *the art* of the clean ask so that intimacy will grow in your relationship
- **How to stay clean** even when your sweetheart asks dirty

STRATEGY 1

The Clean Ask Formula
Feeling + Desire = A Clean Ask

Here is the clean ask formula: Feeling + Desire = Clean Ask.

State your fear (Name It to Tame It); then state your clear desire (I Want…I Don't Want…) to make a clean ask. This is the simple formula of the clean ask. But, as you already know, it's anything but easy.

Most often when communication is challenging, that vulnerable feeling is often fear.

Fear you won't get what you want. Fear you won't be loved. Fear your sweetheart will reject you. But when you name your feeling, you immediately tame it. Getting that feeling out into the fresh air takes the boogieman element away from those feelings that want to hide and haunt.

Fear is stingy. A clean ask is generous, not stingy. Fear will keep sabotaging your ability to ask cleanly. When you can **overcome fear**, you feel generous toward your sweetheart and yourself.

Clarity is empowering. A clean ask is clear, direct, and powered with agency.

Confusion, on the other hand, has no traction. Confusion will keep you spinning your wheels, spraying muddy ultimatums and accusations. When you can **get clear**, you respect yourself and your sweetheart.

Here's my promise: As scary and vulnerable as the clean ask is, it's also magnetic. The clean ask formula will draw you and your sweetheart together and deepen your intimacy. Why? Because we all need to be needed.

When you **ask cleanly** for something you want or need, you're saying to your sweetheart, "I need you in my life." That's cultivating belonging and intimacy.

A clean ask invites your sweetheart to belong in your relationship

When you ask cleanly, you invite your sweetheart into your life. You invite them to be a part of your shared life when you ask your sweetheart to take out the trash, or listen to you while you vent about your bad day. You let your sweetheart know you want them to kiss you. A dirty ask, on the other hand, pushes your sweetheart away. When you make a dirty ask, you alienate your sweetheart with shame, accusation, or control and confusion.

The clean ask invitation lets your sweetheart know you want them, need them, and love them. It's a reach for connection and we all crave the belonging of connection.

Your clean ask is so respectful that it becomes an irresistible invitation.

That doesn't guarantee your sweetheart will always say yes to your clean ask. But your sweetheart will always feel important in your life when you ask cleanly, and you will always feel kind. This pairing makes hearing "no" much easier to swallow.

We're all afraid of hearing "no" in response to our clean ask, but the truth is a *clean no* is much easier to handle than the drama and wounding that result from a *dirty ask*. We'll talk about a graceful and loving "no" in Chapter 5, *Affirm Lovingly*.

Why state your feeling? Because it's vulnerable and vulnerability is at the heart of intimacy. When you're vulnerable, you draw out the naturally compassionate and empathetic humanity in your sweetheart. This opens the door to connection.

Why does it matter to be clear about what you desire? Because your sweetheart has a whole litany of things in their brain that they want you to know about them. Each time you communicate a specific desire, you offer an invitation to your sweetheart to have desires too.

When you share how you feel, then say what you want, it's like inviting the list inside your sweetheart's brain to come out to play. As you each share feelings and desires with curiosity and open hearts, your communication gets filled with vitality and energy.

Be precise so you invite your sweetheart to engage exactly where you are.

Here's some examples of clean asks:

- I'm feeling resentful. I don't want to take out the trash. Could you please do it?
- I feel emotional and fragile. I just need to talk. Do you have time to sit and listen to me for a bit?
- I love you. I want your lips on mine. Would you give me a kiss?

Try This Tool: The Clean Ask Formula

The Clean Ask Formula has three parts: a feeling, a desire, and a question that implies a yes or no answer (though thoughtful responses are welcomed).

Feeling: First tend to your own feelings by naming your feeling. What do you feel? (If it's fear, use the 3 steps to overcome your fear.)

_____
_____

Name It to Tame It:_____
Befriend to Mend:_____
Protect to Connect:_____

Desire: Next, write down what you want. (If you're unsure, use the space below to hone your desire.)

_____

I want…_____
I don't want…_____

Question: Now how can your sweetheart give you what you want? Phrase your ask such that your sweetheart can answer you cleanly with a "yes" or a "no." (Longer answers welcome.)

_____
_____

Example:

I'm lonely and feeling insecure. I'd love it if you'd look me in the eye when you come home and tell me you're glad to see me. Could you make a point of greeting me each time you come home?

STRATEGY 2
Avoid the Dirty Ask
Because a dirty ask inspires alienation and distance

We tend towards the *dirty* ask:
- "Could we get the trash out on time for once?"
- "You should listen to me."
- "You never kiss me anymore."

A dirty ask never gets you what you want. Instead, it alienates your sweetheart, and you're even further from the intimacy you crave.

Remember in Chapter 1 when we talked about fear's many disguises? Now we'll examine how those disguises create a dirty ask.

Fear disguised as avoidance

Remember River and Phoenix and their "conversation" about buying a house? Avoidance is what River used to hide from fear: "Housing prices are dropping around here."

Some people want to hide from feelings because feelings can be overwhelming. But this disengagement makes it challenging to connect with your sweetheart. Your sweetheart can't *feel you* because you are *avoiding feeling*.

There's nothing there. Nothing to connect to.

If you use this strategy to avoid your feelings, your dirty ask will sound something like this:
- Do you know which day the trash gets picked up?
- Whatcha doin'?
- Whatdya think of my new shirt?

Look at how each of these is vague. Your sweetheart could respond to them many different ways.

"Whatcha doin'?" is a perfectly fine question, but not effective if what you wanted was to have your sweetheart listen to you. And yet, we've all done it. See how disguising your fear as avoidance *avoids* getting what you want?

The third example is one I see all the time in my coaching practice. It's a perfectly fair question to ask what your sweetheart thinks of your new shirt. But what you really wanted was a kiss. Did you ask cleanly for that kiss? Nope.

When avoidance is your Dirty Ask Strategy, it's nearly impossible to get what you want in your relationship. After all, you're avoiding it.

Fear disguised as anger

Instead of, "Housing prices are dropping around here," if River used anger to disguise fear, River could accuse Phoenix, "You never do anything around this house."

We use anger and accusation to hide from feelings because it gives the illusion of power. We feel powerless to get what we want, so we blame and accuse. This strategy of dirty asking alienates your sweetheart.

I have never met a person who was inspired to be more intimate because they were accused of failing. Have you?

When you disguise your fear as anger your dirty ask might sound like this:

- You never take the trash out.
- You always ignore me.
- You never show me any kind of affection.

If you hear yourself blaming or accusing on a regular basis, this is a chance for you to get curious about your personal agency and power.

When anger is your Dirty Ask Strategy, you might as well lock tender intimacy in a vault because you'll never access it.

Fear disguised as suspicion

Instead of, "Housing prices are dropping around here," River could see evidence for all sorts of reasons Phoenix doesn't want to buy the house. The two of them are at the hardware store and Phoenix doesn't want to buy mouse traps. *Aha!* thinks River, *Phoenix doesn't care if our home gets overrun with rodents because Phoenix has no plans to stay with me long term.*

We feel unworthy, so we stack up thousands of reasons we can't have what we want and then imagine our sweetheart is the culprit doing the stacking. It's a magical moment in my coaching practice when I can help a person like this laugh at that ridiculous tower of imprisonment that they have built all on their own. Laughter is a great tool to unlock suspicion.

This strategy drives your sweetheart away because they just get *this feeling* that they're doing something wrong. So, your sweetheart backs away. From you.

When you disguise your fear as suspicion your dirty ask might sound like this:

- What message are you sending me when you don't take out the trash?
- Why are you making that face at me?
- Wait. Why are you kissing me? What do you want from me?

When suspicion is your Dirty Ask Strategy, your sweetheart will always feel like the enemy hiding in your home. As a result, you make it difficult to *receive* the love your sweetheart offers.

Fear disguised as control

Instead of, "Housing prices are dropping around here," River would say, "We have an appointment with a realtor on Saturday at 11:00am."

Control as a Dirty Ask Strategy gives the illusion of, well, control. And, you may have control, but what you don't have is intimacy. This is because you're the boss of your sweetheart's choices, agency, or imagination.

This strategy erases your sweetheart. It will keep you safe maybe—until true disaster strikes—but very, very lonely.

When you disguise your fear as control, your dirty ask may sound like this:

- Take the trash out. Now.
- Listen to me. No. Not like that. I said, LISTEN.
- Kiss me. Ew! Not like that.

When control is your Dirty Ask Strategy, you'll reduce your sweetheart to a shadow. You'll feel the brunt of every chore, and you won't be able to truly relax, because then you'd lose control.

We all make dirty asks on a regular basis. This is because it takes mindfulness and practice to ask cleanly. I recommend you notice your Dirty Ask Strategy. Don't get too worked up over your dirty asks. Name them. Wave at them. Laugh at them.

Naming is much like the Name It to Tame It strategy to overcome fear. When you name a dirty ask, it's like turning on the light to see the

Try This Tool: Identify Your Dirty Ask Strategy

It helps to know yourself better. When you know yourself better (including your dirty ask strategy) you can behave better.

Which of the above best describes your go to strategy? (Avoidance, suspicion, anger, or control)

_____

When you can notice your dirty ask—with a scientist's objectivity—it will reduce shame and invite compassion. Recall a moment when you asked dirty and write that here:

_____
_____

Name: Now liberate yourself from the dirty ask. Start by naming your fear or your hidden desire here:

_____
_____

Wave: Continue to free yourself from the toxicity of your dirty ask by waving—which is really just noticing—at it and offering yourself compassion. Why are you afraid? What else are you feeling? What do you want? And why is that desire understandable?

_____
_____

Laugh: What's funny about this situation? What's funny about your dirty ask style? Notice how laughter reduces shame. Notice how much gentler you feel when you can laugh at your dirty ask. Write down why your dirty ask style is funny here:

_____
_____

lump in the chair is a blanket, not the monster it appeared to be in the dark.

Waving is like Befriend to Mend. Have compassion for yourself and why you made a dirty ask. Maybe you're hungry, or tired, or this is not the first time you've asked. When you are gentle with yourself, you're more gentle with everyone else.

When I make a dirty ask these days, I laugh almost immediately. "That was your hungry wife talking," I say. "We better get her fed before she bites your head off."

Laughter frees you from most dirty communication (with the exception of sarcasm). When you can laugh, the gentle part of you is wide awake. Gentle people don't make dirty asks. So, find a way to laugh at your dirty ask.

Walk yourself through that same dirty ask. Use the Name-Wave-Laugh tool to increase your tenderness.

Your dirty asks will fade as you name, wave, laugh, and offer tender compassion.

Then turn your attention to designing your clean asks.

STRATEGY 3

Design a Clean Ask

How to stay in your own business and stop arguing with reality

In this section we'll examine how to clean up a dirty ask. I'll give you some examples of a dirty ask, then, together, we'll explore how to apply the tools you've gotten so far in this book to clean up those dirty asks.

Let's go back to the two tools to help you get clear:
- Is that true?
- Stay in Your Own Business

Let's take a look at how each of these tools help to clean up a dirty ask.

Is that true?

This is a magical phrase for your relationship. It works well to ask your sweetheart, "Is that true?" when they accuse you of something that doesn't feel true to you.

But the real magic of this little phrase is to use it with *yourself*. We all stew and chew on phrases in our brain and then those phrases leak out into a dirty ask like:

"You never take the trash out."

This dirty ask leaked out because you've been chewing and stewing on questions like, *Why doesn't my sweetheart love me enough to know to take out the trash?* Your brain answers the questions you give it.

When you apply *Is that true?* to a thought like this one, it unlocks your anger and resentment. It does this because you are suddenly asking a different question and that engages your curiosity about something different.

"You never take the trash out." Is that true? Never? Absolutely never?

Now your brain serves up a time, 18 months ago, when you were willing to let the trash overflow so completely that there were literally eggshells laying on the kitchen floor. Your sweetheart actually scooped up those eggshells and took the trash out.

The minute you let yourself find a singular exception to "never," your curiosity revs up. *Are there other times my sweetheart took the trash out?* And suddenly you're off to the races and the ask gets less dirty:

"You rarely take out the trash."

This is still far from a clean ask, but you got unstuck. Remember that when your fear gets disguised as anger it's like locking your sweetheart out. Out of the possibility of ever getting it right.

Anger stops the flow of intimacy. By questioning the veracity of "You *never* take the trash out," we've gotten the flow started again.

Now let's look at how we can take "You rarely take the trash out" and turn it into a real live *clean ask*.

First of all, what feeling do you have?

- You feel overwhelmed.
- You feel like it's unfair.
- You feel taken for granted or put upon.
- You feel resentful.

So, let's get that feeling out in the open because a feeling is the first part to a clean ask:

"Sweetheart, you're making me feel resentful."

Close! You've articulated a feeling: *resentful*. But let's apply *Is it true?* here again. Can you be absolutely certain it's true that your sweetheart is *making* you resentful?

Hmm. Tempting. I hear your certainty. *Obviously! It's my sweetheart's fault that I'm resentful because they ~~never~~ rarely take out the trash.*

The magic of the *Is it true?* tool is curiosity rather than certainty.

Once you find the exception and realize your sweetheart MAY have taken out the trash ONCE, you can also get curious about what created a situation wherein your sweetheart was inspired, all on their own, to take out the trash.

You found it! You neglected the trash so thoroughly that your sweetheart finally saw the overflowing trashcan. This begs the question: is your sweetheart MAKING you resentful? Or is it your penchant to empty the trash early that's making you resentful?

I still hear you. *Rebecca*, you're saying to me, *You're being ridiculous. Are you telling me that I have to live with eggshells on my floor all the time in order for my sweetheart to empty the trash?*

No. I'm not telling you that.

But I am asking you to consider that option.

I am asking you to get *curious* about that option. Because it's in this expansive, audacious curiosity where you'll find the clean ask. (And I promise to deal with the unfairness of the overflowing trashcan more in Chapter 6, Build Boundaries.)

When you can get *curious* about where your resentment is coming from, you're able to ask cleanly. Curiosity replaces certainty. You're no longer certain that your sweetheart NEVER empties the trash. And now you're no longer certain that your sweetheart is MAKING you resentful.

Now you're free to find a clean ask:

"Sweetheart, I'm feeling resentful."

This is a great first half of the clean ask formula. You're articulating your feeling. You're owning your feeling. And your feelings can't be wrong.

If your sweetheart disputes your statement, "I'm feeling resentful," I invite you to say, "This is just how I feel. I'm not blaming you. I'm including you in my life. Part of my life is my feelings. I'm feeling resentful."

If you've had a long history of blame in your relationship, it may take some time for this to sink in. Your sweetheart may have built a big brick wall so they feel protected from your angry outbursts and your blame.

Be patient. Keep owning your feelings out loud rather than blaming your sweetheart for causing your feelings. This takes time. Especially if you need to go through a period of reparation.

In the meantime, let's create the second half of the clean ask formula: Feeling + Desire = Clean Ask.

You've got the first half, the feeling: "I'm feeling resentful." Now locate your desire. At first it might still sound dirty:

"I want you to take out the trash for once!"

This is an improvement over "You never take out the trash." It's still shy of a super-duper clean ask. But let's look at the improvement:

"I want you to take out the trash for once" is a desire. "You never take out the trash" is not a desire. It's an accusation.

When you get to this stage of a clean ask – "I want you to take out the trash for once!" – celebrate. Celebrate because your anger is flowing rather than blocked.

Anger is a facilitative emotion. It begs for change. The women's suffrage moment was fueled by anger. The civil rights movement was fueled by anger. Anger announces an injustice and begs for change.

Anger isn't afraid to ask for what it wants. Anger is demanding. Clear. Welcome the clarity that anger offers you.

Then, even as you welcome that clarity, continue to clean up the accusations and blame. Now you've got a clean ask:

"I'm feeling resentful. I want a partner in the chore department. Could you please take out the trash?"

Here's the tricky part: Leave it there.

We want to punish our sweetheart, or justify our own needs. Don't.

You have waited so long to make the clean ask that there is a waterfall of feelings behind it. When you open your mouth to give a clean ask it's like breaking the dam and that entire waterfall of feelings wants to come rushing out. Don't let this happen.

Just stop at the clean ask.

Then watch as your relationship emerges from shame, and blame, and confusion.

My relationship changed radically when I was able to ask cleanly, and then stop at the clean ask. My husband had been afraid of me prior to me learning this skill. I was good at pouring out shame and blame.

When my husband sensed that I wanted something, as a result, he got skittish and withdrawn. He wanted to dodge the accusations he could feel coming his way. I got clean with my asks, and he looked bewildered. Like something was missing.

After a few years of bewilderment—I'd been blaming and shaming for a long time, so lots of recovery was needed—my husband began to engage with me after I made a clean ask. Sometimes he'd protest and say he didn't value paths in the garden getting built. Sometimes he'd say, "Oops! Sorry! I forgot," then get to cleaning the bathroom.

But the biggest reward for me learning to ask cleanly is that on a few occasions my husband wrapped his arms around me and said, "Darling, I'm so sorry I let you down. You've had to ask for that over and over and I wasn't hearing you. Thank you for giving me another chance."

This is transformative interaction. This is the promise of the clean ask. When you take responsibility for your feelings and own your agency when it comes to your desires, you invite everyone else around you to do the same thing.

* * *

Let's try one more: "You never show me any affection." *Is that true? Never? No kind of affection at all?*

When you *question* the universals—"never" and "any"—you see the possibility that they aren't completely true. That brief opening allows curiosity to bloom. Now that you're curious, let's take a look at the next tool—Stay in Your Own Business—to examine "You never show me any affection."

Stay in Your Own Business

Remember the three types of business: Your business, my business, and God's (or the Universe's) business. Let's take a look at what happens when we use this tool to clean up your ask.

"You never show me any affection." Whose business are you in? Your sweetheart's, right? You're telling your sweetheart what they are doing. But you have no power to control your sweetheart's actions.

The thought that goes with this accusation is probably something like, "You don't love me anymore," or the ever present, "You think I'm fat."

If you struggle to see whose business you're in when you say something like "You never show me any affection," just examine the thoughts behind the statement. It's easy to see that "You think I'm fat" puts you squarely in your sweetheart's business, right?

You're telling your sweetheart what they're thinking. You're reading your sweetheart's mind, which is smack dab in the middle of your sweetheart's business.

When you bring this same phrase into your own business, it changes drastically: "I don't feel any affection from you." Here's the first half of a clean ask. See how much blame is washed away when you stay in your own business? Just phrasing it this way opens up possibilities and you might be able to say:

"I miss you. I feel like the affection part of our relationship has gone missing." Can you feel how compelling this shift of language has become. The blame of "You never show me any affection" causes alienation, whereas "I miss you" is an invitation to reconnect.

That's the first half of the clean ask formula: the feeling. Now add the second part: your desire:

"I want you to hug me and kiss me."

Our clean ask becomes:

"I miss you. I feel like the affection part of our relationship has gone missing. Would you hug me and kiss me when you first get home?" How will your relationship change if you learn to turn a dirty ask into a clean ask?

Can you feel how tempting it is to get into your sweetheart's business and wonder, *What are you saying to me when you don't kiss me?* Once you're in your sweetheart's business, your imagination runs wild and you create all sorts of scenarios:

- My sweetheart is telling me they're bored and I wonder if they're having an affair?
- My sweetheart thinks I'm just here to serve them. They want sex when they want it, but they don't think about my needs.
- My sweetheart thinks I'm ugly and fat. My sweetheart is repulsed by me.

Your imagination is brutal when it comes to these scenarios. Can you see how detrimental these thoughts are to your relationship? This is because you're creating both sides of a conversation. Your sweetheart is saying words *inside your head*. But these are words your sweetheart didn't actually say. You imagined them.

I've talked with many couples who have suffered alienation simply because one person is having both parts of the conversation in their head. Then getting mad at their sweetheart for those imagined conversations.

Don't let your imagination go wandering into these fields. Take charge by staying in your own business and create a clean ask.

First notice how you feel:
- You're puzzled: Why doesn't my sweetheart do a simple thing like take out the trash?
- You feel taken for granted: It's not fair that I take the trash out more often than my sweetheart.
- You're tired: I'd rather read my book than take out the trash.

Then state your feeling to your sweetheart. "I'm puzzled." The first half of the clean ask formula.

Now get really clear about your desire. What do you want in this situation? "I want to share chores equitably."

Finally, as clearly and succinctly as you can, tell your sweetheart what you want them to do. "Could you take out the trash the same number of times I take out the trash?"

Putting it all together: "I'm puzzled. I want to share chores equitably. I've noticed that I am the primary person who takes out the trash. Could you take out the trash the same number of times I take out the trash?"

This is a clean ask. See how it eliminates all sorts of dirty implications? You state how you feel. You clarify the kind of relationship lifestyle you want. Then you ask cleanly for action from your sweetheart.

What's great about this clean ask is that it inspires a clean response from your sweetheart: "Oh. I thought I was the recycle person and you were the trash person. I figured that's why you never took out the recycle, because it was my job."

Bingo!

If you can get curious and stay in your own business, you don't accuse, shame, or blame. You simply state how you feel and you state your desire.

This clarity allows your sweetheart to respond in kind, and suddenly you see the entire situation differently. True, your sweetheart ~~never~~ rarely

Try This Tool: Design Your Clean Ask

Think of something you want from your sweetheart.

Feelings: How do you feel when you contemplate this desire?
_____
_____

Feelings: Whose business are you in when you contemplate this desire?
_____
_____

Feelings: What assumptions are you making? Is that true?
_____
_____

Desire: What do you want (specifically, precisely, exactly)?
_____
_____

Ask: Practice phrasing your ask such that there is a "yes" or "no" answer implied.
_____
_____

Put it all together:
_____
_____

takes out the trash, but you'd completely forgotten about the 60-minute round trip errand to the recycle center that your sweetheart takes several times a year.

A clean ask is curious. A clean ask invites the whole story. A clean ask cultivates intimacy, because you stay in your own business and own your own power.

The more you own your own power—and ONLY your own power—the more you invite your sweetheart to own their power. This is the power of the clean ask: it's empowering to both you and your sweetheart.

A dirty ask, on the other hand, makes a power grab.

Your power grab with a dirty ask creates a defensive power move from your sweetheart and your sweetheart in turn makes a power grab with a dirty ask. Suddenly, you're off to the icky races of power grabs instead of a generous exchange of kindness and consideration.

When you're able to get curious about the truth—*Is it true?*—and remain in your own business—*Whose business am I in?*—it's gonna be pretty easy for you to design a clean ask.

The power of "yes" or "no" phrasing

Lastly, a clean ask is framed in such a way that your sweetheart can answer "yes" or "no" to your request.

While most of the time, you want to foster conversation rather than yes or no answers, what makes a clean ask so profound is the clarity of response it inspires.

I'm a proponent of discussions, not demands. However, the clarity of a clean ask frames a discussion with succinct clarity. It blows away all the confusion of a Black Hole. So, practice asking such that your sweetheart's answer is a simple yes or no.

Now let's look at how you can be seated smack dab in the center of your personal power so that you feel capable of asking for what you want.

STRATEGY 4

Sprouting Love

Own your fear. Own your desire. Own your agency.

A clean ask makes your relationship trustworthy. A clean ask cultivates respect. A clean ask is simple: articulate your feeling, then articulate your desire. Then state precisely, exactly, specifically how your sweetheart can give you want you want.

But a clean ask isn't easy.

In order to have your communication filled with clean asks, you need to develop an intentional practice. It doesn't need to be complicated, but consistency will make all the difference.

This practice is all about learning to own your agency when it comes to a clean ask.

Agency is your personal power to influence any given situation. Agency happens when you *Stay in Your Own Business* and when you deal with the reality of your situation: *Is that true?* The more you practice owning your agency, the more empowered you will feel.

The problem is, we forget. We forget to stay in our own business, and we get really confused about the realities we face.

In order to tell you about practicing the clean ask, I'm going to compare the practice to sprouting seeds. Have you ever tried to grow sprouts? Everybody says it's ridiculously easy, but I have failed more times than I can count.

My daughter is amazing at sprouting seeds. The difference between my daughter and me when it comes to sprouting seeds is that she fits the daily steps into her routine, and she hardly notices she's tending those sprouts.

The reason I stink at sprouting seeds is that I've never taken the mental energy to put the steps of sprouting seeds into my life. If you don't create space in your life for practicing the clean ask, you won't get better at it.

Here's the good news: It's not hard. It just takes you deciding that a clean ask is important.

The first step to sprouting seeds is soaking. When you soak a seed, it wakes up the part of that seed that wants to grow. The second step is rinsing the seeds regularly. The last step is draining those seeds so they're not sitting in moisture. After those seeds have sprouted, you get to eat all that green goodness.

After you tend to your clean ask, you get to live in a respectful, tender, kind relationship that fosters intimacy and connection.

The first step to tend your clean ask is to own your fear.

Own your fear

Remember this dirty ask, "You never kiss me?"

This dirty ask is lost in confusion. When Amanda says this to her sweetheart, she doesn't yet know specifically how she wants to be kissed. She doesn't know that she wants to be kissed when her sweetheart gets home after work. She doesn't know that a kiss as she wakes up and says good morning will help her feel connected to her sweetheart all day. She only knows that she doesn't feel kissed.

I've had both men and women tell me their sweetheart never kisses them. For the purposes of this discussion, we'll see what happens to Amanda knowing that Amanda could be any one of us.

It totally sucks to be confused about something as important as physical touch and a sense of belonging. When Amanda feels this way, she does nasty things like blurt out, "You hate me." Or she makes selfish demands, "You owe me dinner and a movie." Or, because she's overwhelmed by the horrible way she feels, Amanda shuts up: her marriage gets filled with a vacuum of emptiness.

Confusion is a yucky feeling, so we want to escape it as quickly as we can. Hence the blurts, demands, and shut downs. But what if Amanda thought about her confusion like the soaking of seeds before they sprout?

Sprouting Love

The Sprouting Love strategy is the opposite of The Pressure Relief Valve. You use the Pressure Relief Valve when you need a break. You use the Spouting Love tool when you need to cultivate connection and grow some patience.

Seeds are dormant until you soak them. Soaking seeds wakes them up. You can't just get the seeds wet. You have to let them *soak*. That means patience and waiting. As the seeds soak, the outer hull softens.

Amanda has built a shell of protection to keep herself safe from her sweetheart who's not kissing her. All this protection is causing confusion. Amanda can't feel her feelings, and she doesn't know what she wants. Amanda's confusion needs a good soak.

Soak your confusion in two ways: overcome your fear, then get clear.

Conveniently, you are holding a book with two entire chapters on how to **overcome your fear** and how to **get clear**.

Let's review. Amanda looks at the above dirty ask and soaks it in our strategies for overcoming fear:

- Naming is Taming
- Befriend to Mend
- Protection before Connection
- Fly into Fear

First, we'd like to name her feelings. But this is hard because right now all she's feeling is blame: *This is her sweetheart's fault.*

I can't ask Amanda to name her fear, because it doesn't yet feel like fear. It's blame. *This is her sweetheart's fault.* There is no agency in this for Amanda. She has given all her power to her sweetheart to control the fate of their kissing relationship.

Our first goal with soaking is to find some agency for Amanda. If you can't name your feeling to tame your feeling—because you can't find a feeling—you need to skip on down in the list of fear-disguising strategies. Let's use the tool *Befriend to Mend*.

I can ask Amanda, "What's the worst thing about your sweetheart not kissing you?"

Amanda tucks her chin and looks at me from beneath her eyebrows. "Isn't it obvious?" she says to me rolling her eyes.

Actually, no. There are hundreds of worst-case scenarios when the people inside a marriage stop kissing. I want to hear *Amanda's* unique worst-case. And, more importantly, Amanda's Inner Lizard wants to hear the worst-case scenario articulated.

Fear is a generalist. It's a brick wall of protection. So, we need to soak that fear. When we get specific, we soften that hull of protection. Then, like our seeds, something has a chance to sprout.

Amanda is mad at me for my stupid question, "No one wants to be in a marriage where there's no kissing."

"That may be true," I say, even though I know of two marriages where there's hardly any kissing and those people tell me they are very happy.

"But, Amanda, what is the *specific* reason *you* don't want to be in a marriage where there's no kissing? What's the worst thing that will happen to your relationship if you spend five years not kissing?"

Amanda looks straight at me, "She'll stop talking to me," she says.

Aha! See why it's confusing? Kissing is somehow, in Amanda's life, a gateway to conversation. This is the power of soaking and letting all those confusing feelings have a chance to soften up. "And what's the worst thing about your sweetheart not talking to you? What will happen to you if she stops talking to you?"

Tears make Amanda's eyes shiny, but her cheeks stay dry as she says, "I'll be so lonely."

Bingo. The feeling that Amanda couldn't find because *this is all her sweetheart's fault* is loneliness.

I hear you. You're thinking, Isn't it obvious that the feeling that inspires a dirty ask like, "You never kiss me," is loneliness? I know. But can you see that Amanda wasn't feeling lonely when she said, "You never kiss me." She was hiding behind a brick wall of protection.

As a result, when Amanda said, "You never kiss me," her sweetheart couldn't feel Amanda's loneliness. The only thing Amanda's sweetheart felt was accused. Which made her sweetheart feel inadequate. Which made her withdraw even more.

See the nasty cycle of a dirty ask? Further alienation. More loneliness for Amanda.

Once Amanda felt the tears of loneliness in her eyes, the brick wall of protection that was causing distance between herself and her sweetheart disappeared.

It's not enough to offer some academic name to your feeling when you use the clean ask formula. Our goal is to speak about the feeling your body is *experiencing*. When you speak a feeling that has been soaked enough to penetrate your body's feeling layer, then your sweetheart will also feel your feeling. Your Animal Body will be communicating.

If you haven't softened up the brick wall of protection, the only thing your sweetheart feels is a brick wall that shouts, "Stay out!"

When I used the worst-case-scenario question to let Amanda get access to her feelings, she stopped walling herself off. Now Amanda is free to offer herself the protection of *nurturance*, instead of the fake kind of protection that is just *avoidance* (or anger, or suspicion, or control).

Remember Protect to Connect? The next fear strategy? The kind of protection that allows connection is nothing like the brick wall of protection your Inner Lizard builds to keep you safe. Protect to Connect allows Amanda (and you) to explore all the ways she (and you) is capable.

"If you and your sweetheart don't kiss for five years," I ask Amanda, "And your sweetheart stops talking to you, what will happen to you?"

Amanda's tears fall. She cries hard. I stay beside her. I don't reassure her that it will be OK. I don't tell her she's up to the task. I just stay beside her while she cries.

"I can see how lonely you feel just contemplating this scenario, Amanda," I say and I continue to stay beside her while her tears soak another tissue.

After a bit, Amanda takes a deep breath. "Wow!" she says to me, "That was horrible!" I know. I could feel her desperate loneliness swirling around the room.

"What did you notice about yourself as you cried and imagined that deep loneliness?" I asked Amanda.

"I didn't die," she said. This is common. Our fears are so large, and so unspecific, and so controlled by our Inner Lizard, that it actually feels like we will die if what we fear comes to pass.

This is why we need to let our confusion have a good soak. That soak that softens our hull of protection so that who we are and what we want for our lives wakes up.

We've located half of Amanda's clean ask: how she feels.

"When you don't kiss me, I feel lonely, and then I get afraid you won't talk to me…like ever again."

When the seed of who you are wakes up, you have a chance to grow into the unique individual you are. You're ready to go looking for your desire. Let's look for Amanda's desire.

Own your desire

The next two phases of growing sprouts are rinsing and draining. It's important to give seeds lots of water while you're rinsing. Lots of water helps keep the seed soft and it provides oxygen. But it's equally important to drain your seeds. Your seeds will mildew if you don't drain them properly.

Similarly, it's important to rinse your fears and feelings. Give them plenty of attention so they don't dry out. Remember how Amanda couldn't access her feelings at first? Then we nurtured those feelings. They got oxygenated and, once exposed, Amanda could begin to rinse them with tears.

We can't overcome fear by climbing over, digging under, or going around. The only way to move from a dirty ask to a clean ask is to go right through the center: feel your feelings. This is rinsing.

Now for draining. Just as it's important to let seeds sit in the stillness of a well-drained environment, it's important to let yourself have space so your desires can bubble up.

I didn't leave Amanda in a heap of tears feeling all that loneliness.

After she'd had time to really notice what that loneliness felt like, and she realized she wasn't going to die, she felt more calm. She could even list ways that she could take care of herself, "I mean I don't wanna do it alone," she told me, "but I see that I'm capable."

Now we were ready to draw from the strategies of getting clear:

- Stay in Your Own Business
- I feel… I want… I don't want…

Let's see what happens for Amanda when we explore these clarity tools.

With Amanda's dirty ask—"You never kiss me!"—she is squarely in her sweetheart's business. I ask her what the subtext of this statement is. "What are you thinking as you say this aloud?"

Amanda makes a list:

- She finds me disgusting.
- She doesn't have time for me.
- She doesn't care about me nearly as much as she cares about the dogs.

Can you see how Amanda is in her sweetheart's business? All these thoughts revolve around assumptions about how her sweetheart is feeling.

I want to bring Amanda back into her own business. "Do you find your sweetheart disgusting?" I ask.

"Of course not!" she says. "Why would I be with her if I found her disgusting."

"But your sweetheart would be with you even though you are disgusting?" I ask. Amanda laughs. "We let ourselves think silly things, right?" Amanda smiles, but I see the tears glistening in her eyes again.

"Do you have time for your sweetheart?" I ask.

"Of course!" says Amanda, but then she pauses, then bursts out laughing. "But I do pet the dogs first whenever I come home." I wish you could be a fly on the wall of my office for one of these moments. It's the moment when all the defenses drain away, and an entirely different truth is somehow suddenly visible. It is often accompanied by laughter.

When you can laugh at one of these realizations, you have offered yourself compassion. Laughter loosens. Shame tightens. Then shame wants to hide more. Let yourself laugh to keep the shame monster away.

"Do you think my sweetheart thinks I love the dogs more than I love her?" asks Amanda. I smile. Connection. Intimacy. I see it right there in the room with us. Her relationship just changed.

In this moment Amanda sees all the things she's feared while the kisses were missing. Then she sees how she might be contributing to the feeling of alienation she has.

We all have so many defenses keeping us safe that it's difficult to find the love that's trying to reach toward us. This confusion keeps us stuck in the land of the dirty ask.

Own your agency

Now that most of Amanda's confusion is gone, I transition to the tool *What do you feel? What are you sure you don't want? What do you want?* This is a great tool to keep rinsing away confusion.

Sometimes you use this for a bit, then realize you've jumped back into your sweetheart's business, so you tend to that. It can feel like rinsing seeds and draining seeds. You don't see much difference for a while. Then, all of a sudden! A green sprout appears and, before you know it, your jar is filled with green yumminess.

I ask, "In addition to feeling lonely, Amanda, what else do you feel? And what is it you want?"

"I don't want my sweetheart to think I love the dogs more than I love her!" Amanda is adamant about this.

"Notice what you're feeling right now," I say, "It looks like a different feeling than the loneliness you were feeling a moment ago."

"It's completely different!" says Amanda. "I feel eager, and brave, and generous. Because I just wanna go home and kiss my sweetheart before I pet the dogs."

What happened to Amanda? She truly glimpsed her own feelings rather than avoiding them, dodging them or trying to find another way to avoid the terror that those lonely feelings represented. Once she felt those feelings, she had room to see things differently.

Before she left, we framed up Amanda's clean ask:

"When you don't kiss me, I feel lonely, and then I get afraid you won't talk to me…like ever again. I realized I always pet the dogs when I first come home. By the time the dogs calm down the moment is gone, and we haven't kissed. I want to change that. I want kissing each other to be part of our coming home ritual. Would you be up for kissing when we first get home?"

Can you feel how clean this ask is? Look at how Amanda owns her agency in every aspect. She owns agency over her emotions: "I feel lonely." It's not her sweetheart's fault. Amanda's not blaming.

She's not arguing with reality: "I pet the dogs." This allows her to see how she has contributed to the thing she fears: the not kissing. When you stop arguing with reality, you see where you can assert your personal agency. You can own your part in the relationship dynamic.

Amanda is also owning her agency when it comes to what she wants: "I want kissing to be part of our coming home ritual." See all that ownership? Can you feel how clean it is?

You can own the agency for your clean ask as well. It just takes a little practice to see where you get tripped up and your ask gets dirty.

The above three are the craft of the clean ask. But there is also an art to the clean ask. The art of the clean ask takes years and decades to hone. The art of the clean ask is where intimacy is developed. Just like the seeds that take rinsing and draining, growth happens over time.

Because it is an art, I cannot offer you boxes to check or blanks to fill in. But I can offer you questions to ponder so you can deepen your ability to reveal to your sweetheart who you are and what you want. I can also offer questions so you can deepen your ability to hear and welcome your sweetheart's fears and desires.

Overcome fear so you're able to feel a clean, well rinsed version of your feelings. Then **get clear** about what you want and what you've been doing to sabotage getting what you want. We all do it. We all need the practice.

Rinse, drain, and let set. Rinse, drain, and let set. Before you know it, your relationship will be filled with green sprouts of love in every corner of your lives.

Try This Tool: The Art of Sprouting Love

Here are things to keep in mind as you practice the art of *giving* the clean ask:
- What else are you feeling?
- When did you first have that feeling?
- How old do you feel when you're experiencing this feeling?
- What will you gain or lose if you don't get this thing you want?
- What is it specifically, exactly, precisely that you want?
- Why do you want that change? How will that change impact your life?
- Have you asked in a way that your sweetheart can answer yes or no? I know you might like a longer conversation, but a clean ask is potently clear. Look for this clarity.

Here are things to keep in mind as you practice the art of *receiving* the clean ask:
- What else is your sweetheart feeling?
- When did your sweetheart first have this feeling?
- How old was your sweetheart when they first felt this way?
- What will your sweetheart lose or gain if they don't get this thing they want?
- What is it specifically, exactly, precisely that your sweetheart wants?
- What will change in your sweetheart's life if they get this thing they want?
- Why does your sweetheart want this change? What will that offer to your sweetheart?
- Has your sweetheart asked in a way that you can answer yes or no? Request this clarity.

STRATEGY 5

Stay Clean Even When Your Sweetheart Asks Dirty

Because one clean asker can change the dynamic in a relationship

Would you like a phrase you can use when you're tempted to ask dirty? Here are a few to choose from:

- I'm confused. I don't really know exactly what I want. I'm tempted to dump my confusion onto you. So, I want to hold up a caution sign. I might be tempted to be mean to you today, but it's just because I hate feeling confused and lost.
- I'm mad at you. I'm not sure why. Until further notice, assume my grumpiness is my problem since I can't figure it out.
- I'm hurt. I don't know why. Can we both remember that, when I get hurt, I behave worst to you…and that's a good thing because that means you're my safety zone? I guess I'm asking you to grant me some extra grace today.
- It would help me if you hugged me right now.

These are all clean ways to deal with dirty confusion. But let's face it, we aren't always clean. What do you do when your sweetheart offers you the blame, shame, or overwhelm of a dirty ask?

You're tempted to blame back. To get defensive. To attack.

Resist the temptation.

Instead, stay clean.

Even when your sweetheart asks dirty, stay clean.

Caveat: If you are in an abusive relationship, don't worry about clean or dirty. In that case, just get as much support as you can so you can figure out how to exit.

Why do I recommend staying clean? Because we all want a clean, healthy relationship. We all want a relationship that is kind, gentle, and full of compassion.

When you stay clean, you raise the level of conversation in your home. Your sweetheart will be seduced by your clean energy. You will, at some point, experience a break through with your sweetheart if you keep asking cleanly for exactly, precisely, specifically what you want.

In the meantime, let me give you several strategies to deal with the dirty asks that come from your sweetheart. (I also want to refer you to Chapter 6, Build Boundaries, because sometimes what's needed with a dirty ask isn't so much the finesse of a clean response as it is a boundary.)

Four tools to penetrate the brick wall of a dirty ask

1. Hug and heal
2. Hunch + Tell Me Where I'm Wrong
3. Laugh together
4. Hear the heal

Let's take them one by one. We'll discuss the first three, you'll get a tool to help you practice, then we'll discuss how you can better hear what needs healing.

Hug and heal

We'd been married a number of years when I felt the power of the hug and heal tool from my husband.

I had many dirty asks in the bank at that point. I'd ask dirty, blame my husband, then feel terrible. I'd apologize, but another day I'd just ask dirty again. Ugh!

So, I began to debrief with David after my dirty ask. I'd say something like, "I'm so sorry I blame you. I'm struggling. I don't know how to do this better yet, but I'm trying. Can I ask one favor of you while I try to do better?"

"Of course!" I think my husband was eager for anything that would shift this dynamic in our marriage.

"When I'm blaming you (I hadn't thought about naming it a dirty ask yet), I feel icky inside. If I'm honest, I feel like a naughty kiddo. You know how when the kids throw a tantrum it's really just a signal that they are tired or hungry most of the time?"

My husband nodded.

I let out one of those under-your-breath laughs that tells everyone in the room you're embarrassed. "When I'm blaming you, I'm wondering if you'd be willing to treat me like a toddler?"

"What does that mean?" asked my husband.

"Could you ask if I'm hungry? Could you realize I'm tired?"

"OK," said my husband, but he looked mystified. He didn't know how to do that.

Honestly, we had the above conversation for a long time, through the course of many fights. I'll tell you the truth, it was years. It won't be years for you though, because you're reading this book.

Here was our pattern: life went along pleasantly enough until there was a need—the snow plow needed fixing, or there was an issue with the insurance—and I didn't know how to ask cleanly (or maybe it was that David didn't know how to respond cleanly, who knows?), and I wouldn't get what I wanted: a working snowplow, freedom from the barrage of emails from the insurance company.

So, I'd revert to the dirty ask of blaming and shaming.

Then I'd apologize and remind David it would help in that moment when I'm blaming him, if he could treat me like a toddler. He'd say he'd try. But the next time I blamed or shamed him, he would freeze. Understandably. I'm scary when I attack.

This was our pattern.

But one day, when I began to blame him, David walked over to me and tried to hug me. I pushed him away as any good self-absorbed-angry-person is wont to do. But he persisted.

He said, "I know you don't want me to hug you now. But in a couple hours you're gonna be apologizing and telling me you wish I'd hugged you. So here I am hugging you so that at least you can't blame me for that part of this situation."

That was a watershed moment in our lives. I laughed a little. Then I let him hug me. Sort of. I was very stiff and wouldn't really let his hug in. Thankfully, my husband is a tremendous hugger. He doesn't talk a lot, but he hugs loudly.

He just kept holding me. I softened. He hugged me some more. I softened more. Then I began to cry. I felt all his tenderness. No matter how tangled up our marriage could feel at times, I knew in this moment that my husband loved me. And I loved him.

We were both trying to do better. And our efforts would pay off big time.

The first strategy when your sweetheart is asking dirty is to hug the "toddler" inside of them that doesn't want to face a grown up's responsibility.

Hugging your sweetheart when they are behaving badly isn't tolerating bad behavior; it is how to extend unconditional love.

(Quick disclaimer here: sometimes hugging is just a co-dependent desire to make the pain go away. If you wonder if this could be you, give a listen to episode #27 of my podcast, *Habits for Your Happily Ever After*. The episode is called: Don't Let Your Inner Child Sabotage Your Relationship.)

Then, after the hug, you can ask for what you want cleanly. Or, you can use the next technique to clean up your sweetheart's dirty ask.

Hunch + tell me where I'm wrong

If you coach with me, you'll hear this phrase several times in each of our sessions: *tell me where I'm wrong*. This phrase allows me to guess at what you're feeling or what you want.

I learned this magical phrase from my teacher, Martha Beck.

The idea is to guess at what your sweetheart is feeling or guess about what they want. Then say, "Tell me where I'm wrong." Why does this help? Because fear is holding your sweetheart hostage. If you can make guesses about your sweetheart's desires, you cut through the bonds of fear. While he was hugging me, my husband could have said, "I'm guessing you're frustrated with me about the plow still being broken. Tell me where I'm wrong."

When he says this, it wipes away a host of fears that I maybe didn't recognize I had: Fear that he'd never fix the plow, fear that I have to do all the adulting in our relationship. Fear that my husband doesn't love me enough to keep his promises.

So, when your sweetheart is stomping around the house, lugging the vacuum up and down the stairs, you could say, "I think you'd like me to help with the cleaning. Tell me where I'm wrong."

See how you made a guess, then served the agency for the behavior back to your sweetheart with the *tell me where I'm wrong* phrase?

This is a subtle way to say, "Hey, you can just ask me cleanly to vacuum rather than stomping around this house, all the while offering me the cold shoulder."

When you call out the bad behavior directly—"You're acting passive aggressive!"—you don't leave your sweetheart room to save face. (Again, sometimes that's exactly what you need to do, and we'll get to this in Chapter 6, Build Boundaries.)

It may be that your sweetheart asked you to vacuum three times and you said you'd do it, but here it is: company arrives in an hour and you still haven't vacuumed. We all do it, right? We all forget to vacuum, and we all stomp around when we don't feel heard.

A guess and a *tell me where I'm wrong* also works well when you're having an argument and you can't agree. If your sweetheart seems to be talking in circles because they're overwhelmed, offer them the gift of a guess: "I think you don't know where you want to spend Christmas because you want to be with your family, but your family also drives you crazy. *Tell me where I'm wrong.*"

Can you see how your clarity might be a relief for your sweetheart who doesn't want to admit her family drives her crazy, but once she can hear that out loud, it relieves all the confusion bombarding her inside her head?

Sometimes we can't see what we want, and it really helps to have our sweetheart—who knows us so well—guess. It's even better when that sweetheart says, *"Tell me where I'm wrong,"* so that we can feel in control and can disagree or refine the statement.

Your guess allows your sweetheart to say, "Well, my family doesn't *always* drive me crazy. But frequently. And I so want to have a peaceful Christmas. What should we do?"

A moment like this, by the way, would be a great moment for you to hug your sweetheart. Just sayin'.

Laugh together

There is nothing that cleans up a dirty ask better than laughter. But you have to find your moment.

You don't want to tease your sweetheart when they are banging the vacuum around. Remember, you are the one who forgot to follow through and vacuum before the company arrived.

You don't want to tease your sweetheart if they've had a wretched day and they're exhausted and hungry.

You don't want to tease your sweetheart if you sense they feel fragile.

But in all other circumstances, I recommend laughter.

"Oh! You found the vacuum! I went looking for that the other day, and couldn't find it under the sink. Thanks for finding it for me. I told you I'd do the vacuuming. Do you mind if I take over?" See how you're making fun of yourself?

Of course, you never looked under the sink. How could a vacuum fit under the sink?? But this joke allows you to save face even as you take responsibility for messing up. We all need to forgive ourselves and start over.

Teasing allows both of you to save face and it's great way to clean up a pattern of dirty asks.

If your sweetheart is famous for "You never kiss me" type dirty asks, you could say, "Well, you never kiss me either," then take off running and shout over your shoulder, "If you catch me, I'll kiss you."

This laughter and playfulness lightens the very heavy dirty ask. It brings a waterfall of freshness.

It's an art to learn how to use laughter to diffuse a dirty ask. Be gentle with yourself. If your sweetheart uses laughter to dodge the messiness of a dirty ask, be gentle.

We all use laughter for many different things. Sometimes laughter helps us hide from our shame. We're ashamed so we make fun to shake off the shame.

But when your sweetheart uses laughter to try and help you shake off shame, it might sting. Be gentle. Be gentle with yourself. Be gentle with your sweetheart. Keep your eyes on the biggest picture of love and open communication you're trying to create.

After that first hug that David offered me and I resisted, he began to tease me. "I'm gonna hug you now because I can sense the blame waterfall is about to pour out of your mouth."

This stung the first time he did it.

If I'm honest, it probably required more than ~~once~~ a dozen times before I could also laugh. But even though giggles didn't make it out of my mouth, I was borrowing his laughter. When David teased me, it was like he was believing in me. Believing that there would be a day when I didn't blame him. I could feel his tangible belief in his laughter. It felt hopeful.

He knew I didn't *want* to act like a toddler. He knew he was to blame in some measure. He also knew that laughter would heal both of us. I wasn't capable of initiating the laughter, but I recognized it when I saw it and I felt the potential of the healing.

When you're able to laugh—with compassion, not with sarcasm—you offer gentleness to your sweetheart. When your sweetheart is able to receive that gentleness, they will want to ask more cleanly.

This is a dance. Be patient. Keep trying.

Try This Tool: Stay Clean by Rewriting History

A great way to reduce the conflict you have and increase the intimacy in your relationship is to reimagine a past moment. This time, however, as you remember that historic moment, add in details that are more likely to give you the desired outcome.

Think of a persistent conflict between you and your sweetheart. Write your remembered scenario here:
_____
_____

Imagine what would happen if you hugged your sweetheart during that conflict. Write your imagined scenario here:
_____
_____

Imagine what would happen if you offered your sweetheart a hunch about how they're feeling during that conflict. Write your hunch, then write your imagined scenario here:
Hunch: _____
Scenario: _____
_____

Now imagine what could help you laugh during that conflict. Write your imagined scenario here:
_____
_____

How do you think imagining these different scenarios will help you manage conflict differently in the future?
_____
_____

Hear the heal

You will try the laugh together method for cleaning up a dirty ask and it will backfire sometimes.

It will backfire because your sweetheart is in a bad mood, or because your sweetheart feels fragile and you'll hurt your sweetheart's feelings.

Don't be discouraged. Listen. Then listen more. Keep listening. But don't give up on your attempt to use laughter to lighten the communication.

Meanwhile, listen for that part in your sweetheart that feels discouraged, overwhelmed, embarrassed, or even like an imposter.

When you can name the part of your sweetheart that feels discouraged, overwhelmed, embarrassed, or imposter-y, you feed your sweetheart oxygen so they can breathe better.

After I blamed David, and after I apologized, and after his hug of tenderness, what I really needed was for him to get curious about why I had this pattern. To let me know he expected me to communicate with him in a healthy adult fashion.

The part of me that blamed him (and many other people) was a wounded little girl.

David was a safe place for that wounded little girl to show up in hopes of getting healed.

But it *never* felt gentle for David. It was wretched for him. I was scary.

So, we sought the help of a skilled therapist. She helped both of us listen more effectively.

She helped us unravel our patterns. Remember how I struggled with the unmade bed? I thought I was asking cleanly, but I wasn't. David couldn't identify the dirty ask; he just felt the *pain* of the dirty ask.

David couldn't hear exactly, precisely, specifically what I wanted, because I didn't know how to ask cleanly. I asked dirty because I was wounded from my parents' divorce. I constantly polluted my ask for a made bed with the baggage of my then-belief that all marriages break.

I was confusing a tiny thing—making our bed—with a big thing—our happily ever after.

This happens all the time, and it's one of the biggest reasons you can't get what you want in your relationship.

You think you're being clear: "David, why don't you care enough about our relationship to make the bed?"

Can you hear how dirty the ask is? I'm wrapping up David's care for our marriage with making the bed. I'm not telling him how I feel. I'm not saying, "I feel like a made bed is a signal of the health of our marriage."

I'm not telling him what I want. "I want each of us to tend our marriage."

And I'm definitely not asking clearly for what I want David to do. "Could you make our bed if you get out of it after I've gotten up?"

When you ask dirty, your sweetheart hears something completely different than you intend to say. My husband heard *my wife is constantly telling me I'm not enough.*

Can you understand why he hears that? "David, why don't you care enough about our relationship…" He hears that I think he's a failure. He hears I'm not getting what I want. What he doesn't hear is how he *could* give me what I want. So, he's lost in guessing land. He feels helpless. He's left with a feeling of emptiness.

Communication has two parts: speaking and hearing. Giving and receiving. You can say things over and over, but that doesn't guarantee that your sweetheart hears what you *think* you're saying. That's why it's crucial to **get clear** about what you want and what you fear. Then **ask cleanly**.

You're probably suffering right now because you feel like you've communicated so clearly. But your sweetheart is hearing something very different than what you're saying.

In the early draft of this book, I wrote the above sentence differently. I wrote, *Your sweetheart is* **healing** *something very different than what you're saying.* This Freudian slip could not be more true.

Your sweetheart is busy *healing* and learning to clarify their own desires. Because of that, they will HEAR your words through the lens of the HEALING they're trying to do on their own.

We all do it.

We all **hear** what we're trying to **heal.** What your sweetheart *hears* may have nothing to do with what you're *saying*.

When David didn't make the bed, I heard, David doesn't care enough about tending our marriage to make our bed.

We all hear what we're trying to heal.

Dear Reader, now that I know better, I can promise you that my husband never even knew there was a connection between tending our marriage and making the bed.

Try This Tool: Phrases to Help Unearth a Clean Ask

Use these phrases when your sweetheart asks dirty.

- *Remember, I'm on your team. I want to help.*
- *I want you to feel my love. What's happening right now that you feel so alienated from me?*
- *I'm feeling defensive. I don't think you want to be attacking me. Can you say that a different way?*
- *Please don't blame me. I want to hear what you want. If you blame me, I'm not gonna be able to hear you clearly because I'll get defensive.*

As you get clearer, you up your chances that your sweetheart will hear the same thing you're saying. Ask as cleanly as you can. Then forgive your sweetheart because your sweetheart is asking as cleanly as they can.

Improvement is happening.

So how do we listen in the meantime while our sweetheart is healing? And how do we stay clean when our sweetheart is asking dirty?

You can help your sweetheart ask more cleanly when you help them excavate their fears and their desires.

To help your sweetheart heal, you want to hear their suffering, and you want to hear how they wish life were different.

The following phrases are an attempt to reassure your sweetheart that you love them. These phrases help you to get distance from the yuckiness you're hearing, and, instead, get in touch with the yuckiness your sweetheart is feeling (and needs to heal).

When you are a curious listener, you provide a safe place for your sweetheart to heal.

However, you are not your sweetheart's therapist. You might need the help of a skilled professional and an objective space where you and your sweetheart can explore the healing vs hearing conundrum.

Our therapist asked me the question, "How old do you feel when you have these blame sessions with David." I paused. I always thought I was a frustrated wife who couldn't get my husband to help me, but when she asked this question, I realized I felt very helpless. Very young.

Our therapist expected me to be an adult and explore all the things that contributed to my desire to blame.

Because I believed everyone divorces eventually, I polluted my ask with that belief. But that had absolutely nothing to do with David.

When David was able to listen—with an open heart—to the reasons I believed our marriage would fail, he didn't feel blamed, but he saw why I wanted to blame *someone*.

When David could see the reasons I wanted to blame, he got very compassionate. He saw the healing I was trying to do. He stopped hearing me blame *him*—as if he wasn't *enough* as a husband—and he heard my fear that we would divorce.

This wound I was trying to heal was somehow tied up in his attentiveness to our made bed.

When he heard what *I* was trying to heal, he stopped hearing what *he* was trying to heal.

He stopped hearing that I didn't think he was enough. Instead, he heard that little girl inside me that was so scared.

You also have wounds. These wounds impact how you hear things.

Likewise, your sweetheart has wounds that impact what they can hear.

When you ask your sweetheart to examine their dirty asks, you are believing in the adult inside of them that wants to heal from those childhood wounds. This accountability feels like love. You and your sweetheart are asking each other to heal.

The sprouts are the perfect analogy because they need to be rinsed. And drained. Then there's some growth. Then more rinsing. More draining. More growing. Until they can feed you and they look nothing like the seeds you started with.

This is how you create your happily ever after: one clean ask at a time.

Chapter Review

- **The Clean Ask Formula.** Pair the soft vulnerability of your feelings with the powerful agency of a specific desire to ask cleanly. Feeling + Desire = A Clean Ask.
- **Avoid the Dirty Ask.** Recognize how fear disguises your feelings and causes confusion. When that fear is disguised, it can create a dirty ask.
- **Design a Clean Ask.** Clean up your dirty ask one step at a time. Use these two phrases: *Stay in your own business*, and *Is that true?* A Clean Ask has a "yes" or "no" implied response.
- **Sprout Love.** Own your feelings and desires in order to create a Clean Ask. A Clean Ask is less "polite" and more direct. The directness deepens the intimacy in your relationship.
- **Stay Clean.** Even when your sweetheart asks dirty it's important to stay clean because a Clean Asker can change the dynamic in a relationship. Four tools to stay clean: *hug, offer a hunch, laugh* and *offer compassion* when your sweetheart is *healing instead of hearing*.

You've just taken in a lot of information.

To make real changes, you need time to synthesize.

What will help you turn what you just read into a habit you can practice?

Part II
Receiving

Conditions
Affirmations
and how to build a kind
Boundary

First of all, congratulations for reading this far. Most people buy a book and it sits on the shelf. You've read the entire first half. Hooray you!

The thesis of this book is that communication involves two things: giving and receiving. That's not complicated, right?

But even though it's simple to articulate, it's not easy in practice. In the first half of the book, we talked about how to tidy up the communication you *give* by asking super cleanly. This second part of the book we'll turn our focus to the communication you *receive*.

As a reminder, communication has two basic parts: speaking and listening. Giving and receiving. What you've already read will improve the *speaking* part of your communication.

Because you've learned strategies to **overcome your fear**, you'll be more apt to pause in a conflict and notice how your fear is getting in the way. Your awareness of your own fear will help you give differently in a communication.

You've learned how crucial it is to **get clear** on what you want so you can articulate that clearly to your sweetheart. Confusion is so often the thing that ignites conflict.

Overcoming fear and getting clear sets you up to **ask cleanly**.

Ahhhhh.

A clean ask provides relief for your relationship. A clean ask is a key component in reducing conflict.

Great! So now you've got the tools and you've begun to up your relationship communication in the speaking/giving department.

Now let's shift gears and concentrate on the listening/receiving side of the relationship communication equation.

Part 2—Beware Conditions, Affirm Lovingly, and Build Boundaries—will give you strategies to aid you as you receive or listen to the communication your sweetheart gives to you.

Notice that I said, aid *you* as *you* listen to your sweetheart.

Remember the most important tool of relationship communication? *Stay in your own business.* There is absolutely nothing you can do to change the way your sweetheart communicates.

But you have all the power in the world to change the way you communicate. And when you change, your sweetheart will need to change because the dynamic is different.

While you will use overcoming fear and getting clear all your life, they are particularly important for the *falling-in-love* stage of your relationship.

Now, in the second half of the book, we'll focus on the *landing-in-love* stage of life.

What do I mean by *landing in love?*

When you first move in together, it's novel to put pictures on the wall and decide which cupboard your dishes belong in. Because it's new, that originality is fun.

Later, the pictures have dust on them and the dishes are in the sink rather than in the cupboard. Setting up a home is like a game, whereas living in a home, and creating a lifestyle can feel dull and monotonous.

Let's reframe those words: dull and monotonous. Living with your sweetheart for years and decades is filled with predictability and stability. But, let's be honest, sometimes predictability can feel dull. And stability isn't super sexy.

This stable phase of a relationship is when you truly get a chance to land in love, however. For what it's worth, I think landed love is ten times more satisfying than the twitterpation of falling in love.

Why? Because I feel wholly myself. And I feel wholly loved. Turns out that is a holy feeling. Safe. And sacred.

But there's a transition between the two: You haven't yet landed, but you've fallen.

You don't feel cozy-blanket-safe-from-stability yet, but your knees are skinned from the fall. It's a tough stage of a relationship. I hope just knowing it's normal for that to be tough gives you some encouragement.

Now you wake up to the realization you're in a long-term relationship developing a home life where you try to figure out who's gonna get those dishes from the sink back into the cupboard.

Add to this that your home of origin or other life experiences may have wounded you. As you create a home of your own, those childhood wounds show up in unexpected places.

Those wounds affect your hearing. Those wounds affect how you receive love.

We are all healing in one way or another. Our wounded spots act like the BLEEP police on network television, blocking out all the words that trigger us.

When words your sweetheart says get bleeped by the wounds of your childhood, you aren't able to hear what your sweetheart is actually saying. This means you can't receive the love your sweetheart is offering.

The second half of this book addresses your ability to hear more accurately. So you can truly receive the love you long for.

How so?

The wounds you've experienced affect your feeling of worthiness. When you don't feel worthy, you accept conditions on love. You even *expect* conditions on love. We will tackle this in Chapter 4, Beware Conditions.

Your childhood also gave you a bunch of habits. You learned habitual responses to habitual behaviors. Maybe each time the sink was full of dishes, you got blamed or shamed. In Chapter 5, Affirm Lovingly, we'll discuss those habits and how you can choose to change your habitual response.

One more wound you may have gotten from your childhood home or society at large is a host of rules for how The Game of Life is supposed to be played. In Chapter 6, Build Boundaries, we will examine how these rules get projected onto your marriage and how you can fence them out.

Just like we did in the first half of the book, we'll take each of these steps one by one, so we can illuminate the traps and foibles, but remember that life is messy and these three will show up in your life overlapping and tangled together.

STEP FOUR

Beware Conditions

We impose conditions because we think the rules of love will keep us safe.

It's risky to accept conditions on love. Have you ever felt like your sweetheart will love you *if* you're thin? Or *if* you're rich? Or *if* you say yes instead of no?

Conditions on love try to slip in without being noticed. Conditions are a shortcut, and we're all tempted to take that shortcut: *Love me the way I tell you to love me.*

It feels safe to have rules. But rules don't allow the magic of unconditional love to flourish.

We taste and cultivate truly intimate love only when we're seen and cherished for precisely who we are right this minute.

If you can resist the shortcut of conditional love and cherish your sweetheart instead, you will be capable to receive the love your sweetheart genuinely has to offer you. This is rich, unfettered love. Not manipulated. Not sanitized by your rules. If feels wonderful. But the path to this love is risky. That's why we're tempted to avoid it.

We want to avoid the risks of vulnerability. But we cannot live without love. So, we impose conditions that are rules of how we demand to be loved. We've all done it.

The purpose of this chapter is to carefully examine the conditions you accept or impose. Examination leads to recognition. When you can recognize conditions, you're able to question them, and employ strategies to help you let them go.

In this chapter…

You'll learn to give and receive communication with open-hearted generosity.

- **Recognize conditions.** I'll tell you a story from my marriage because conditions aren't always obvious
- **Recognize your worthiness.** Worthiness is a tender shield of protection that empowers you to resist conditional love
- **Listen to your body.** Get familiar with the signals your body sends. Your body recognizes conditional love better than your mind
- **Cherish yourself.** Use two meditations to do this
- **Untangle conditions that hide.** Conditions are messy little buggers; you'll get some worksheets to help you untangle them
- **Turn hidden conditions into transparent agreements.**
- **Agree to disagree.** Learn to disagree without conditional love

First, let's get a clear understanding of conditions:

A four-year-old knows what it's like to want a lollipop. A four-year-old also knows how to ask clearly: "Please, please, please can I have the sucker?" And when they hear no, they ask again: "But I really want it!"

A parent can offer the treat without conditions and hand their four-year-old the lollipop. The parent gets joy when they see their child happy, and the child's desire is satisfied. There are no conditions in this situation.

But sometimes a lollipop comes with a multitude of conditions: "Give me a hug first," "You can have the lollipop after you eat your lima beans," or implied conditions that the child can feel but can't articulate: *If I give you this lollipop, your job is to love me more than you love anyone else.*

Suddenly the lollipop isn't as tasty. The child wonders if the conditions are worth it.

These conditional pairings enter into our adult lives as well.

You've seen marriages built on conditions: *I'll give you the security of a house if you'll build my ego and dote on me.* Or *I'll make a nice dinner, but then I expect to get lucky in the bedroom.* We are a little ashamed to ask for the trade out loud, so instead, we go covert ops and weave these unwritten rules into the fine print of our love contract.

Don't take the bait. When you fall for the rules hidden in the fine print, you will feel as empty as an all-day sucker.

The deep oneness you long for is built on compassion and a deep feeling of worthiness. You will learn how to cultivate compassion—for yourself and for your sweetheart—with curiosity and transparency. That compassion will replace your desire to keep score and soften your urge to have so many rules when it comes to love.

STRATEGY 1

How to Recognize Conditions

An example of conditional love from my marriage

Wanna hear about the conditional love I imposed?

Many years into my husband's education I took a weekend away from my family and went to a writer's retreat. I felt rested for the first time in years. I was happy driving home and eager for a reunion with my kids. For the first time in a long time, I was imagining a sexy encounter with my husband.

During the years of his schooling, I mostly functioned like a single parent and I kept a tight ship: healthy food meant the kids didn't have sugar meltdowns. A clean house meant I didn't feel overwhelmed by chores.

I walked through the door anticipating hugs and, "We missed you!" I was sure my husband was going to see how difficult my job was since he'd been doing it all weekend.

Instead, I found my family quietly settled at the table eating pancakes for dinner. They all said hello, but there was no sign they'd missed me. I felt the palms of my hands get hot. How come they don't seem excited to see me? A pang of insecurity bit at the inside of my gut.

As I looked around the kitchen, there were piles of dishes. Suddenly resentment mixed with the insecurity and I said, "You're eating pancakes? For dinner?" I chewed on the inside of my lip.

These kids were gonna be wired for hours. I stayed up late the night before I left and made chicken soup. I made this easy for him to do the right thing and give these kids wholesome food rather than sugary pancakes. Why didn't my husband feed them the soup?

The kids were beaming. My son said, "And dad let me put powdered sugar *and* jam on mine." I turned to my husband cocking my head. He got my message: he'd done it wrong.

I asked what they'd done that weekend. "We watched *The Princess Bride* and had a *Reading Rainbow* marathon."

"You watched TV all day?" I wasn't asking. I was accusing. My husband looked away. "Did you guys go outside at all?"

They hadn't. Both my kids were still in their jammies. And, to top it off, there was a pile of laundry in the hall.

I felt sorry for myself. I was the maid who did the laundry. It was up to me to tire the kids out. And there'd be no lingering kisses for my husband and me: these kids would be sugar-wired for hours.

I wanted David to take care of the kids and the house according to my standard. When he didn't, I withdrew my love. In a matter of four minutes and three questions, I managed to ice him out. He failed.

He failed as a father. And now, he wasn't worthy of my love.

Maybe you relate to my struggle that day. Maybe you think I did the right thing by icing my husband out. Afterall, why should I do all the work and he get to watch all the movies and feed our kids pancakes?

I know. I bet you're tired, too. That's because living life is filled with moments of exhaustion and overwhelm.

The first person you get frustrated with when you're exhausted and overwhelmed is your sweetheart. That's natural.

But let's look at this snippet of time from David's perspective. The week prior to this Saturday movie fest he worked 2 36-hour shifts. 36 hours! Twice! And while at those shifts, he cared for a man who was stabbed, a drug overdose, a stroke, and a three-car accident. My husband had to tell the surviving gentleman in that accident that his wife and one of his sons had died.

My husband started that weekend wrecked, but he was eager for me to get a break. So, he did what he could and cozied up on the couch, putting a kid in each arm and snuggled his kids while they watched TV so he could snooze off and on.

We were *both* tired.

If you're lucky enough to live with your sweetheart dozens of years, you will encounter a situation similar to this multiple times.

When you're tired, you think only of yourself and you think your way of living is the only way. You lose perspective. You can't see that there are lots of ways to live and love and be in the world.

I lost perspective. When David didn't do things my way that weekend, I withdrew my love. If he didn't do it my way, he didn't *deserve* my love. My love became conditional, and, although I didn't say it aloud, my body sent him a message as I headed down the hallway to sort laundry with a vengeance: *David, you don't deserve love unless you parent our kids according to my criteria.*

Do you know what he did? He called down the hallway after me, "We were happy until you came home."

Ouch.

But it was a good wakeup call for me.

David rejected my conditions on love. He knew he'd been a loving father to his kids.

He had been loving to himself as he rested and inhaled the scent of each of his children, still alive, able to be held and snuggled.

He'd been a loving husband to me to say, "Go to your retreat; I've got this," even though he was exhausted.

I put conditions on my love for David because I thought I knew the best way for him to love me and to love our kids. But I was wrong.

The best way for David to love our kids that weekend was to hold onto them and be grateful they were alive. That restored him as a father who suddenly felt vulnerable because he'd had a front row seat to watch how an instant could change the life of a family.

Try This Tool: Just Notice (Gently)

This week, try just noticing ways that you might be offering or accepting conditional love.

Don't ask yourself to make any changes. Noticing is powerful. Let that be enough as you take this first step toward eliminating conditions.

What conditions do you tend to put on your love?
_____
_____

What conditions are you accepting?
_____
_____

Note: Noticing gently leads to compassion. Noticing to blame leads to shame. I invite you to be gentle as you notice conditions on love.

STRATEGY 2

Recognize Your Worthiness

How compassion, curiosity, and transparency will help you avoid conditions on love

You can choose to accept or reject conditions on love.

Fortunately for my marriage, David chose to reject the conditions I put on my love that day when I arrived home filled with agendas.

When he rejected my conditions, I was forced to question them. I couldn't manipulate David into behaving the way I wanted by withholding love, so I needed to rethink those conditions.

How you rethink love's conditions is the critical element. If you ask yourself questions like:

- Why should David feed the kids healthy food? or
- Why should I feel justified in my anger?

you're going to get answers that *increase* your compulsion to employ more conditional love.

This is because conditions on love are built on a scaffolding of fairness, justice, and righteous anger.

You will recognize the breeding ground of conditions in *why-questions* and the word *should*. Why-questions typically look for an answer that will justify your conditional love. Why-questions have a basic premise: *Why am I right?* (The implied other half to this question is *Why is my sweetheart wrong?*)

When you *should* all over your sweetheart, you're applying your rules of love to their life. We all have a long list of things we think our sweetheart should do. But guess whose business you're in when you tell your sweetheart (even in your own mind) what they should do?

Reminder!

The most important tool in your marriage is to:

Stay in your own business.

I wasn't wrong to want David to feed the kids healthy food, or get them outside to play so they'd be tired when bedtime arrived. But when I meditate on the RIGHTNESS of my request, it only inspires me to dig my heels in deeper and tighter.

Instead of focusing on justice, open a discussion (even if it's only in your mind) about compassion. Rethink your conditions with a wash of compassion.

Compassion is cultivated with curiosity and transparency.

If I had been transparent about my feelings—*Hey, none of you seem happy to see me*; or *Hey, I really missed you guys*—there would have been a completely different vibe in the household.

Try This Tool: Remember Differently

Remember a time in your relationship when you felt that little-kid-voice swell inside you, "But this isn't FAIR!"

Revisit that moment in history with transparency and curiosity to cultivate compassion. Notice how your body feels when you approach the situation with transparency and curiosity rather than blame or shame.

Transparency:
- How are you feeling in that moment in history when life didn't feel fair?
- What is it, precisely, that feels unfair?
- What do you make that mean?
- What story are you telling yourself about this moment and your sweetheart?

How does your story change?

_____

_____

Curiosity:
- How is your sweetheart feeling in this moment of unfairness?
- What is it, precisely, that feels unfair?
- What does your sweetheart make that mean?
- What story is your sweetheart telling themselves about that meaning?

How does your story change?

_____

_____

That different vibe—one of openness and transparency—may have inspired David to tell me about his struggles at the hospital and why he so desperately needed a weekend of quiet relaxation holding his kids.

If my openness didn't inspire David to reveal what was happening for him, I could have gotten curious: *What made you choose pancakes when I had prepared chicken soup?* Or, *You typically love being outside, what made you choose a day of jammies and TV?*

When you can remain transparent about your feelings and curious about your sweetheart, you invite compassion. Compassion is a huge ingredient in cultivating worthiness because compassion erases shame. Compassion embraces human frailty. Compassion invites loving kindness.

Loving kindness will erase the Me-vs-You tendency to argue, and instead foster the WE of your union. Compassion—and the loving kindness it creates—will perpetually build your relationship as ONE unit, rather than constantly weighing whose *turn* is it: mine or yours?

Rethinking helped me to see I'd been unfair. I saw that I wasn't offering my love unconditionally. I was trying to change David. With his rejection of my conditions, he was telling me, "I'm worthy. Right now. I'm worthy of being loved."

You, Dear Reader, are worthy of unconditional love. Right now. Your sweetheart is also worthy of unconditional love. Right now.

You do not need to change in order to be more loveable, and neither does your sweetheart.

Unconditional love is magic. It's healing. It beckons the best part of you to wake up over and over.

Assume you and your sweetheart are both lovable. Right now.

If I had walked through that front door assuming David was worthy of my unconditional love right now, I would have seen the messy dishes and the pancakes and gotten curious instead of accusatory.

You cultivate compassion, and thus worthiness, when you are transparent and curious. I would have asked about his weekend. "Are you OK? I noticed you didn't do the dishes, is something wrong?"

When you assume your sweetheart is worthy of your unconditional love, you are curious first about their well-being rather than being curious first about all the ways your sweetheart let you down.

Now, because my husband isn't as reflective as I am, he would probably have said, "I'm fine." He wouldn't have told me about the accident and the husband whose wife died. And then I'd be tempted to return to conditional love, resenting a person who's "fine" but unwilling to step up and be a contributing partner.

That's when it's crucial that you also remember *you* are worthy of unconditional love. That's when you extend unconditional love to yourself. I could have said:

I came home eager to see all of you, but when I saw the dishes and the pancakes, my eagerness turned to resentment. I feel alone in this project of raising kids while you're at school or gone so much, David. When I see dishes undone, and I see you taking the easy path with dinner, I feel disrespected. Then I feel lonely.

Clients regularly tell me they have to put conditions on their love or they'll never get help with the chores around the house.

However, consider the flavor of the love you receive when that's the bargain you make. Condition-laden love is transactional. You and your sweetheart will simply accrue a tally sheet.

Sometimes you'll feel owed "love." Sometimes you'll feel like you are the one in debt and you'll toss some "love" your sweetheart's way. This kind of love, though, is transactional, and if this is all you offer or receive, you'll never swim in that gorgeous, soothing ocean of abundant love, freely given.

How to cultivate compassion with curiosity and transparency

Let's use a water analogy to talk about conditions on love. Imagine a hose. Water runs easily from one end to the other. But if you take that hose and bend it, that kink lets less water flow. Conditions on love are like kinks in the hose.

I had a list of things David needed to do in order for me to feel loved by him. Each time he failed to live up to the list, I placed a kink in the love-hose I could feel from him.

- Did David feed the kids healthy food? No? OK: kink number one.
- Did David do the dishes? No? Kink number two.
- Fresh air? No? Kink three.
- Laundry? NO! Kink. No flow.

This love-hose has so many kinks I can't feel David loving me at all.

Isn't it interesting how I was the one imposing the conditions, but it was also me that couldn't receive love from him because of those conditions? This happens. All. The. Time.

Let's imagine that you are able to focus on cultivating a compassionate relationship; a relationship where both members' needs are considered. In order to do this, you need to let go of your just-and-fairness mindset. You need to stop keeping score.

David, I think I had some expectations I didn't speak out loud before I left. I expected you to take care of the details like dishes and laundry. I expected you to avoid sugary foods that mess with the kids' mood-regulation.

And, what's funny is I didn't think I needed to speak those expectations aloud. I thought those things would be obvious. But you didn't do those things, so my expectations weren't obvious. Can we talk about how that feels for me?

Speaking like this assumes I'm worthy. It also assumes David is worthy. We simply have a misunderstanding. When you start with worthiness you remove the kinks or conditions and your love can flow freely.

Worthiness falters when you get unresourceful. Maybe you're tired. Maybe you're feeling financial or emotional stressors. We forget we're worthy when we're tired or unresourceful. And we really forget our sweetheart is worthy.

Exhaustion is a prime ingredient for conditional love. The more exhausted you are, the less flexible or resilient you are. When you get tired, you send the message: *You're not living up to my standard. You're not loving me the way I want to be loved. So, it's your job to change.*

This is the implication of conditions: you want your sweetheart to change.

You want to be loved your way, according to your list, *or else*. This doesn't leave room for your sweetheart to have their own needs, or their own list of ways to demonstrate they love you.

When I put conditions on love that weekend, I was saying, "David, in order for me to feel you loving me, I need the dishes done." I couldn't feel his love because I had so many restrictions on how I could receive his love.

Look what I missed out on as a result: As a girl, I dreamed of a Whole Family. I wanted that one unit where parents and kids were all snuggled together in the same home, on the same couch, watching the same movie.

David was embodying my childhood dream when he took the pain he felt from the hospital and wrapped his arms around his children to comfort himself. He was living my dream.

But I couldn't feel his love and my dream coming true because I was lost in conditional love.

When we don't *feel* loved, we're tempted to withhold our love.

Try This Tool: Cherishing and Educating

Where are you tempted to keep score in your relationship?
- Chores?
- Money?
- Sexual initiation?

List three specific situations where you have kept score in the past:
1. _____
2. _____
3. _____

Education: What did your sweetheart not know about this situation?
_____
_____

Education: What did you not know about this situation?
_____
_____

Cherish: How could you cherish yourself in that situation?
_____
_____

Cherish: How could you cherish your sweetheart in that situation?
_____
_____

Compassion is magical in these moments. The instant I understood what David was going through, I no longer needed help with the dishes. I was actually glad he left them in the sink and rested.

I felt the irresistible love David had for our children. I began to tell myself a different story. *My husband loves our family so much he just needed to spend his weekend holding them.*

The problem was, he didn't tell me about that accident and the wife who died for several weeks. David wasn't transparent about his own feelings. When your sweetheart doesn't reveal their feelings, it's difficult for you to cultivate compassion.

Remember the importance of clarity when it comes to communication? I didn't even know he needed my compassion. When David didn't clearly communicate about his experience at the hospital, I made assumptions that he was "fine."

Yes, curiosity will help to fend off conditional loving. But it was also important for David to be transparent and reveal his situation and feelings to me. You can't know things your sweetheart doesn't share with you.

It's not enough to be curious instead of accusatory when it comes to avoiding conditional love. You also have a responsibility to be transparent and revelatory about your circumstances and mood. When you each behave with curiosity and transparency, you set yourselves up for compassionate love instead of conditional love.

Compassionate love vs conditional love

In a lifelong relationship there are tons of times it's tempting to offer conditional love. Here's a list of ways you might want your sweetheart to change so they are more lovable:

- Wipe your crumbs off the counter.
- Listen to my story.
- Have sex with me.

I hear you: But Rebecca, all those demands sound reasonable in a loving relationship. I don't wanna clean up after my sweetheart's crumbs. Isn't it right that I should expect my sweetheart to listen to me? Sex an important part of a marriage after all.

Yes. All those things are important. But *withdrawing love* when they don't happen is conditional and, thus, toxic.

Instead, I challenge you to cherish your sweetheart and yourself. To assume you're both worthy of love even when your behavior needs an education or an upgrade.

Behavior doesn't determine your worthiness. You are worthy of love because you were born.

We've all felt annoyed at our partner when there's a pile of crumbs we didn't create. We've felt lonely when our story goes unheard. And we all know it's painful to have a sexual advance rejected.

But conditions on love take that annoyance, loneliness, or rejection and pollute the love with punishment and "prove it" tally sheets.

The best way to stop imposing conditions or accepting conditions is to notice conditions when they appear.

Replay those scenarios using transparency and curiosity to cultivate compassion for both yourself and your sweetheart. Look for the ONEness rather than the Me-vs-You tendency.

The dishes. The pancakes. The all-day-movies. These are all behaviors my husband had. Behaviors are a symptom of the person behaving. Lousy behavior signals a lack of resourcefulness or education.

When I took time to cherish myself, I was able to ask for what I need: *I really wish you could have done the dishes.*

When I took time to cherish David, my need for clean dishes evaporated because I saw his suffering and exhaustion as well as my own.

We will talk about boundaries in Chapter 6. In the meantime, I want to say this: Building boundaries in your relationship is easier when you cherish your sweetheart and cherish yourself.

But how? How do you cherish that person who has disappointed you or hurt your feelings? First, let's take a look at a few ways to uncover conditions that are hiding in your heart. This next section will help you tune into your body to find conditions that aren't obvious.

STRATEGY 3

Listen to Your Body
Get familiar with the signals your body senses

Conditions are sneaky and they like to hide as righteous indignation. We all want to impose conditions on love when our sweetheart is "doing it wrong."

How do you recognize the fine print of conditions?

You'll recognize conditional love because you can feel the if/then implications that are rarely spoken aloud. There's a difference between conditions and agreements. Agreements are stated clearly and both you and your sweetheart can talk about them.

Conditions, on the other hand, try to hide so you can't see them, but you're forced to abide them if you want to get the love you crave. Think of conditions as the fine print of your unspoken love contract.

Let's imagine your ability to love like a pond filled with water. Imagine how it feels to scoop up a cool, clear drink from that pond when you're hot and thirsty. You feel refreshed. Hydrated.

This is how unconditional love feels: pure and energizing.

Now let's take that pond and let it sit, stagnant for months. A film of scum grows on the top of the pond. Lily pads emerge and block out the light. The water gets so murky you can't see through it. Drinking from this pond? It feels slimy and toxic. You'd rather go thirsty than drink from it.

This is how conditional love feels. Icky and toxic.

The problem is we can't survive without love, just like we can't survive without water. If you get thirsty enough, you'll drink that pond-scum-water, even though it's icky. So too, if you are deprived of love long enough, you'll swallow conditions even though they're toxic and pollute your soul.

Notice your body. You might be *imposing* conditions on love if you:
- Feel tight. In your throat, chest, or gut.
- Lean in. Like you're trying to push your agenda.
- Lean away. Like you're trying to dodge something.
- Fold your arms across your chest. Cross your legs. Any posture that sends the stop-sign signal. "Ain't no love getting through this wall."

Notice your body. You might be *accepting* conditions on love if you feel:
- Slimy. Or like there's something on your skin you wish you could wipe off. Manipulation or confusion can cause your body to feel like there's a film between you and the world.
- Like you want to hide. Shame, embarrassment, or a feeling of unworthiness can cause you to want to hide.
- Like you're running to catch up. When you feel indebted, it feels like nothing you do will ever be enough.

Try This Tool: Clue into Conditions

Notice your body as you recall a time when you felt huge conditions placed on the love you wished to receive.

Recall a specific memory and write that memory here:
_____
_____

As you remember this moment in time when you feel icky, conditional love, recall what the room or outdoor space smells like. Recall the quality of light. These specific sensory memories help your body to be transported back to that time. Write down specific sensory memories of smell, light, and sound here:
_____
_____

Once you feel steeped in that memory, notice your body. What is the strongest feeling in your body? Notice how your skin feels. Notice your gut and your heart. Notice your throat and your face. Write down 1-3 specific feelings in your body here:
_____
_____

This is your body's way of signaling conditional love. Give this feeling a name that will help to remind you to notice conditions:
_____
_____

Ex: The bottom of the driveway feeling

This is your body's template for conditional love. When you're struggling or can't figure out how to adjust your behavior in a conflict, consult your body's template for conditional love. What do you need to do in this moment to feel more worthy so you can reject the conditions, or to soften the conditions you're imposing?

Sometimes it's difficult to feel your body's signals. This is normal when you're confused or when you've grown up with so many conditions on love that your body has grown accustomed to the feelings associated with conditional love.

You know what helps? Cherishing yourself. When you cherish yourself with unconditional love, you wake up your body's willingness to feel.

Let's talk next about how to cherish yourself and nurture your ability to love unconditionally.

STRATEGY 4
Cherish Yourself
Unconditional love for others begins with unconditional love for yourself

When we are deprived of love—from ourselves or others—we're willing to accept (and impose) more conditions. Therefore, the more worthy you feel, the fewer conditions you'll accept or impose.

How do you feel more worthy? You focus on love instead of on fear.

Your Inner Lizard is always afraid and focuses entirely on *what's wrong*. You need to refocus your attention on all the positive things in your character and world. When you meditate on beauty and all you have to be proud of, your need for conditions diminishes.

The Proud Meditation is an exercise to cherish yourself and help you feel more worthy of love. When you feel worthy, you receive love more easily. When you receive love with ease, you feel lighter, freer, and—total bonus—you give love more freely as well.

Let's try another way to cherish. Instead of the focus being on yourself, try focusing on something you find beautiful. It may be a painting you see in the museum you visit, or the tree you pass on your way to work, or the dog who lives next door.

Try This Tool: Proud Meditation

Think of a time you were really proud of yourself. Describe the details of what made you feel proud here:

___

Ex: Formatting this book that you're reading was hard, and outside my comfort. But I'm proud I stuck with it. I believe my love and care show in the details.

Now, reflect on the core traits you have that allowed that proud moment to happen. List those core traits here:

___
___

Ex: patience, breaking the giant job into small tasks, showing up for the work

Now, reflect on how those core traits have impacted your life. Let yourself notice the gratitude you feel for the person that you are:

___
___

Ex: I'm grateful for the people I've met as a result of having my work in the world

Try This Tool: Beauty Meditation

Bring to mind (or better yet, go gaze at) something you find beautiful. Describe your beautiful thing in detail here:

___

Ex: the way my horses's ears flicker back and forth.

Now, reflect on the core traits that inspire the beauty you see. List those core traits here:

___
___

Ex: my horse picks up every tiny sound and signal I send.

Now, reflect on how those core traits have impacted your life. Let yourself notice the gratitude you feel for the beauty all around you:

___
___

Ex: I feel grateful for the unconditional love I feel from my horse and the bond we have.

These cherishing exercises wake up your tender, loving heart. Cherishing is the antidote to conditional love. Cherishing promotes a loving mindset.

This open, cherishing mindset may help you to do the exercises in the following strategy with an open heart that is ready to be transparent, curious, and full of tender compassion.

STRATEGY 5

Untangle Conditions that Hide

Worksheets to help you untangle what feels so messy inside

Sometimes you just need a little help to identify your conditional thinking. The following worksheets will help you look at the way you behave a bit differently. We're asking specific questions to uncover conditions.

Warning: In these exercises you're going to violate The Most Important Strategy in Relationship Communication: *Stay in Your Own Business*. We're violating this rule for a specific reason: we want to make *explicit* what is happening *implicitly* in your relationship.

I invite you to enter this space as an explorer, rather than as a project manager. You want to explore all the ways you're in your sweetheart's business (or your sweetheart is in your business) so you can map it out. You want to see the landmines.

You are not entering into your sweetheart's business so you can tell them what to do or prove how right you've always been.

If/Then

This is the most common way for conditions to hide. Use the following prompt to get the conditions your sweetheart offers you out of hiding.

If I do/don't _____ then my sweetheart will_____.

Example:

- If I spend "too much" time with my friends, my sweetheart will punish me by getting concert tickets to my favorite band and not include me.
- If I don't kiss my sweetheart when he gets home, then he will give me the silent treatment for the rest of the evening.
- If I spend more money than my sweetheart thinks is appropriate, my sweetheart will cancel plans we had saying, "Now we can't afford it."

Your turn to identify if/then conditions your sweetheart imposes. Think of a situation where your sweetheart withholds love from you:

Try This Tool: Identify If/Then Conditions

Identify the if/then conditions your sweetheart imposes. Fill in the following blanks using moments from your history.

If I do/don't _____, then my sweetheart will _____.

If I do/don't _____, then my sweetheart will _____.

If I do/don't _____, then my sweetheart will _____.

Now, ask yourself these questions:
- How does your body feel when you notice these conditions on love?
- How do you behave towards your sweetheart when you feel the weight of these conditions?
- Do you want to continue to accept these conditions on love?
- What patterns do you notice?

What did you discover as you explored? Now that you see where the conditions are hiding what feelings do you notice? How can you be transparent about those feelings with your sweetheart?

How can you get curious about your sweetheart? Reminder: you're not the project manager trying to get things RIGHT. You're the lover, the partner, and the friend who wants to connect with your sweetheart and understand their motivations.

Now let's give you a chance to spot conditions that you are tempted to impose. Use the following series of blanks to get your conditions out of hiding.

Remember, you're an explorer. You are worthy of both compassion and unconditional love. These questions will help you to discover how you're in your own way when it comes to cultivating a home filled with unconditional love.

If my sweetheart does/doesn't _____ then I will _____.

Examples:
- If my sweetheart doesn't wipe up their crumbs, then I'll infantilize them by telling them what a slob they are.
- If my sweetheart doesn't listen to my story when I want to tell it, then I'll roll my eyes and stomp out of the room.
- If my sweetheart doesn't have sex with me, I'll punish them by talking about the hottie at my work so they'll feel threatened.

Your turn to identify if/then conditions you impose. Think of a situation where you're tempted to withhold love if your sweetheart does/doesn't behave according to your rule book:

Try This Tool: Identify If/Then Conditions

Identify the if/then conditions you impose on your sweetheart. Think of a situation where you're tempted to withhold love if your sweetheart doesn't behave according to your rule book.

If my sweetheart does/doesn't _____, then I will _____.

If my sweetheart does/doesn't _____, then I will _____.

If my sweetheart does/doesn't _____, then I will _____.

Now, ask yourself these questions:
- How does your body feel when you impose these conditions?
- How do you behave towards your sweetheart when you impose these conditions
- Do you want to continue imposing these conditions on love?

Cultivate Compassion

There are as many ways to love conditionally as there are human beings. We love conditionally because we are scared. We apply conditions to love because we think the rules of love will keep us save.

There are no rules when it comes to unconditional love.

Unconditional love is just love.

You are worthy of love because you were born. The more you cultivate unconditional love in your life the more freedom and ease you will feel.

You cultivate unconditional love each time you refuse to accept conditions, and each time you refuse to impose conditions. You simply let love be love.

The antidote to conditions is compassion.

Try This Tool: Cultivate Compassion

When you encounter conditions try this repetition to cultivate compassion:
1. Reveal more feelings.
2. Request more information; get curiouser.
3. Reveal more feelings.
4. Request more information; get curiouser again.

Then trust your body. If your body relaxes and heaves a sigh of relief, let yourself receive the unconditional love your sweetheart is trying to give. Or let yourself give the unconditional love you're long to share.

Receiving love is a practice. We think we aren't worthy, so we push unconditional love away.

Notice the times you're tempted to push love away.

Breathe.

Breathe again.

Practice letting go of conditions—both those you impose and those you accept.

If, however, your body gets tight, or rigid, or you feel your head spinning in a cycle of confusion, trust your body. This is your body giving you the signals of conditional love.

Sometimes conditions are so ingrained that vulnerable feelings and curiosity don't unlock them.

Believe your body in these moments. See those conditions for what they are. Name them. Take those conditions out of hiding. Because what you deserve and what you were designed for is *unconditional* love.

We will talk more about this in Chapter 6: Build Boundaries. For now, just trust your body's signals. And name conditions for precisely what they are: polluted love. Kinks in the hose.

Take conditions out of their hiding place to unkink the hose of your love so it can flow freely. Next, let's look at how you can wash those conditions away.

STRATEGY 6

Turn Conditions into Agreements
Overcome fear. Get clear. Ask cleanly. Then cherish.

Cherishing your sweetheart washes conditions away. You do that when you remember that both you and your sweetheart are worthy of love. Right now. You can also wash conditions away with a Clean Ask.

In the first half of this book, I named three steps for communicating better with your sweetheart—**Overcome Fear, Get Clear, and Ask Cleanly.**

In this section, you're going to see why those three steps prepare you to **love unconditionally.** You'll also see how when you skip those first three steps, you set yourself up to poison love with conditions.

In order to visualize how these steps work in concert, let's imagine a 3-step car wash: the kind you drive through and at each station your car gets attention. These three steps are a review of previous Try This boxes.

First stop you get rained on by the colorful, foamy soap, and the giant spinning rollers scrub the sides of your car. Next, your car drives through the rinsing waterfall. And finally, you enter the cave of blowers that dry everything up.

How the Fear-Clear-Clean Wash allows you to let go of conditions

When you are imposing or accepting a condition on love, take that condition through the Fear-Clear-Clean Wash until the condition is washed away.

Try This Review: Fear-Clear-Clean Wash
Stop #1 Overcome Fear

First stop: Overcome Fear Naming is Taming. Imagine that foamy, colorful soap that is your condition. Your condition imposes rules on love to keep you or your sweetheart safe. See the condition as clearly as you see that soap dripping on your windshield and name it.

Example: David is entitled to my love if and only if he cares for the house and kids in the way I've prescribed.

Just naming the condition helps me loosen my grip on it because, as soon as I say that out loud, I realize I don't really believe that.

Use this space to name the condition you're feeling from your sweetheart:_____

Use this space to name the condition you're imposing on your sweetheart: _____

Befriend to Mend. Conditions show up because they think they're being helpful. Remember your Lizard Brain that's trying to keep you safe? Conditions are simply fears hiding. Employ those spinning giant rollers at the car wash to unearth the whole fear you feel.

Example: I'm afraid David's gonna take advantage of me if I don't set really strict parameters. I'm afraid I'm gonna end up doing all the work in this family.

Now that you can see the fear, it loses some of its captivating powers and you can…

Get Curious about your fear's—or your condition's—premise. *Hmm… Is David actually a slacker?* No! Not even.

Use this space to state why you feel your condition is righteous or needed. If you have trouble articulating that, state the worst-case-scenario you fear if you don't impose your condition:

_____
_____

Protect to Connect. We all want a fanciful Prince Charming to come and carry us away from the things that are difficult in life. We crave ease. But true intimacy isn't easy, and there are times it's quite uncomfortable.

Example: I was exhausted. David was exhausted. Being able to understand each other when each of us was completely unresourceful strengthened our capacity to love.

Intimacy is delicious and worth the effort. Take a moment to notice why intimacy—true companionship—is worth a little discomfort on your part. Use this space to notice how you're up to the task.

_____
_____

Try This Review: Fear-Clear-Clean Wash
Stop #2 Get Clear

Second stop: Get clear. The second stop in the Fear-Clear-Clean Condition Wash is to get clear about what you want. Clarity invites agency and empowerment. You feel worthy of your desire because you can feel the truth of it in your body.

Imagine that rinsing waterfall clearing away all distractions and hydrating you (and your car) so you can easily see specifically, precisely, exactly what you want.

Example: *I want David to do all the things I would have done while I was gone: the dishes, the healthy food, and the outdoor play. And I realize if he had done these three, I wouldn't even care about the laundry.*

Specificity sets you up to notice the precise behavior you want from your sweetheart.

Use this space to clearly articulate all the things you want your sweetheart to do to "earn" your love:

___

Try This: Fear-Clear-Clean Wash
Stop #3 Ask Cleanly

Third stop: Ask Cleanly. Now you're ready for the finishing power of those big blowers and you can ask cleanly. Remember the Clean Ask Formula? Fear + Desire = a Clean Ask.

Example: *David, I just shoved conditional love at you because I walked into this house and saw all the work ahead of me. I'm afraid you'll take me for granted. I wish you would have washed the dishes and fed the kids better food so I don't feel like I'm the only one being a parent around here. Would you wash the dishes now?*

Conditional love hides in non-verbal cues. When you ask cleanly for what you want, you take the conditional love away and replace it with a proposed agreement. Now your sweetheart can actively or passively disagree with you.

Use this space to formulate your Clean Ask. Start with your feelings. Then clearly state your desire. Then follow it up with a direct question.

___

What conditions do you need to speak—out loud—to your sweetheart?

How can you say that clearly and cleanly, staying in your own business?

STRATEGY 7

Agree to Disagree

Because you won't always agree, learn to disagree without conditional love

After you've noticed the feelings you have that give birth to a condition on love—and this is a practice that might take years to hone—speak those feelings out loud. The advantage of this is that your sweetheart can hear them directly rather than the unsaid, slimy way of communicating with disdain and disapproval that is the pattern of conditional love.

Example: Rather than keep my kid-care agenda silent and invisible, I could have made it clear before I left in the morning: "The kids will do better with a big serving of protein at mealtime. Getting outside will put them in a better mood and will help them fall asleep more easily tonight. Would you be willing to feed them and tire them out?

Dave could then choose to agree or disagree with me, but it would be out in the open rather than an invisible condition on love.

Speaking your conditions aloud helps you to own them as yours. When you keep them invisible, you're more likely to see them as *universal laws* rather than *personal desires*.

This goes back to the Most Important Strategy in Relationship Communication: *Stay in Your Own Business.*

The bummer about speaking your conditions aloud and proposing an agreement is that your sweetheart might disagree. This is why we're tempted to keep them invisible: so that our assumptions about how the world should work don't get challenged.

Even after I told David why I was upset, and clumsily revealed my conditions in order to get his agreement, he disagreed.

Dave chose to honor his own exhaustion and have a restful weekend snuggling his kids. When he served a mountain of pancakes and watched dozens of movies with the kids, he was modeling self-care for his kids and they felt bathed in the safety that he had no expectations of them.

The worthiness of a disagreement

When you turn a condition into a fully transparent agreement, you treat your sweetheart with respect. Here's the rub: your sweetheart can disagree. Clearly and firmly. This makes you very vulnerable.

And it might hurt. A lot.

It's this hurt we try to avoid when we side-step the confrontation of a spoken agreement. But our body wants what it wants, and so those non-verbal cues sneak in and create conditions that are felt, but not articulated.

If you impose conditions, you keep yourself from the softness love has to offer. We impose conditions because we think the *rules* of love will keep us safe. The opposite is true. It's only when we can surrender to the reality of the moment that pure love is able to flow and foster intimacy.

If you accept conditions, little by little you're giving away your personal integrity, trying to fit yourself into a box created by someone else. This weakens your personal foundation, and thus, your relationship.

When conditions are not spoken aloud, your relationship gets mired in confusion. Confusion makes your relationship tentative and unhinged.

You will find abundant love when you can transform conditions on love into agreements that can be discussed.

- First you need to notice where conditions are hiding.
- Then speak those sneaky buggers aloud.
- Stay in your own business rather than trying to change your sweetheart.
- And be willing to disagree rather than accept conditions on love.

While you risk losing control when you give up conditions, you'll open yourself to the flood of unconditional love coming your way.

We'll talk more about what happens when you can't agree in Chapter 6: Build Boundaries. The critical distinction between conditions and boundaries is that conditions withhold love. Boundaries, on the other hand, preserve love.

When you and your sweetheart are able to turn conditions into agreements, you'll feel your intimacy grow. You'll liberate yourselves from the fine print and the "rules" of love and embrace the glorious feeling that you are worthy of love right now.

Chapter Review

- **Recognize Conditions.** Notice and name places where you are tempted to impose or accept conditions on love in your marriage.
- **Recognize Your Worthiness.** Both you and your sweetheart are worthy of unconditional love. Right now. Transparency and curiosity cultivate compassion which dissolves conditions.
- **Listen to Your Body.** Create a template of conditional and unconditional love so your body recognizes how they feel. Now tune into the conditions you're tempted to accept or impose.
- **Cherish Yourself.** Overcome your negativity bias to increase unconditional love. Two meditations—Proud & Beauty—refocus your Inner Lizard and reduce conditions on love.
- **Untangle Conditions that Hide.** Worksheets help you untangle conditions that try to hide in righteous indignation.
- **Turn Conditions into Agreements.** Take your conditions through the Fear-Clear-Clean Condition wash to see conditions clearly, then turn them into transparent agreements.
- **Agree to Disagree.** Because you can't control your sweetheart, and because you won't always agree with your sweetheart, agree to disagree without imposing or accepting conditions on love.

You've just taken in a lot of information.

To make real changes, you need time to synthesize.

What will help you turn what you just read into a habit you can practice?

STEP FIVE

Affirm Lovingly

Intentionally offer a counterweight to your negativity bias.

Affirmations are the way to keep the fire of your relationship tended.

Have you ever had to start a fire without a match? How could you create enough friction between two sticks to ignite a spark? It's tough enough to seem almost impossible, right?

Imagine your relationship is a fire. If you let the flame go completely cold, you're constantly doing the difficult work of starting that fire from scratch every time. But if you keep the fire banked and the coals protected, all that's needed is some fresh tinder against those coals and you've got flames again in seconds.

In order to keep the fire of your relationship banked and protected, you need to be vigilant about feeding it. Think of affirmations as the way to keep the fire of your relationship tended.

Two things threaten the fire of your relationship. The first thing is your negativity bias.

Your Inner Lizard, whose job it is to keep you safe, will constantly be alerting you to all the scary stuff about being in a relationship. This is your negativity bias at work. With every warning your Inner Lizard offers you, it's like pouring water on the fire of your relationship:

- Is she mad at me?
- Crumbs on the counter again?!
- He stinks. I wish he'd take a shower.

You won't be able to get rid of your negativity bias. It's programmed deep inside your brain to keep noticing what's wrong. That's what kept your ancestors safe from the sabertoothed tiger.

Chapter 5, Affirm Lovingly, therefore, is a way to keep your relationship fire tended as you put positive communications into your relationship. Think of those positive communications like sticks that keep the flames of your relationship warm. This counteracts the natural inclination to focus on the negative.

In this chapter, you'll get several strategies to counteract that natural negativity bias, as well as a strategy to help you apologize if you've had a relationship explosion.

The other thing that threatens the fire of your relationship is complacency. So, the other reason to affirm lovingly is to make the invisible visible. When your relationship fire is burning brightly, it's easy to take it for granted and stop feeding the fire.

When you first move in together, you notice how fabulous it is to wake up in the same bed. When your sweetheart leaves for work, there's a moment of connection, "OK, so what time will you be home today? And what should we make for dinner?"

It all feels sparkly because you're getting to intertwine your life with the person you love most.

You communicate a lot because everything is new, so you want to comment on it. It's easy to keep your relationship fire stoked during this stage of your relationship.

However, once you've lived with your sweetheart every day for a couple of years, you take it for granted that you sleep in the same bed. You know what time your sweetheart comes home. You have a rhythm—more or less—about how dinner unfolds.

All those moments that were full of verve in the beginning have lost their sparkle. They become invisible because they're so familiar.

But here's the thing: if your sweetheart died, research indicates it is these invisible moments that are missed most wholeheartedly. Each daily habit you have—like bumping into each other in the bathroom as you brush your teeth—becomes a thread in the giant tapestry of your shared life.

If your sweetheart disappeared from your life, their threads would go missing from your life's tapestry, and you'd feel cold and lonely by comparison. The task in this chapter, as a result, is to wake up your senses to what is so familiar that is disappears, and to mindfully want the thing you already have.

How does this help your communication? It keeps your communication warm, friendly, and tenderly awake.

When you affirm your sweetheart lovingly, you're stoking the fire of your relationship. You're noticing the tapestry of your shared life that is keeping you warm.

In this chapter...

You'll learn four concrete strategies to affirm the love between you and your sweetheart.

- **Make the invisible visible.** We want things until we have them. But once we have what we yearn for, it disappears into everyday normalcy. The trick with this strategy is to continue to *want* the things you already have
- **Turn yes-but into yes-and.** This one-word-fix untangles one of the chief fumbles people make when they *think* they're being supportive, but they're not
- **Apologize well.** There is an art to crafting a good apology
- **Demonstrate your belief.** Your sweetheart will gain confidence when they feel that you believe in them. Confidence promotes intimacy

STRATEGY 1

Make the Invisible Visible
The power of hello, goodbye, and thank you

Does it matter how you say hello to your sweetheart? How about goodbye?

Think for just a minute. Does your hello say, "I'm glad to see you!" or is your hello flavored with the taste of goodbye. "I'm busy."

The way we say hi and bye is so invisible that it's tempting to think those moments in life don't matter. But moments like hi and goodbye matter as much *if not more* than the big events in your life.

Why? Because hi and goodbye are transitional moments and transitional moments have a particular power in your relationship. You're in between. In-between moments can help us feel grounded, like we belong, or they can cause the ground under us to feel unstable, like at any minute life will crumble.

I'm gonna tell you a story about hello in my marriage and why changing just that single welcoming moment made an enormous difference in my marriage.

Let me remind you of my disposition: I'm a rollercoaster of emotion. My laugh is so loud that once the people in front of me at the movie theatre got up and moved. And that laughter and joviality make me the life of the party.

But I'm not always laughing.

When I'm crying or mad or just sad, that emotion is just as big as that laughter that made the people in front of me get up and get outta there.

My husband, on the other hand, isn't a rollercoaster. He's rock steady.

Sometimes he'd come through the door and I'd toss my arms around him and plant a big kiss on his lips. Of course, he loved that. And for the first while in our relationship I think he even loved it when I was an emotional mess because he loved feeling like he could comfort me.

But how many times can you ride a rollercoaster and still enjoy your stomach turning over?

All those excitable emotions became a wave of chaos drowning my husband.

He didn't know what to expect when he walked through the door. It was unpredictable.

This was that in-between moment. How do you think he felt when his transition into his home was chaotic?

My rock-solid-husband became unsteady.

I didn't see my husband crumbling right away. But over time, it looked like he was walking on eggshells trying not to make noise. In his head he was silently asking the question, *Is she gonna love me today?*

This nervousness on his part made me sad. Of course I loved him. I was just overwhelmed. I was caught up in my own experience.

And THAT is the essence of why hi and goodbye matter so much.

Because it's natural for us to be caught up in our own experience. Especially when life is serving up something that's overwhelming.

But moments—repeated moments—provide the texture of your life. The house, the job, the friendships: they can all be smooth and wonderful, but if the moment your sweetheart welcomes you home is rough, you will feel like a little bit of your skin was just scraped off with sandpaper.

The emotional power of routine

When I talk to couples who've been married a long time it's teeny tiny moments that make them feel safe and loved. The smell of toast cooking each morning, the predictable sound of toothbrushing just before bed.

Seeing a kind face, hearing familiar sounds will fill your home with a sense of belonging.

That's what I wasn't doing. I wasn't saying, "Welcome home. You belong here."

Maybe my husband wondered where he belonged.

So, I started an experiment. No matter how I felt, I was gonna greet David in a way that said, "I love you. I'm glad you're home."

However, I didn't wanna put pressure on myself that it had to be some grand big gesture. Just a small pause in whatever BIG feelings I had for just a moment to say, "Hi Lovey."

Then I gave myself permission to be my rollercoaster self. If I was bubbling over with excitement, I let myself rattle on. If I was frustrated, I let myself tell him all about it. If I needed to escape, I handed over the baby and left.

But not before I filled the air around him with welcome home energy.

The welcome home experiment

I paused for a purposeful hello for 30 days. And do you know what happened to his eggshell-terror?

Absolutely nothing.

Everybody loves this part of my story because it's real, right? We all work so hard at something that is so big and feels so transformative *and the people around us don't notice at all.*

But to my credit, I didn't give up.

I kept at it. For another 30 days. And probably more than that, because, let's face it, when you're learning a lesson, it takes much, much longer than you realize.

Then one day, I saw my husband walk in the house and the eggshells were gone and in their place was that rock solid gaze that told me he wanted to know about my day.

I didn't even realize how much his rock-solid-gaze is what helped me feel like *I belong*. That his calm demeanor told me, "You're my person, Rebecca. I'm glad to be home with you."

This is how fundamental a habit can be. I'd created a sandpaper moment that made my husband felt raw.

I could read that raw feeling on his face. His face said a mixture of things, one of which felt like he was saying, "Oh, um you're here again. OK."

I hadn't realized that the ping-pong nature of his eggshell feeling and how it was making *me* feel insecure.

I carved out a moment for hello and it helped my husband. But it was also a way for me to give *myself* some rock-solid stability. And, bonus, I saw again that look in his eyes that said, "I'm glad I live with you."

It wasn't a long moment. But it was mindful. And powerful. And that moment anchored ME.

And with me anchored, our marriage was anchored. This is the big impact of a tiny, loving affirmation.

The magic of this strategy is that noticing is enough to create a change.

Try This Tool: Notice Your Hello and Goodbye
Run your own hi & bye experiment.

Notice the character of your hello.
Notice the character of your goodbye.

Then notice how they each change because of your mindfulness.

Notice Your Hello and Goodbye is a great strategy to use if your relationship communication needs a reliable touchstone to keep the invisible visible. The next strategy helps to keep each of you aware of the invisible contributions you make to the relationship.

The power of thank you
Your marriage communication will get a giant boost if you simply employ the words "thank you" more frequently. It's a great way to make the invisible work your sweetheart does—and thus your sweetheart who feels invisible—become visible again.

This is a simple way to affirm your relationship, but we all forget it do it. How do I know this? "Thank you" tops the list of things my clients wish they heard more often from their sweetheart.

My clients complain that their sweetheart doesn't notice all the contributions they make to create a nice home and/or life. We all want to feel seen, and saying "thank you" makes your sweetheart feel seen for their efforts while, at the same time, affirming that you need them in your life.

When I felt taken for granted, I asked David if he'd try to find one thing each day to thank me for. (Gold star to me making a clean ask, right?) He appreciated things I didn't expect:
- "Thanks for walking me to the door."
- "Thanks for cutting my hair."
- "Thanks for calling the kids so much."

I didn't expect any of these thank yous. I wanted him to thank me for cleaning the kitchen, but what amazed me is how much these affirmations buoyed my spirits. I felt tenderness grow where the resentment was sneaking in.

I still wanted to be thanked about the kitchen though, so, I refined my clean ask, "David, I enjoy taking care of our house. I really like the combination of writing and domestic chores. So, I'm not complaining. But I think I need to feel appreciated for the chores I do. Could you thank me for some of the invisible work I do so I can keep enjoying it rather than getting resentful?"

Here's the next list of things I got thanked for:
- "Thanks for lighting all these candles. It looks so cozy in here."
- "The white board is a great system. We never run out of things." (That's where we keep the grocery list.)
- "Thanks for going to the gym."

It was really sweet to hear my husband appreciate the lighted candles and the great systems we have. But still, no kitchen thanks. I decided to ask directly, "David, how come you don't thank me for cleaning the kitchen?" (By the way, not a clean ask, right? A clean ask would have been, "Could you thank me for cleaning the kitchen?")

He answered the question I asked however, "I don't want to thank you for cleaning the kitchen because I don't want you to think that's your job."

Oh. Wow. That surprised me. I know it's not *my job* to clean the kitchen. But this was a newsflash: David thought if he thanked me for cleaning the kitchen that he was telling me cleaning the kitchen was my job to do.

This is a great distinction to make. I felt the opposite way. I felt like the more he thanked me, the more he was saying, "The kitchen is a shared job. Thanks for taking a turn doing it."

When you make "thank you" part of your habitual vocabulary—asking cleanly for the thank yous you want as well as giving thank yous regularly—you create a space for deeper understanding with your sweetheart.

Questions to ponder about "thank you" at your house:
- How often do you say/hear "thank you"?
- Is there a reason you don't say/hear thank you in your home as often as you'd like?
- Maybe you weren't raised with thank yous so they don't come naturally to you.
- Do you, like my husband, hesitate to say thank you because you worry it will send a message that you expect that chore in the future?
- Are you worried you'll draw attention to a task you don't want to do?

Try This Tool: Say "Thank you" More

What can you do to increase the "Thank yous" in your relationship? Here's three ideas:

- Have a conversation with your sweetheart, and ask cleanly for the thank yous you'd like to hear.
- Go on a treasure hunt to see how many different kinds of thank yous you can offer to your sweetheart.
- Give yourself a challenge to say "thank you" once a day for 30 days.

Whether it's a shared task, or you and your sweetheart tend to divide and conquer, tasks are often a way to live into your values. Living into your values, however, takes work. When you have the help of your sweetheart, it feels easier.

Perhaps you value creating community or you want to create a strong and stable home life, but your follow-through is lacking. This provides a great opportunity to thank your sweetheart for those actions that foster your values. Say "thank you" when your sweetheart helps you choose the bigger life.

There are things your sweetheart does that might seem like they take away from your relationship. My husband takes more adventure trips than I care to take, so he goes without me.

I sometimes get lonely while he's gone, so it would be tempting for me to get resentful of those trips. But David being adventurous is one of the things that attracts me to him the most. So, I've learned to thank him for feeding that part of his soul… and bringing all that wonderful energy back home to me.

"Thank you" is affirmational because it lets your sweetheart know you appreciate them in your life. It also sometimes highlights how much you need your sweetheart, and we all like to feel needed.

"Thank you" is additive. When you say thank you, you bring attention to an invisible part of your relationship dynamic. You're highlighting something that would otherwise go unseen. It's a great way to keep the fire of your relationship tended and glowing.

Sometimes, though, our negativity bias sneaks in without invitation and we unintentionally pour water on the fire of connection in our relationship.

Try This Tool: Up Your Thank You Game

Here's some prompts and lists to help you up your thank you game.

Thank your sweetheart for routine tasks:
- "Thanks for cleaning the bathroom." Cleaning chores are notorious for creating invisibility, so saying thank you helps enormously to make your sweetheart feel seen.
- "Thanks for changing the oil in the car." What are the other vehicle maintenance tasks your Sweetheart does to keep the wheels turning?
- "Thank you for getting the mail and keeping up with all that stuff." (This is my most onerous task and David doesn't mind it, so I thank him several times a year that he's taken it completely off my plate.)

Thank your sweetheart for things that are valuable to you.
- "Thanks for sending thank you notes. I don't do that, but it's important to me, so I'm very grateful you are so good at that."
- "Thanks for organizing our family vacation. I value getting together with our siblings, but the job of organizing is often too much for me, so I put it off. When you just do it, it feels like magic to me."
- "Thanks for making dinner, and going grocery shopping. Having a meal around the table is valuable to me, but I am often so tired at the end of the day, I'm tempted to grab food and sit down to watch something. When you create a real meal, it makes things feel like a special occasion."

Thank your sweetheart for taking care of themselves.
- "Thanks for going to the doctor. I want you to live a long time."
- "Thanks for joining me for Sober January. It's a great way for me to reset after all the December parties."
- "Thanks for going to the gym. Your butt looks great!"
- "Thanks for writing. When you engage your creative brain, you are ten times happier and it's so wonderful to live with you. When you don't write, I can feel how empty you feel." (Guess who thanks me for this?)

Next let's look at a common word that can unwittingly chill the warmth of your relationship.

STRATEGY 2

Turn Yes-But into Yes-And

Why saying yes-but kills connection & how to switch to yes-and

You say *yes*. Your sweetheart hears *no*. What happened?

You've been invited to dinner with some friends. You ask your sweetheart if they want to go. "OK. But I really wanted to stay home and watch a movie," is the reply.

"Why don't you want to go?" you ask.

"I said I would go," your sweetheart says in that tone that tells you to back off.

You feel confused, hurt, and rejected.

Your sweetheart said, "Yes." But it feels like "no." What happened?

You've been yes-butted. The word "yes" when followed by the word "but" is a contrarian's delight. Tina Fey says this "yes-but" answer will destroy the energy in a comedy scene. It will also kill the connection in your marriage.

Why saying yes-but kills connection

"But" sets up a contradiction, and because we are neurologically programmed to focus on negative information, the negative message is what your sweetheart will hear. When you **say,** "I'd love to go to the beach, but I'm afraid of sharks." Your sweetheart will **hear**, *I don't want to go to the beach.*

When you **say,** "I love movies, but I hate the smell of theaters." Your sweetheart will **hear,** *We're not having date night this week*.

When you **say,** "I'd love to have sex, but I'm really tired." Your sweetheart will **hear,** *I think you're ugly.*

"But" cancels out anything before the word "yes." Then it feels like we just *lost* whatever was offered with the "yes."

If you're given something and it's taken away, it's much more painful to lose than if you were never given it in the first place. Don't believe me? Which upsets you more: holding airline tickets and having them ripped out of your hand, or never having plans to visit the beach?

We *hate* losing things or missing out. When you say "yes," you've given your sweetheart tickets to the beach. Then your "but" grabs those tickets away.

"But" pours water on the fire of your relationship. If you keep butting, soon your warm, glowing fire is cold and dark. You'll lose trust and alienate the person you love most.

> ### Try This Tool: Notice Your "Buts"
>
> This week notice each time you use the word "but" in a sentence after the word "yes."
>
> Just listening for that three letter word is going to change how often you use it. In this case especially, awareness is enough to make a big shift.

You're saying yes-but more often than you think

You want to do things, so you say, "Yes." But then your Inner Lizard wakes up and is terrified of all the ways you'll get hurt because of saying "yes." Imagine your Lizard deep inside your brain as it quickly attaches a warning flag to the "yes" you just said. Suddenly the word "but" is pouring out of your mouth.

"But there might be sharks!"

"But I'm worried about getting sick."

"But I don't have any energy."

It's your Lizard's job to keep you out of trouble, and "but" is a great restraint to keep danger at bay.

The intention is good. You want to keep yourself and your sweetheart safe, but it's not working. See what I just did there? I mentioned your good intention: you want to keep you and your sweetheart safe. Then I used the word "but" to warn you that your intentions are not enough.

Let's look at an example: My stepfather was a "yes-but" person. He was conservative in every sense of the word except with his love. He loved people by keeping them safe and provided for, and he was great at it. But I had trouble feeling his love because it was delivered with so many "buts".

As a result, I didn't *feel* loved. I felt restricted. Stopped. Demoralized. Interestingly, it was the "buts" he offered my mother that caused these feelings. She'd say, "Let's play a game."

"**But** dinner is almost ready," he'd reply. My mom knew dinner was only a few minutes away, but she wanted to seize the moment.

Ever the idea person, my mom would suggest, "Let's take a vacation! I want to see the Pacific Ocean."

"That would be nice, **but** I'm not sure we can afford it," was his quick reply. He was a provider. That's how he showed love to his family. He worried about the roof over our head and money for food so we didn't have to.

His intentions were always good. In the days before bill paying was automatic, he made the most of every penny by waiting until the last minute to pay a bill. He had a stack of envelopes with a date each should go into the mail. This way he was never late with a payment, but the money stayed in the bank account, earning interest, until the last possible second.

His nurturance was a FORCE in my childhood that I only see in retrospect when I'm paying my own bills and making my own dinners.

At the time, his "but" energy sucked the joy out of the room.

In addition to good intentions, you need to employ skill. Fear—and the "but" that signals fear is nearby—will sneak its way into a multitude of moments in your relationship. Fear attracts your sweetheart about as well as a skunk inspires snuggling.

Try This Tool: How "Buts" Signal Fear

As you continue to notice the word, "but" after you say "yes," ask yourself:

"What am I afraid of?" Write that fear here:
_____

"What am I trying to protect?" Write that here:
_____

You and your sweetheart want to build a life together and that certainly includes all the basic stuff like a roof and food. You'll probably worry at times about how you're gonna make ends meet. So be aware of your language.

When you use the word "yes," you open the window for joy. When you use the word "but," you put bars on that window. Let the love you share be full of fresh, unrestricted air.

Why does this work? Because now you're going to hear yourself saying "but" and you'll hear your words differently. This gentle way of changing: simply offering your *attention* to your *intention* is enough. In fact, it is the most important thing you can do.

How to shift to saying yes-and

The next step, after reducing the number of times you say "yes-but," is to substitute the word "and" for "but."

"I'd love to go to the beach, **and** I'm afraid of sharks." Now your sweetheart hears, Can you help me be watchful for fins?

"I'd love to have sex, **and** I'm really tired." Now your sweetheart hears, I think you're so hot, I'll never get enough sleep again.

See how "and" *embraces* your desire to say "yes" rather than contradicts it? With the word "and" your Lizard fears are welcomed gently. Instead of pushing your lover away with the word "but," you're using the word "and" to connect you.

Try This Tool: The "But" Pause Switcheroo

Learn to pause when you hear yourself say "but," then switch to "and."

When you hear the word "but" coming out of your mouth, **pause.**

Switch instead to the word "and." How does it sound now?

Notice how just the character of the word "and" inspires a different feeling in your body. Instead of fear or contradiction, notice how your feelings change: to revelation or invitation.

It's as if "and" is the word that glues your human frailty to your hope for deeper connection with your sweetheart. "I long for the beach **and** I'm afraid; will you help me?"

"I think you're so sexy **and** I need sleep; would you be willing to wake me up with your kisses?"

You reveal you're afraid of sharks: Revelation draws you and your sweetheart closer. You're both confident and vulnerable when you say you're tired: vulnerability, mixed with confidence, is the magic elixir when it comes to sex.

But what if you actually want to say no?

Remember how the "but" after you say "yes" cancels out the agreeable nature of your "yes"? Well, "but" can do the same with the word "no," canceling out the negative nature of the word.

Sometimes you want to say "no," like when your sweetheart invites you to sit through a 45-minute video detailing how to use a chisel. But you like the bowls your sweetheart carves.

When your sweetheart invites you to sit down to watch the 16th YouTube video of a guy spinning a bowl, holding a chisel, say, "No thank you. I'm not patient enough to watch a chisel at work, **but** I adore getting to use the bowl that is the result."

The magic of "but" when paired with "no" is that you are able to tell the truth about what you enjoy doing, but you don't risk alienating your sweetheart.

This is the opposite of conditional love. You're naming, clearly, the thing you don't want, while simultaneously emphasizing a reason you love the person.

We can smell the truth. Your sweetheart knows when you don't want to do something. Most communication is nonverbal anyhow. When you try to hide your negative energy with the word "yes," your negative feelings come flooding in to backfill, and they override any positive energy "yes" tried to inspire.

It's better to speak your truth. When that is "no," then say, "No" to the request.

Then offer "but" as a reach of connection.

"No-but"—as opposed to "yes-but"—leaves room for you to connect and affirm your sweetheart even when you don't want to do the same thing.

Listen to these:

"No, I don't want to go to the beach because I'm afraid of sharks, **but** I'd love to set up a beach umbrella in the backyard and drink umbrella drinks with you there." Now your sweetheart hears, *I may not like the beach,* **but** *I like you.*

"No, I'm too tired for sex now, **but** I'm going to rest up because you deserve to be loved when I'm wide awake." Now your sweetheart hears, *I'm willing to adjust my life* **and** *I want to give you the best I've got.*

Use "but" to your advantage when you start with "no" and watch your love deepen quickly.

Can a single word really make that big of a difference in your relationship? Yes! But only if you follow the spirit of "yes-and" energy.

Try This Tool: Use "But" to Link Up Your "Yes"

Sometimes you want to say, "No." You can use "but" to powerfully send a message of "Yes!" to your sweetheart.

1. **Notice the "No."** Notice when you want to say "no." Sometimes this is a practice all its own.
2. **Name.** Name, specifically, what is in the request that you don't want.
3. **Yes.** Ask yourself what you do want. Be specific. This is your "yes."
4. **"No" but "Yes."** Use a "but" to link the "no" you found with this "yes."

Example:
1. **Notice the "No."** No. I don't want to go out to eat.
2. **Name.** I don't like the noise of a crowded restaurant.
3. **Yes.** I want to encourage my sweetheart's invitation because I love date night, and it thrills me that my sweetheart invited me out to dinner.
4. **"No" but "Yes."** No, I don't want to go out to eat, but I'd love to have a special date night. How about we order sushi and eat it in front of the fire?

The reason this exercise works so well in your marriage is because communication style matters. Am I *affirming* my sweetheart? Or am I trying to *warn* my sweetheart?

I challenged my stepfather to stop saying "but." I told him he was always shooting down my mom (I was clearly a relationship coach even at 15), but I was sure he loved her.

"But" disappeared from his vocabulary. He was the living embodiment of "yes-and." Years later, when the two of them would go to the rec center together, people stopped them almost every day. "You're always holding hands," strangers would say. "You really look like you love each other."

My mom was always the one to answer, "I've never been loved so well in my life."

You can learn to use "and" instead of "but" when you say "yes" and banish alienation from your marriage.

You can also learn to use "but" after "no" to affirm your sweetheart, and even those places where you disagree can become opportunities for your marriage to grow more tender every year.

While eliminating but from your relationship vocabulary will reduce lots of your conflict, you'll still probably disagree. And some of those disagreements will require a tender apology to repair your relationship. Let's look next at the power of a good apology to deepen the intimacy you feel.

STRATEGY 3

Apologize Well
Counteract the vulnerability & doubt that arise after a conflict

Every relationship has conflicts. That's inevitable, right? A key ingredient to keeping your relationship communication healthy, therefore, is how you *affirm* your sweetheart after one of these conflicts. Another key ingredient is to *allow* your sweetheart to affirm you.

A quick word on allowing: Part II of this book is all about *receiving*. Apologies—those you give and those you receive—are all about letting your sweetheart back into your heart after a tangle. This is huge personal development work. Be patient with yourself and your sweetheart.

The way you recover from a tangle impacts your relationship communication disproportionately. Do you give each other the silent treatment for a few hours/days? Then, eventually, you need to communicate about something logistical, and so you're back to talking?

Or do you have a specific way to affirm your connection after a conflict?

Think of the conflict like it's opening a door on a new room in your relationship. Are you gonna put locks on that door because it was painful to walk through it? Or are you gonna dive deeper into that new room to explore what's there?

You're hurt after a conflict, and it's hard to trust again. When you purposefully re-enter that "room" and try again, you affirm your sweetheart.

I had to learn to apologize well. I was like anyone else I know: I wanted to be right. I wanted to feel justified about my behavior. I hated eating the humble pie of admitting I'd behaved badly.

But wow! When I learned to apologize well, it transformed my relationship.

In most romantic relationships, the biggest conflicts center around chores, finances, and sex. That was true for me. I looked for the common denominator among those three categories when I was behaving badly and it was easy to spot how I shame and blame:

- "I always have to do all the work around here. You can't even manage to empty the trash."
- "Why do you get to spend willy-nilly and I always have to be the responsible one?"
- "You don't ever show me you love me. I'm always initiating sex."

Can you see the damage I was wreaking in my relationship? As a result, my husband felt scared of me as well as disempowered.

In this strategy, we'll imagine a way of behaving differently. Want to hear some other examples of success?

A client of mine was a blurter. Anytime something bothered her, she blurted it out. This was disruptive to her partner. She apologized over and over until she came upon a solution that would help her. "I'm putting up this Blurt Board. When I need to blurt, I'll write it here. But would you promise to talk with me about what's on the blurt board once each day?"

Another client's bad behavior was using hyperbole: Always. Never. "I'm sorry. I can't seem to stop saying these hyperbolic things!" We realized he wasn't going to stop until he could laugh at himself. Laughter is a great method to unlock hyperbole. So, he promised to do something goofy each time. Whenever he used hyperbolic language, he stood on his head.

This strategy will help you come up with a plan for changing your bad behavior, whether that is mindfulness like I used as I talked to my husband

> ### Try This Tool: Identify Your Bad-Behavior-Go-To
> Think about the conflicts in your relationship. What are the common denominators in the way you talk to or treat your sweetheart? What is your bad-behavior-go-to?
>
> Do you offer the silent treatment?
>
> Do you use humor so you can't get "caught" when you spear your sweetheart's heart?
>
> Do you simply avoid the troubled subject, pretending it doesn't exist?
>
> Do you shame or blame your sweetheart?
>
> Write your bad-behavior-go-tos here:
>
> _____
>
> _____

about money (more on that below), external cues like the Blurt Board, or a goofy gesture like my client's headstands.

When your sweetheart sees you trying hard to change your behavior, you affirm the love and connection between the two of you.

You'll refer back to this bad-behavior list in the following steps as you learn to apologize well.

Here are the four steps that helped me learn to apologize well:
- "I'm sorry"
- "I did…"
- "You feel…"
- "I want to do better, so my plan is…"

Let's take them one by one.

"I'm sorry"

These words matter. You could also say, "I want to apologize," or "Hey, I think I've been treating you badly," or "I haven't been living up to my values." Any of these words work well because they all announce that you're taking responsibility for your behavior.

We all feel a softening in our heart when we hear these words because we know we've messed up too. Your sweetheart *wants* to give you another chance. In fact, when you apologize, you're also modeling to your sweetheart how to apologize to you.

The first step, therefore, is to use words that alert your sweetheart you've hurt them. This is huge. Don't skip this step.

Here's what it sounded like at my house:

- "I'm sorry for the way I've blamed you about the trash."
- "I don't like the way we discuss money. I haven't been my best self."
- "I've unwittingly put pressure on you when it comes to sex, and I want to do this differently."

When you say you're sorry, you invite your sweetheart to offer you compassion. This is because when you take responsibility for behaving badly, your sweetheart instantly tunes into your vulnerability and remembers times that they've behaved badly too.

We all behave badly sometimes. Compassion is a huge ingredient in feeling the flow of love, so invite it into your relationship by saying, "I'm sorry."

Two quick words of caution about the word sorry: Only use this word when you're *truly apologetic* and have some bad behavior you want to turn around.

Some people use "sorry" reflexively:

- "I drank the last of the orange juice, sorry."
- "I want to watch something funny instead, sorry."
- "I exist, sorry."

Don't use "sorry" to apologize for living, taking up space, or existing. This is a symptom of feeling unworthy. I've had a lot of success with clients that use "sorry" this way when we simply eradicate the word from their vocabulary.

Save the word sorry for true apologies and bad behavior.

The other caution I have about the word sorry is to only use it if you want to heal a relationship and take ownership for your bad behavior.

I have had several clients who use the word sorry when what they really want to say is:

- "Please stop talking about this, it upsets me."
- "Please stop being mad at me."
- "Please be happy instead of angry (or sad, or disappointed)."

If you can hear yourself using "sorry" in place of the above phrases, I suggest you stop. Using "sorry" in these ways is really saying, *I hate conflict, so please let's get past this.*

If this is the way you feel, you're terrified of conflict. Using "sorry" in this way can cause deep wounds in a relationship because you're avoiding the conflicts you need to solve in order for intimacy to feel safe to bloom.

If this is you, I suggest finding a good therapist to help you negotiate conflict so it's no longer so terrifying. I do this work for a living, so you know I study, and ponder, and suggest ways my husband and I could do better. But nothing was as effective as finding our therapist.

Our therapist has impartial eyes and ears and she pointed out things neither of us could see precisely because we are both so partial to our relationship. Please don't hesitate to get help from a skilled therapist. After you've been, you'll wonder why you waited.

Try This Tool: Words that Say "I'm Sorry"

Using the list of bad behaviors you created above, practice finding words that help you start your apology.

I'm sorry…
I haven't been treating you well…
I'm embarrassed of how I acted…

Using the prompts above, find your words to start the conversation about your bad behavior:

_____

_____

Now let's look at how to fully accept responsibility for your bad behavior by articulating it along with your "I'm sorry...."

"I did..."

After you say, "I'm sorry," the second step in a good apology is to accept ownership for your bad behavior. When you articulate your specific bad behavior to your sweetheart you validate their hurt feelings. You're not trying to excuse your behavior or justify why it was fair. You're simply owning the behavior as yours.

I cannot overstate how profound this is. When I told David, "I've been treating you like a little kid when it comes to money," I watched his face change. I was naming the precise behavior that hurt him.

So, I continued. "When you spend money and I rant about how irresponsible you are, I have this shower of words that disrespect you. Then I further shame you by talking about how *now I'll have to fix this situation*. I wasn't treating you like a grown ass man. I'm so sorry."

We are all ashamed to name our bad behavior. This is because we're embarrassed. We want to hide from our bad behavior because we want to think we're better than that. We are ashamed of ourselves, but instead of owning our own foibles, we project them onto our sweetheart.

We all do it.

This bad behavior, however, precludes you from cultivating the relationship you long to have. You want to be loved unconditionally. You long to be loved even though you behave badly sometimes. You hate the feeling of how unworthy you feel when you behave badly.

Announcing your behavior aloud is like confession. Confession is simply an admittance of our guilt.

Your body longs to confess. Do you know how I know this? I once spent time in the department of youth corrections teaching writing to those young people. No matter the writing prompt I offered them, their confession leaked into their story.

They longed to confess over and over.

Once, I offered a writing prompt about an animal they loved. Along with the story about the stuffed elephant his uncle brought him in the hospital when he was nine years old, one 19-year-old prisoner wrote about the murder he committed. The two stories had nothing to do with each other.

These kids wanted to see if I'd come back next week after I heard about the horrible things they'd done.

Some place inside you, you want to know if your sweetheart will continue to love you if you tell the truth about your shortcomings. But you're scared. You're scared your sweetheart won't come back. Won't continue to love you. You feel this way because it's difficult to love *yourself* when you really look at what a schmuck you've been.

Tell the truth. Practice confessing. Own your behavior.

Then watch as something magical happens in your life.

When I told my husband that I'd infantilized him in the way I talked to him about money he said, "Well, I wasn't acting like an adult. I wasn't being very responsible."

Try This Tool: Own Your Bad Behavior

Use the list of bad behaviors you created above to find the words that help you name your bad behavior. Be patient with yourself. None of us like to talk about the ways we behave badly.

If your go-to-bad-behavior is blame, be sure to use the word "blame" when you say *"I'm sorry…"*

If your go-to-bad-behavior is forgetfulness, be sure to acknowledge that you don't want to forget.

If your go-to-bad-behavior is to think only about how things impact you, be sure to mention your self-absorption as you say, *"I'm sorry…"*

Name your bad behavior here:

_____

_____

When you own your bad behavior, you invite your sweetheart to do the same. It's a gorgeous exchange of vulnerability and shame begins to melt away in a sea of understanding and compassion.

I can't promise your sweetheart will respond in kind right away, but if you keep owning your bad behavior, you're modeling the way you want to be treated.

Conversely, when you don't own your bad behavior, you invite self-righteousness and distance into your relationship. You lose out on love because you're determined to be right.

It's lonely to be right all the time.

Instead, I invite you to experience deeper and deeper intimacy. Affirm your sweetheart by describing the way you have treated them. This has the cleansing effect of confession. When you tell your sweetheart you've behaved badly, you're affirming that your sweetheart is *worthy* of clean love.

This is a practice. It takes time. Allow yourself to dip your toe into the little ways you behave badly. Hopefully you'll be able to receive compassion and forgiveness from your sweetheart and this will increase your trust to try again with another bad behavior.

Now let's look at the third element of the apology formula: describe the way you imagine your sweetheart feels when you behave badly.

"You feel…"

After you've described your bad behavior and taken ownership for it, now let yourself imagine and speak aloud how these behaviors impact your sweetheart. Name the feelings you imagine they have.

"David, when I act like the shaming mother, scolding you for the way you spend money, I imagine you feel embarrassed and want to run away."

The look on my husband's face tells me I'm not wrong.

I'm able to see the dynamic in our relationship. I see how my behavior has contributed to this dance we have around money and spending. My husband feels infantilized. He wants to prove he isn't beholden to me. So, he buys something just to prove he can. That I'm not the boss of him.

I want to remind you that I'm writing this book to help YOU feel empowered in your relationship. I'm mentioning this now because I can hear some of you wanting to come to my emotional rescue. "Rebecca, if he's spending wildly, you need to treat him like the kid he is."

As you explore the dance between yourself and your sweetheart, it's tempting to justify your own actions because of the bad behavior of your sweetheart. Resist that temptation.

Why? Because if I just sat here and complained about my husband's spending whose business am I in? My husband's, right? I have no power there.

You have no power when you're in your sweetheart's business.

Here is a clue you're in your sweetheart's business:

- "Should." When you use the word should, you are telling your sweetheart how they should *behave.*
- Instead, imagine how your sweetheart *feels.*

This idea of naming the way your sweetheart feels is tricky. It's hard. It might even trigger you to behave badly. This is because you probably picked your sweetheart because they have things to teach you.

Come into this moment. Right now. Not the future. Not the past. Let yourself imagine how your sweetheart feels when you behave badly.

As you imagine how your sweetheart feels, you're leaning into the lessons of your relationship. This is Big Work. So, stay with me here, and stay with the struggle to truly examine *your part* in the *relationship dynamic.*

It helped me to give a color and texture to the energy that I created as I scolded David. It was brown, muddy, and sticky. I could see this icky stuff oozing out of my pores and infecting the air between David and me.

So, I name that. "David when I talk with you about money, I might use polite *language,* but I can feel this sticky, muddy, brown energy emanating from me and raining down on you. I imagine it's tough for you because I *sound* so mature, but then I'm infecting you with this icky energy that makes you feel slimy. It must feel terrible to get such a toxically mixed message."

The relief my husband feels is palpable. He looks straight into my eyes. He reaches to hug me.

What happens in this moment is the magic I want for your relationship.

"Davey," I say quietly into my husband's ear as he hugs me, "when I send those mixed messages, I act high and mighty as if I'm better than you. I'm more mature. I have my act together. But it doesn't seem very mature to send you the message that you're a loser. I bet it's so confusing for you."

The air felt clean between us.

I washed that icky, sticky energy away. And that allowed David to feel into his own heart. This is why he reached to hug me. He was feeling two things simultaneously: gratitude to me for wiping away the ick, and keenly aware of his part in our money conflict.

He reached to hug me because he felt seen and that provided relief from the shame I'd been heaping upon him, but he also felt genuine embarrassment for the way he'd acted.

The magic of a clean apology is that you invite your sweetheart to own their bad behavior as you own yours. Your sweetheart may not accept this invitation. But if you keep offering clean apologies, you're modeling the type of relationship you want to have.

Try This Tool: Guess at Your Sweetheart's Feelings

Imagine the energy that pours out of your pores when you behave badly.

- Give that energy a color and a texture. Notice how it lands on your sweetheart or in the space between you.
- Then describe that energy to your sweetheart.
- Make a guess at how that feels to your sweetheart, then ask them to correct you about their feelings. This is similar to the "Hunch + Tell Me Where I'm Wrong" tool we used in Chapter 3.

What color and texture is the energy you create when behaving badly:

_____

How do you imagine that energy impacts your sweetheart?

_____

Either way, *you feel better* because it feels good to own your actions 100%, and to apologize for where you've behaved badly.

Every apology implies that you want to change. Now let's examine that step in our apology process.

"I want to do better"

The last step in an apology is to imagine yourself behaving differently out loud.

"David, I want to stop pouring icky energy out of my pores when we talk about money. I want to treat you with respect. This is a pretty engrained habit in our relationship, so it's gonna take some time for me to shift. But I'm going to try to stay mindful of the energy I'm raining down on you."

Notice how I didn't promise to change overnight. I knew that my bad behavior was triggered by David's behavior. I couldn't change him, but I could change my responses to his behavior. This was a big ask of myself, so I gave myself room to learn that new behavior.

After two years of trying hard to respond differently, we had a pretty significant conflict about money. I tried hard the entire time to stay clean and to stay in my own business. I'd had the advantage of truly practicing this pattern for two years.

When we finished the difficult conversation, I asked my husband, "How did I do?"

David asked, "Whatdya mean?"

"I've been trying to do better when we discuss money. Did you feel shamed today?"

"No," said my husband as he shook his head.

"Did you feel like I was treating you like a kid?"

"No," he said. "Thank you." My husband is a man of few words, but the way he enveloped me in his arms after the very difficult conversation we just had told me we had come to a new place of discussing money.

Try This Tool: Promise to Do Better

Imagine, specifically, what you can do in the future.

- When you actively imagine yourself behaving differently, you have taken the first step toward that behavior change.
- Regularly practice imagining yourself behaving in this different way. The car is a great place for these imaginations.
- When you articulate your promise with specifics, it shows you have an actual plan rather than simply wishing for a different future.

What specific behavior change will you make in the future?
_____

What cues can you offer to yourself to help make that change happen?
_____

My husband and I relate completely differently now when it comes to money. This is a whole story of its own that I'll tell you in Chapter 6, Build Boundaries. The promise I want to offer to you right now is that when it comes to the biggest fights in your relationship, if you treat them like a room to be explored with curiosity and personal growth, your relationship will deepen and that intimacy will blow you away.

When you learn to apologize for your bad behavior, completely owning what you did, your relationship will shift. When you imagine how your sweetheart feels when you behave badly, and articulate that aloud, your relationship will shift. Finally, when you determine to change your behavior, you're keeping a promise to your sweetheart.

This way of affirming your sweetheart is like saying, "I want to be a better human because I'm with you." Wow!

STRATEGY 4

Demonstrate Belief
Show your sweetheart you think they're great

When you demonstrate your belief in your sweetheart, you affirm them. I have a great story for how my husband believed in me.

On one of our vacations, we went to raft the Alsek River in Alaska with a dozen other friends. One of the hikes on the trip wound up and down through the tundra and, near the end of the hike, we were headed up a big sandy hill.

David and I were the last two people to climb the hill and all the other hikers were at the top of the hill. As we started up the hill, I realized I was comfortably ahead of him, so I turned on the steam to race him to the top.

David was getting close to catching up, but maybe he wasn't absolutely certain he could beat me to the top. So, he grabbed my ankle and pulled. I went down face first in the sand and every single one of our friends saw it and gasped.

I was delighted.

That might sound like a funny way to feel when my husband trips me in front of a huge group of people. But the message I received was that he believed in me. He didn't think I was fragile. He knew I could take a joke.

I am very independent and like to be self-reliant. When he tripped me, oddly I felt empowered. I knew my husband thought I was strong enough to handle it.

When you show your sweetheart you believe in them, you affirm their self-worth. You strengthen their confidence.

I've spoken with many clients who've lost their job. One man who'd been struggling with his confidence in our sessions came in one day uncharacteristically beaming.

I asked him if he'd found a job. "Nope," he told me. "I found something much better."

I asked what he'd found. "My wife sat me down this week and said she loved me. She told me she doesn't love me because I'm top of the sales heap. She loves me because I'm her person. She told me she's happy to sell the big house and live a whole different life. She just doesn't want to live without me."

There it was. The power of affirming lovingly. When you affirm who your sweetheart is, you build their confidence and you further cement your relationship.

Here's a few other ways to demonstrate your belief in your sweetheart:

- Tell a friend about your sweetheart's skills. It feels great when your sweetheart believes in what you do enough to recommend you. "My wife knows every trail in the valley. She can recommend a great hike to you."
- Ask for a favor from your sweetheart. "I have to bring something to the office potluck. Would you be willing to make your spectacular chili so I win the prize for best dish?"
- Show them that you trust them. "I know you've been wanting to take a tantric sex class and I've been resisting. But I've been noticing how much our relationship has improved with your other suggestions. So even though I'm radically uncomfortable at the idea, I trust you. So, I'll try it."

How can you display belief in your sweetheart?

- What is your sweetheart good at? How can you showcase that to your corner of the world?
- Where is the intersection between what you need and your sweetheart's strengths/loves? Ask for help where you find those two things meet.
- Where is your sweetheart insecure, but you know they've got this? Rather than encouraging, how can you make it obvious you know

your sweetheart has this locked up? (When our sweetheart takes our skills for granted, that inspires confidence.)
- Laugh spontaneously at your sweetheart's insecurity. Nothing calms my nerves like my husband's laugh that says, *I can't believe you're afraid of that.* That's when I ride his belief in me until I find my own.

Try This Tool: Demonstrate Belief

Practice a re-do of a moment in your past.

Look at the two lists above and find two moments in the recent or distant past when you know your belief in your sweetheart would have offered them a pick-me-up.

Describe your moment in history:
_____
_____

Now imagine your re-do. How could you demonstrate belief in your sweetheart in that moment?
_____
_____

When you practice a re-do of the past, you set yourself up to change behavior in the future. Rewrite your history in the way you wish you'd behaved and practice "remembering" the moment this way.

Then notice when a moment like that returns and how you demonstrate belief in your sweetheart just like you practiced.

Chapter Review

- **Make the Invisible Visible.** The longer you live with your sweetheart the more comfortable you become. We don't see things that are familiar because they disappear. You affirm your love by consciously waking yourself up to the things that are so familiar they've disappeared. Two ideas to help you: Pay attention to your hi and goodbye, and offer an intentional thank you.

- **Turn Yes-But into Yes-And.** When you say "yes," your sweetheart opens the door to receive that yes. "But" slams the door shut. Notice when you say "but" and change the "but" into "and." This tiny transformation allows you to honor the concern contained in your "but" while still inviting your sweetheart into your "yes."

- **Apologize Well.** A solid apology is a huge opportunity to affirm your sweetheart after a conflict. The four steps in a good apology: 1) Say "I'm sorry." 2) Tell your sweetheart about your bad behavior. 3) Imagine how your sweetheart feels when you behave badly. 4) Articulate your plan to do better aloud.

- **Demonstrate Your Belief.** Use tangible evidence to show your sweetheart you think they're great. Tangible evidence strengthens your sweetheart's confidence and cements their strengths into your relationship.

These are HiByeHearts.

I give these away so you can create a game of noticing the character of your hi and goodbye.

Hide the heart in your sweetheart's shoe, in the coffee grounds, or taped to the mirror.

If you'd like a HiByeHeart, send me an email (rbcamullen@gmail.com) and put "HiByeHeart" in the subject line.

Include your address (US and Canada only), and I'll send you a HiByeHeart to help you to make hi and goodbye a fun part of your relationship communication.

You've just taken in a lot of information.

To make real changes, you need time to synthesize.

What will help you turn what you just read into a habit you can practice?

STEP SIX

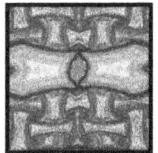

Build Boundaries

Conditions withhold love.

Boundaries magnify love.

Many people who coach with me do so "because I need to learn how to set some boundaries." Then we talk about their **fears**. And they **get clear** about what they want. Really truly clear. Clear enough to **ask cleanly**.

They see how they've been loving **conditionally**, and they unravel that tangled mess. They learn to **affirm** their sweetheart because we often take our sweetheart for granted.

After we've done all of that, mostly, the boundaries take care of themselves.

There're usually just one or two niggling things where their sweetheart is honestly—if unintentionally—violating my client's boundaries. How about you? Have you investigated all the other steps to improve your marriage communication?

For a boundary to feel loving, you need the investment of those first five steps.

Boundaries fail because *you* aren't yet *truly clear* about what you want. Or because your *fears* are still running the show.

OK. Enough. I've warned you that this chapter is to be taken into consideration only after you've dug in deeply to the other steps.

Now let's talk about why you still might need a boundary.

If you and your sweetheart have made an agreement, and your sweetheart isn't living up to the terms of that agreement, a boundary is your way of saying, "I'm worth it. This is my standard for how I will be treated in this relationship."

In this chapter...

You'll feel empowered to build a kind and loving boundary.

- **The invitation to build a boundary.** How do you recognize when a boundary is needed?
- **Avoid takesies backsies.** Learn to recognize (and clear up) the mixed signals you're probably sending now
- **The Full Stop.** There is power in a Full Stop when enforcing a boundary
- **Receiving The Full Stop.** What do you do when you don't like a boundary your sweetheart has drawn?
- **Identities and payoffs** are essential to understand because they make building a boundary challenging
- **Wishing, willing, and worthiness.** Why wishing for a boundary isn't enough, and how to go from wishing to willing. Hint: it's about worthiness
- **Pick your battles.** Learn how to pick your battles when it comes to building boundaries
- **Beyond identity.** What happens to your love and relationship beyond identity?

You need a boundary where your sweetheart isn't willing or able to accept responsibility for what is clearly theirs.

A boundary is clear and consistent. A boundary tells you and your sweetheart that the love you share respects *both* of you.

A boundary doesn't mean you stop loving your sweetheart, or that you love them up to this line. No. A boundary isn't conditional love.

A boundary helps to *magnify* the love and intimacy in your relationship.

You want to be clear why a boundary will help strengthen your relationship, as well as know how to kindly assert your own boundary. Finally, you'll realize how to recognize a boundary your sweetheart is offering to you.

STRATEGY 1

Invitation to Build a Boundary

A story about a fence, a dog, and a neighbor who doesn't take responsibility

When your sweetheart is unwilling or unable to accept responsibility for what is clearly their responsibility, your sweetheart is inviting you to build a boundary.

A boundary is kind. A boundary is fixed and doesn't move or waver. A boundary builds a firm line between what you are responsible for and what your sweetheart is responsible for. Finally, a boundary is not emotional, it just *is*.

To offer you a clear example of where a boundary is needed and how a boundary is built, I'll tell you a story about my neighbor.

My office is in a mixed-use neighborhood. That means in addition to businesses, there are also residences where people live.

My next-door neighbor had a dog. There were a few flimsy wires that simulated a fence between our two properties. That dog regularly lunged at me as I walked from where I parked my car to my office door. That poor dog got tangled in those flimsy wires every time he tugged against the force of the chain that held him.

I am a dog person, so I simply went over to untangle the dog and return him to his own yard.

Then he bit me.

I went to the front door of my neighbors' home and knocked. "Your dog was in my yard. When I tried to return him to your yard, he bit me."

"He's a handful, that one," said my neighbor. Not, "Sorry," or, "Are you OK?" Nope. My neighbor wasn't taking any responsibility for her dog.

I tried to make an agreement. I tried to say *could you please keep your dog in your yard?* But the only discussion my neighbor wanted to have was about her health and how badly she felt.

My neighbor wasn't going to take responsibility for her dog.

Sometimes your sweetheart isn't ready, able, or willing to take responsibility for their portion in the world. This is when you need to build a boundary. A boundary says, I won't take responsibility for your portion.

I needed to draw a clear boundary with my neighbor, so I built a fence.

Let's use this dog and fence analogy to get really clear about what a boundary is, when it's time to create a boundary, and how to build a boundary.

I was clear: I don't want to be afraid of this dog, and I CERTAINLY don't want my clients to have to deal with this dog.

I think we can all agree it was my neighbor's responsibility to keep her dog out of my yard. It was also clear that she wasn't going to accept this responsibility.

When a person isn't willing to accept the responsibility that belongs to them, you need to build a boundary. Your boundary is a fence that says, *I won't accept responsibility for what's yours.*

My neighbor wouldn't accept responsibility for her dog, so, I needed to create a boundary.

Maybe your sweetheart lacks communication skills. You may need to draw a boundary around the silent treatment you receive when your sweetheart doesn't communicate effectively.

Maybe your sweetheart has an addiction problem. You may need to draw a boundary that tells your sweetheart you won't be in the same room when they are under the influence.

Maybe your sweetheart is secretive about spending. You may need to draw a boundary around trust and transparency.

First, review the other five steps

When you examine the first five steps, you'll get clarity about the type of boundary you need.

Overcome Fear: It was easy to identify the fear I felt. I was afraid this wild dog would scare—or worse, bite—me or my clients as we walked from the parking space to the door.

Relationship fears that might need a boundary include:
- I'm afraid of how my sweetheart punishes me when I don't meet expectations.
- I'm afraid of the damage wreaked by my sweetheart's addiction problem.
- I'm afraid my sweetheart will bankrupt us.

Your fears alert you to where and when you might need a boundary. Listen to your fears for the messages they offer.

Get Clear: It's true that I wanted my neighbor to deal with her wild dog, but she wasn't willing or able to do that. So, I needed to get clear about what I would tolerate.

My clarity about the boundary I needed: I needed a boundary that kept this dog out of my yard.

I wasn't willing to deal with a dog over and over. I needed a strong fence. This is my boundary to say, *I'm not willing to deal with your dog.*

Relationship clarity that highlights the need for a boundary might include:
- I won't tolerate punishment from my sweetheart for expectations I didn't know about.
- I won't continue to interact with my sweetheart when my sweetheart is under the influence.
- I want total financial transparency and accountability with my sweetheart.

Clarity about precisely, exactly, specifically what you want helps you to claim your agency. This clarity gives you the reason the boundary is important.

Ask Cleanly: I asked my neighbor to keep her dog out of my yard. It's important not to skip this step. I knew my neighbor probably wasn't going to rein in her dog, but asking cleanly sets the stage for the boundary I would draw after I noticed the response to my clean ask.

A clean ask—for precisely, exactly, specifically what you want—invites your sweetheart to accept or dismiss your request. This allows you to see how much you need a boundary. These clean asks might include:

- "I feel confused, and sometimes angry, when you give me the cold shoulder. I want to know your expectations ahead of time, rather than finding out what you expected after I've already disappointed you. Could you please state your expectation clearly so I know exactly what you want from me?"
- "When you drink, I feel like you're far away. I want a relationship of emotional connection. Could you stop drinking altogether?"
- "When I can't see your credit card statement, I get nervous we aren't keeping up on payments. Because we are married, legally I am responsible for everything you spend. I want to see everything you're spending. Will you give me access to your account?"

Asking cleanly allows your sweetheart to know precisely, exactly, specifically what you want. Your sweetheart's response to your clean ask determines whether or not you need to create a boundary.

If your sweetheart responds to your clean ask positively, you've got all that you need and you don't really need a boundary. If, however, your sweetheart dismisses or ignores your request, or they change the subject, or they are suddenly "busy," keep going with the remaining steps.

Beware Conditions: I didn't treat my neighbor better or worse depending on whether the dog lunged at me as I walked from my car to my office door. I simply went straight to her and had a frank conversation.

However, ultimately, I had no power over where the dog was, or how the dog was treated. I needed to find my agency: Where I could exert control? I needed a fence.

It is crucial that you examine how you treat your sweetheart when they don't behave the way you want them to. Examples might include:

- When your sweetheart gives you an undeserved cold shoulder, you give them a taste of their own medicine and give one right back.
- You personalize your sweetheart's substance abuse problem and say, "If you loved me, you'd stop."

- When your sweetheart spends irresponsibly, you grab the credit card and spend twice as much as your sweetheart just to prove you can.

When your sweetheart disappoints you, be aware of your temptation to retaliate with conditional love.

Affirm Lovingly: My neighbor example isn't as appropriate here. But it was important to me not to punish her. I told her I was sorry she felt so poorly and suffered so much. AND, I built a fence.

In your relationship with your sweetheart, however, affirmations of love are crucial, especially as you're enforcing a boundary.

- "Sweetheart, I love you. I love having a wonderful date night with you. I don't think we have a system for planning dates. Would you like to take turns planning a date night? That way I know exactly when it's my turn to plan the who, what, where, and when of how we'll spend time together so I make sure I have time and space to show you how much I love you."
- "Sweetheart, I love you. I have fun with you when we are able to both be emotionally present. When you drink, you aren't emotionally available. I don't want to be around you when you drink."
- "Sweetheart, I love sharing a life with you. I want us to build more trust. It would help me build that trust if we talk openly about money."

Affirmations put a fence around the love you have with your sweetheart. They make an announcement about why your boundary is so important.

It is my most sincere belief that boundaries magnify love *only* when these five steps are taken first.

Regarding my neighbor: my husband and I built a fence. The dog—who no longer had to be chained up—calmed down significantly. Even when the dog was barking, the fence safely held him at bay and my clients and I were able to walk to the door without concern.

Regarding your relationship: a boundary is what you put in place when your sweetheart isn't capable of or willing to engage in creating an agreement. Or, a boundary is what you put in place to uphold an agreement that you've made with your sweetheart.

Try This Tool: Purposefully Review First 5 Steps

Doing this creates a firm foundation for the boundary you will build.

Overcome fear: Name your fear to tame it.
_____
_____

Get clear: What is your precise, specific desire?
_____
_____

Ask cleanly: Write your clean ask here (feeling + desire = clean ask).
_____
_____

Beware conditions: What conditions are you tempted to impose if your sweetheart doesn't comply with your clean ask and how can you avoid them?
_____
_____

Affirm lovingly: How can you affirm the love you have for your sweetheart as you make your clean ask?
_____
_____

STRATEGY 2

Avoid Takesies Backsies

How to avoid sending mixed signals as you create a boundary

If you're inconsistent, it's not a boundary.

When I was a little kid in the lunch room my classmates would put their food up for grabs, "Who wants a peanut butter sandwich?" When I offered my chips for their sandwich they'd say, "No takesies backsies."

A boundary is when you let someone have or own the consequence of their actions.

No takesies backsies.

This is harder to do than you think. Because once you truly give your sweetheart the responsibility that is actually theirs, you may not like what they do with that responsibility. You like having some control. And with a boundary, you relinquish control.

We all want to feel powerful and have things our own way. So, we try to control a situation. How is setting a boundary different from being controlling?

Your sweetheart agrees to take out the trash. This wasn't a casual agreement. You stated a clear desire, asking cleanly, "Would you be in charge of seeing that the kitchen trash makes it to the curb for the trash truck to pick up?" And your sweetheart agreed to make the trash their job.

But right now, as you're peeling the potatoes, you notice the kitchen trash is overflowing.

Your sweetheart isn't keeping the agreement. This is the first time the trash has overflowed, and you want a happy home, so you tease your sweetheart, "Looks like somebody's slackin'."

Your sweetheart jokes back, "Actually, there's all this room over here in the corner." Your sweetheart smooshes in the potato skins and takes the trash to the curb.

A week later, however, there it is again: a full trash can and this time you're holding that messy filter with yesterday's coffee grounds. Your sweetheart is nowhere in sight.

You're frustrated. You had a clear agreement.

Depending on your relationship history, it might be most gentle and kind to try the teasing method a time or two more. But don't let yourself get resentful. Only tease to lighten both of your moods.

Don't tease if what you really want to do is yell and be mean, because that meanness will slide into your teasing and that can feel meanest of all.

Instead, guide your sweetheart to the trash. Clearly state, "You agreed to do this. This is the third time the trash can has been full when I'm trying to throw something away. What's up?"

This is clean. Clear. You're affirming your sweetheart's ability to solve this problem on their own.

When you point to the full trash can and expect your sweetheart to figure it out, you empower your sweetheart and you create the expectation that *we're both adults in this house. I'm sure my sweetheart will figure this out.*

This is a tangible boundary. And this boundary works with most partners.

But it's tempting to handle this full-trash-can moment differently, isn't it? Here's a couple other choices you might be tempted to make:

You take the trash out yourself

While this isn't necessarily a problem, you are also violating the agreement you made with your sweetheart.

Never thought of it that way? It's easy to want to avoid the conflict of the moment or the hassle factor of waiting until your sweetheart sees the full trash. But this is takesies backsies. You're taking back the task you agreed belongs to your sweetheart.

This sends a mixed signal.

One of the crucial elements to a good boundary is clarity.

Takesies backsies muddies the waters. You're sending the message, "I agree that you'll take out the trash except when I see the full trash can first."

Instead of taking the trash out yourself, wait for your sweetheart to take the trash out in their own time.

You infantilize your sweetheart

The second way you might be tempted to practice takesies backsies with the trash can moment is to belittle your sweetheart.

"I can't believe you can't do a simple thing like take out the trash!" We've all done it, right? This does a great deal of long-term damage to your relationship.

This is criticism. It's what relationship scientists John and Julie Gottman term one of the four horsemen of the apocalypse, and it spells danger for the long-term health of your relationship.

The Gottmans are famous for their Love Lab where they study couples. They bring couples in to the Love Lab where the couple simply interacts while scientists study their behaviors. The Gottmans can predict, sometimes within 90 seconds, whether the marriage will last a lifetime or end in divorce.

Criticism attacks the person, rather than focusing on the behavior. When you focus on the behavior, you empower a person to change that behavior.

However, when you attack the person, you weaken your connection to your sweetheart. A good boundary doesn't weaken connection. It strengthens connection.

Instead of criticizing your sweetheart's character, stick to the facts of the trash can.

You drown your sweetheart in solutions

The third way you might be tempted to send a mixed signal about the trash can moment is to provide a menu of solutions to your sweetheart. You try to solve the problem for them.

You have great ideas for how your sweetheart can get the trash can emptied. "Sweetheart, how about you take out the trash right after you empty the coffee grounds. That way you won't forget."

You are brilliant! You have the solution for everything!

Except that the reason your sweetheart drinks coffee in the morning is that their entire mental capacity depends upon it. They have zero ability to take out the trash until that coffee kicks in.

You may think you're helping your sweetheart by giving them all sorts of ideas for how to stick to the agreement, but the truth is you're meddling. You're doing the opposite of empowering your sweetheart. This is not a clean boundary.

Instead of offering lots of solutions, trust your sweetheart to figure it out. Out of all the fabulous people in the world, you chose this phenomenal human being. Trust your choice. Trust your sweetheart.

You make the trash can moment omnipotent

The fourth way you might be tempted to handle the trash can moment is to make your sweetheart's lack of emptying that trash can mean the end of your relationship.

You tell yourself a story about how your relationship is doomed because see! My sweetheart won't even empty the trash. My sweetheart couldn't truly love me if they can't do a simple thing like take out the trash.

Again, we've all done it. We catastrophize tiny moments. We make things mean more than they actually do.

This might be because you're tired, or because you and your sweetheart haven't had a fun relaxing day in a long time so your friendship is a little rusty. It might be because you haven't had sex in a long time.

Don't believe me about the sex? Think of a time you were upset at your sweetheart and then, after you had a wonderful sexual encounter, suddenly that huge thing faded and was no big deal. This is because of all the happy hormones that flood your body after sex. It's real.

A good boundary is just a tiny thing. Don't let it be more powerful than it is. When you infuse a boundary with all kinds of emotional weight, the situation gets confusing. You lose your clarity. Let the trash can just be about the trash.

Instead of getting into your sweetheart's business making the trash can mean more than it does, call your sweetheart's attention to the full trash can or wait until they see it and tend to it on their own.

Try This Tool: Take Back Takesies Backsies

You'll stop sending mixed signals when you clearly identify your tendency to practice takesies backsies.

Remember a clear agreement you have with your sweetheart. Write it:
_____
_____

How did you send mixed signals about that agreement or practice takesies backsies?
_____
_____

The way we do one thing is the we do most things. When you can spot the mixed signals you give in one area of life, it will help you spot your tendency all over the place.

It's not a boundary if you're not consistent. Avoid sending mixed signals by asking for precisely what you want. Then: no takesies backsies.

Now let's talk about what comes after that space where you are not taking it back. How do you come to a Full Stop and let your sweetheart deal with the figurative trash can (or the real trash can) in their own way?

STRATEGY 3

The Full Stop

How to shut your mouth and let your boundary do the talking

The best way to enforce a boundary is with Full Stop attention and *belief* that your sweetheart is capable.

You kindly ask your sweetheart to look at the full trash can. Then you say, "Sweetheart, do you remember our agreement about you taking out the trash?"

Then wait. Full stop.

Your sweetheart might just hustle to take out the trash, apologizing as they do. Ask them to wait a moment. "Sweetheart, this is the third time I've reminded you and I'm getting irritated. What do you need to do so you can stay on top of this?"

Then wait. Full stop.

It's tempting to go into a rant about how you do everything around here, and all you're asking is for your sweetheart to take out the lousy trash. "Do you have any idea how much I do around this house?!" you want to exclaim.

Don't.

Just wait.

Full stop.

This is scary! This stopping is so... potent.

Yes. It is potent. When your boundary is potent, it works.

This is the moment you are enacting your boundary. People think it's when they make an agreement. No. That's the moment of an agreement.

This moment, when you wait—Full Stop—this is the moment of your boundary.

What you are communicating in this moment is, "I'm worth it." You and your sweetheart had an agreement, and now you are standing firm to say, "Honor me by honoring our agreement." Because you *are* worth it. You're a catch! Your sweetheart needs to keep the agreements you've made together.

The other great thing about this just-wait method is that it is enormously empowering to your sweetheart. You aren't taking out the trash for your sweetheart. You aren't offering your sweetheart suggestions about how to stay on top of the job. And you're not making the trash can more important than it is.

If this seems challenging, that's because it is. I picked the trash because it's important to practice with tiny things so you get better at the potency of just waiting. Full stop.

Practice with the Full Stop method is important for building your emotional fortitude and for building trust in your relationship. Practice with small, tangible things.

You will need the skill you learned when more difficult moments present themselves.

- Like when you make an agreement about your mother-in-law who keeps popping by unannounced.
- Or when your child's begging over and over and over is so seductive.
- Or when your sweetheart keeps talking about the job market in Seattle even though you've said you absolutely will not move to Seattle.

See why practice is essential?

How to tuck your emotion away so you are capable of the Full Stop

You realize it's true: You need to come to a Full Stop and let the boundary stand on its own. *But how?* How do you do this when it's the 22nd time your sweetheart hasn't emptied the trash?

You tuck or vent your own feelings in your own way. You tend to yourself.

Your emotion doesn't need to be shared with your sweetheart.

If the emotion isn't wildly out of control (because it's maybe only the second or third full trash can that's been neglected), you can experiment with tucking your emotion. Here's how I teach clients to do this:

- Notice the emotion you're feeling by naming it silently to yourself.
- Imagine you're scooping up that emotion with your hand, then take it and tuck that emotion into your armpit.
- Return to your emotion later. (We'll discuss options for this in the epilogue: The Marriage Meeting.)

This works well when the emotion is certainly felt, but it isn't out of control.

When you're feeling crazy with emotion and you can feel you're about to explode, take yourself away from the situation so you can vent your feelings in a safe place. Go for a walk. Pound on something to let the anger you feel vent its way out of your body. Scream (outside, AWAY from your sweetheart).

Some of my clients are very reticent to experience anger. Anger scares them. If this is you, please understand you're normal. And. It probably will help you—on occasion—to have a safe way to TRULY vent that anger.

I've taken these reticent clients who struggle to vent their angry emotions into the woods near my house. I teach them to throw rocks, to pick up giant sticks and slam them to them to the ground, causing a zillion splinters to fly through the air.

As they learn to let their body vent the emotion, I have them pair grunts and later words to these physically charged actions. "F*&k you!" and "D@^n you to h*!!" are common phrases that garner a great feeling of release.

Anger is a healthy emotion. It's telling you something is unjust. It needs an outlet. Let your anger find release, but don't pound it into your sweetheart.

When you can let your anger vent itself in an appropriate forum, it doesn't explode onto your sweetheart and blow up your marriage.

I hear you saying, "But isn't it right that I should be angry when my sweetheart has violated our agreement 22 times?" YES! Absolutely you'll feel angry. Totally justified.

I want to draw a distinction between anger that is used to fuel your boundary and anger that explodes your relationship. When you blow up all over your sweetheart about the trash, the conversation becomes about your blowing up rather than about your sweetheart's inability to follow through on your agreement.

What you need is a safe, predictable place to talk about your anger. We will discuss this in the appendix: The Marriage Meeting.

For now, realize your anger is yours to vent. Once you feel the power of the rock-throwing, stick-breaking anger-venting, you'll realize the peaceful place of the Full Stop boundary.

With the Full Stop, you're simply returning the responsibility for the trash can (or whatever is your boundary struggle) to your sweetheart. You're staying in your business, and giving your sweetheart full trust they will stay in their business.

The reason you need a boundary in the first place is that your sweetheart is struggling to accept their own responsibility. The Full Stop says, "This is yours. I trust you to figure it out."

Other benefits of the Full Stop boundary

Think of a situation where the boundary in your marriage is clear. One of my clients told me she learned to put her shoes away because if she left them in the middle of the room, her husband threw them away. That was their agreement. And he followed through.

When the consequences of your actions are clear, you feel calmer. Your sweetheart feels safe. So do you. There's less friction in your home because you're not regularly faced with a choice of how to act. "Will I get away with it this time?" or "Do I bring it up this time? Or hope my sweetheart is just forgetting and will do better next time?"

We're tempted to think that full permission to act in any way we choose is freedom, but the opposite is true. It's not fun to live in a home where your sweetheart's mood determines the amount of happiness you feel.

Agreements, therefore, are key. To keep an agreement, sometimes you need a boundary.

Strong boundaries will let you and your sweetheart feel safer, healthier, and fall more in love. The strongest boundary is the Full Stop which simply draws attention to how your sweetheart is failing to comply with your agreement.

Try This Tool: Imagine The Full Stop

When you can imagine yourself making The Full Stop, you're much more likely to be able to enact The Full Stop.

Think of an agreement violation between you and your sweetheart.
_____
_____

Remind yourself of the agreement you've made together. (If you don't have an agreement, that's helpful to notice. Try making one.)
_____
_____

Now practice The Full Stop by imagining yourself coming to a Full Stop. What do you do with your hands? What is your posture? What are the words you're NOT saying?
_____
_____

Notice how your body feels. Uncomfortable, right? Use your breath to practice remaining in The Full Stop even though you're uncomfortable. Inhale. Exhale. Stillness is a practice.

STRATEGY 4

Receiving The Full Stop

When you don't like the boundary your sweetheart has drawn

Sometimes a boundary is action-oriented and tangible, like my client who left her shoes out and they got thrown away. Easy to see. A clear line of demarcation.

Sometimes, though, a boundary is invisible and unannounced.

Sometimes you want something from your sweetheart that they are not giving. Your sweetheart may not know how to give you what you want. Or, perhaps, your sweetheart doesn't want to give you that thing.

Your sweetheart may have drawn an invisible boundary.

Here's an example: I wanted my husband to tell me stories about his work day. I wanted to feel like we share the details of our lives.

But he was always "too tired." Or "nothing interesting happened that day."

Then, one night we were out with friends and my husband told this harrowing story about a difficult case he had at work. It involved him leaping up onto a moving gurney to give CPR as the gurney was being wheeled through the emergency room. My husband is the least dramatic person you could meet, so if he needed to leap onto a moving gurney, that sounded pretty darn exciting to me.

As we drove home from our dinner with friends, I teared up. "What's wrong?" asked my husband.

"I feel left out of your life. Why didn't you want to tell me that story?"

My husband paused. He took a deep breath. I got nervous because I could feel his disappointment with me hanging in the air. I was suddenly aware he was about to tell me why he didn't actually *want* to tell me his stories.

"You always want to fix everything. You're really good at your job, and you can fix a lot of relationship things. But what upsets me at work doesn't have a fix. I just feel more worn down after telling you a story."

Ouch!

But true.

My husband had drawn a boundary I didn't know about. *If you won't listen to my story and give me what I need, I'm not gonna tell you my stories.* That was his invisible boundary. He'd been enforcing that boundary for years.

Sometimes your sweetheart is speaking to you with their actions rather than words. Let's imagine your sweetheart, who typically is in charge of dinner, makes a singular PBJ and begins eating it without saying anything. Can you get curious about the PBJ?

Maybe you promised to share dinner duty, but each night you've had dinner duty, you're busy or you grab take out even though the agreement was for home-cooked food.

Your sweetheart tried to have conversations about sharing the dinner duty, but, even though you agreed to the shared-dinner-duty, you have yet to cook. So, your sweetheart's Full Stop method says, *I'm not interested in making you dinner today.*

Saying nothing can be a powerful boundary. (Just beware of passive-aggression; passive-aggression is conditional love rather than a clean boundary.)

David chose not to tell me his stories. Because I "fixed" instead of listening, he needed to build a fence; a boundary.

This is what his unwritten and unarticulated boundary sounded like: *Don't tell Rebecca your stories because, if you do, she'll try to fix the situation and that will make you feel worse. Then you'll be annoyed with her. You hate being annoyed with her, so, instead, just avoid the stories in the first place.*

My husband put up this boundary to *preserve* our love.

He knew he would get irritated with me if he kept telling me stories only to have me attempt to fix things; that he'd blow up. Or, worse, exit our marriage. So, in order to preserve our love, he built an invisible boundary.

I was sad.

I wanted more from our marriage. I wanted to share the stories of our days.

Then I watched myself for a few months. It was natural for me to ask questions that pointed at fixing. I like relationship problems and I like digging into the nitty gritty, to see what can be improved.

While that might be what makes me a great coach, it was making me a lousy wife.

I shifted my behavior and slowly, slowly, slowly my husband began telling stories again. When he opened up and told me about a struggle he

Try This Tool: Uncloak Invisible Boundaries

What invisible boundaries do you feel from your sweetheart? Notice the places you tend to blame, and get curious instead.

Try this phrase, "I feel left out of _____ area of your life. Is that on purpose? Is there anything I could do to make you feel comfortable including me in _____ part of your life?

Your turn:

_____

_____

_____

was having with a co-worker, I listened. I nodded. I said, "Ick. That sounds awful."

My husband hugged me and I said, "How did I make you feel?"

"Whatdyamean?" he asked me.

"Well, a while ago you told me you didn't like telling me work stories because I tried to fix you and that felt yucky to you. I'm wondering if I made you feel fixed just now."

"Oh," said my husband who doesn't ponder these sorts of things the way I do, "No. That felt nice. Thank you."

What would happen if you let your sweetheart know you'd prefer a different way of interacting? How can you frame a discussion about that that doesn't accuse your sweetheart?

Sometimes when you're not getting what you want, you lash out. I did this with David. "You never tell me about your day," I'd complain. I was blaming him. This only further served to anchor David's no-stories boundary.

It was only when I was tender and *genuinely curious* that our discussion became real. I noticed he was willing to tell our friends the gurney story. It was obviously something about me that made him reluctant to tell me that story.

This realization made me sad.

My sadness made me curious instead of greedy for his stories or angry that he was withholding. My sadness inspired enough humility that I asked with interest instead of accusation. "Why don't you want to tell your stories *to me?*"

It was a genuine question. I think my husband could feel my willingness to change if I could. This willingness to change is critical when you're on the receiving end of an invisible boundary.

Are you willing to change? Do you want to ask your sweetheart about this boundary you sense with an open heart? Are you ready to examine how you might be contributing to the situation?

When you can have an open-hearted discussion, your sweetheart will want to trust you. Remember, your sweetheart chose you for a reason. Trust that your sweetheart loves you. And get curious.

Then look for ways you can change so that invisible boundary isn't necessary.

Maybe change isn't possible in this particular instance, however. That's very normal. If change isn't possible, you may be experiencing a *Necessary Loss*. Read on to learn if there are any Necessary Losses in your life and how you can grieve them.

Learn to grieve the Necessary Losses

Judith Viorst wrote a book called *Necessary Losses*. If you want to live with your sweetheart for your entire lifetime, you will experience a few of these Necessary Losses.

In grade school, we think we're Wonder Woman or Superman, and, as we age, we experience tiny losses that result from realizing we're not as powerful as we dream. In addition to losing people and the chance at experiences, we lose dreams and identities we once thought were so fixed.

There might be a disconnect between what you want from your sweetheart and what your sweetheart is capable of giving you.

When I was in my 20's and 30's I needed to talk. A lot! I got frustrated with David because he would get tired while I was in the middle of talking. It hurt, and I felt lonely.

Try This Tool: Grieve Your Necessary Losses

Identify the boundary your sweetheart has that won't let you in.

_____

Can you change? It's critically important that you ask this question with curiosity and compassion rather than tantrums and blame. How can you offer curiosity and compassion both to yourself and your sweetheart?

_____
_____

If you cannot change, identify the wound this boundary is creating for you.

_____
_____

How can you give yourself what you need elsewhere?

_____
_____

Consider creating a grieving ritual, recognizing this as a necessary loss.

Then one day, after I noticed aloud that, *yet again*, he seems like he's zoned out while I'm talking, he says, "I'm so sorry. It's just that my ears are full."

It was such an innocent thing to say.

Gone was my hurt: he wasn't doing this *to me*. He just didn't have the same capacity for long, emotional discussions that I have.

Your sweetheart may not have the ability to give you what you want. This might feel like a canyon so enormous that it's a vast ocean between you and your sweetheart.

When you bump up against one of these boundaries, I encourage you to grieve that loss.

Desires like this, if not acknowledged, then grieved, can cause toxicity to fester. Even if it's just a dream that you and your sweetheart will dance together.

Once you have grieved the Necessary Loss with your sweetheart, ask yourself, "Where else can I go to give this important thing to myself?"

You want what you want. Your desire is powerful, as we've discussed. Rather than deny your desire, grieve the part of your desire that can't be quenched by your sweetheart, then explore alternative ways to give that to yourself.

Then, do one more thing. Ask yourself *Why might it be a good thing that my sweetheart can't give me this thing I want so very much?*

I am a talker. I talk for a living. People like to talk to me. When I asked myself this question I was surprised when the answer arrived: *I chose David because of all the contented quiet he brings into my life.* I didn't expect that. I thought I wanted a husband who talked to me. But this quiet realization has brought a whole different layer to my life.

OK. We've looked at the most straightforward approaches to boundaries: The Full Stop and Invisible Boundaries. You've also learned how to grieve the Necessary Losses. Next let's go a level deeper and discuss all the reasons it's difficult to create a boundary.

In the next section, I'll offer you an interlude of sorts to explain these deeper layers and what they look like inside a relationship dynamic. Then I'll get practical and offer you a couple concrete strategies for dealing with all the complexity.

INTERLUDE

Identities & Payoffs

Why boundaries are difficult to form and enforce

Boundaries are complicated. They are difficult to enforce consistently. One of the reasons for this difficulty is that we all want to rush to the boundary and we neglect the first five steps in this book.

This is normal. But it's not facilitating the kind of deep, intimate, trusting love you crave with your sweetheart.

We don't have what we want, so we rush to create a boundary, when what we really need is to examine how our *fear* is getting in the way of receiving what we want.

Or we don't want to *enforce* a needed boundary because it might mean we have to sacrifice an identity. Or maybe we actually get a side-line payoff when we don't uphold a boundary. In this section we'll explore reasons it's difficult to enforce a boundary.

Of course, I have a story to tell. It's about how I clung to an identity in my marriage: *I am the frugal, responsible saver, and my husband is the impulsive, irresponsible spender.* It turns out neither of us were fused to these identities, but it was a journey to let these identities go.

A strong boundary is the only thing that helped our money negotiations. That strong boundary—that at first felt alienating and punitive—actually magnified the love we feel for one another.

What issue causes the biggest and most predictable conflicts in your relationship? Think about your primary source of conflict as I tell my story. We all struggle. You're not alone.

I'm a saver. My husband is a spender. We tangled over money.

On paper, we agreed. We both wanted to pay for vacations with cash rather than credit cards. "Great!" I said, "I'll start a savings account."

I love putting money into a savings account, do you? I really do like that feeling of watching money grow. I have the spreadsheets to prove how exciting it is.

My husband loves eating dinner out, do you? Occasionally, on Friday night he'd say, "Let's go out to eat." He loves good food and that feeling of *It's A Date*.

On a typical Friday, I'd feign resistance, "Well, I don't think we should spend the money." But as I said this, I was putting on my shoes. There was nothing obvious to make for dinner. We were hungry. Going out was easy.

So, we went out.

Then, the next morning, as we were both getting ready to leave, I'd casually say, "I'll have to transfer the money we spent on dinner last night out of savings and into checking so we can pay the credit card."

I wasn't outright nasty, just a tad regal in the way I pointed out that *I had saved the money* and *David had taken us out to eat*.

This is not a boundary. This is blame. It's toxic for your relationship.

Let's look deeper into the relationship dynamic at work here. I truly was good at saving most of the time. I grocery shopped with cash, and, when there were more groceries than dollars, I put things back. I hid a $20 bill in my coat pocket so I could find it later and feel suddenly rich. I opened three different bank accounts for three different savings goals.

Consequently, I got a reputation in our family as frugal.

David was a fabulous spender. He loves quality and he's happy to pay for it. He's a tool-guy who holds three chisels alternately in his hand and buys the best one, not even glancing at the price. He's a gear-guy and makes sure everyone in our family has a rain coat, a fleece, and a puffy jacket, because there's a coat for every kind of weather.

So, David got a reputation in our family as a spendthrift.

I remember a camping trip we took and David came home the night before we left with a new tent. I got angry with him because we hadn't talked about this purchase. "We've agreed, Dave! We don't make big purchases without talking about them."

But guess what? We took that tent camping, and we had a glorious time.

Not only that, but I raided the three savings accounts *to save the day* and pay off the credit card. Again.

See how our identities are forming? David is Mr. Fun and gets to buy things. I am Ms. Responsible and get to save the day. *We all* go camping in style.

But I don't get to own the joy of the new tent. And David has to bear the shame of being irresponsible.

With this, there's no real boundary around money in our relationship. It's just a pattern of "break the rules" followed by a storm of shame.

This is wishing for a boundary rather than willing a boundary into place. A pattern like this forms in your relationship because you want something, but you're not ready to dig into the transformational power of a *true* boundary.

The payoff for keeping things in the status quo is too great.

Let's look at the payoff both David and I got. I get to look like the responsible person because I complain about eating out and buying a tent. I get to blame David for how these things come into my life. Let's be clear, though: *I do get to eat out, and I do get to sleep in the new tent.* These are my payoffs.

What is it costing me, however? Joy. I never sat at the restaurant table gushing over how delicious my burger was. I swallowed each bite with the bitterness of blame at the back of my throat. I never snuggled into my sleeping bag listening to drip-drop-drip of the rain on the tent and thought, "I'm so dry. This is so cozy."

The payoff of an identity—Ms. Responsibility—was too seductive for me to resist. I couldn't let myself desire those dinners out, nor the cozy tent. David got to have all the desire. I was the one who kept our family in line. So, *no joy for me!* (*Do you know this Seinfeld reference?)

What are the costs for Dave? He never got to feel like the hero of our family, even though he earned the money to pay for the tent.

David's payoff identity—Mr. Fun—may have given him the freedom to indulge, but he was never treated like an adult in our home. So, *no respect for him!*

We lived this way for years—me without joy, and David without respect—until there was something I truly wanted that we couldn't afford.

I wanted to pay for our kids' education. I was always willing to be frugal with myself. But I never wanted to deprive my children of anything. It gave me great joy to see my kids happy. Joy I wasn't willing to defer to keep my Queen of Frugality title.

Have you ever had an experience like this? You're willing to live inside a prison of your own creation until you see that your prison impacts someone you love? Then suddenly, the captivity is no longer tolerable.

This is common. It's why I often ask my clients, "What would you want for your dearest friend?" A question like this opens wide the door of kindness and permission. Worthiness takes root more easily when we offer it to someone else.

David also voiced that he wanted to pay for our kids' college. Then he trusted me to make it happen.

I couldn't.

There was no way I could save that much if we continued to spend like we were.

System breakdown.

Most of us won't do the difficult work of creating a boundary until there is enough pain to give up the *payoff* we receive when the rules are flimsy and weak.

If that fence we built to keep the dog out was flimsy and weak, I'd still be getting bit. A boundary is only a boundary when it holds the thing it's supposed to hold. A dike is not a dike if it leaks like a sieve.

If your boundary is leaking, it's not yet a boundary.

The arguments David and I had about money intensified. The dream that we would be able to help with the kids' college funds began to look like a fantasy. I got angrier. I fought dirtier. David felt more shame. He retreated deeper.

Read on to understand the power of releasing an identity and a payoff in order create the intimacy that a boundary can offer you.

STRATEGY 5

Wishing, Willing, & Worthiness
Why it's worth it to stay the course, even when it's really hard

We all want to push away the responsibility that a boundary requires. How do we make it palatable to accept responsibility for the consequences in our lives?

Short answer: Find the worthiness in your request.

A diamond is formed when carbon, deep inside the earth's core, is exposed to intense pressure and heat. Similarly, your relationship might undergo intense heat and pressure before you are willing to do the work of setting a firm boundary.

But wow! will your relationship sparkle when you do.

I didn't realize how unworthy I was treating myself until I felt the pinch of that college fund. Suddenly, I wanted more power over that money that flowed through our bank account.

Prior to that moment, when David would spend beyond our budget, I felt insecure. *Was the money he made equally mine?* He earned more than I did. What right did I have to go to the mattresses over his expenditures?

On top of that, when I tried to convince David of the importance of dedicated savings accounts, he'd *say* yes, then *do* something different.

I personalized his actions, and imagined that he was thinking, *This isn't your money, Rebecca. You can't tell me how to spend it.* (See how I'm in his business?)

But once I felt my desire was *worthy*, I had no trouble pushing back.

I'm embarrassed to say it took my children's needs for me to stand up and realize my desires were worthy, but whatever it takes, right? And now that I've crossed that threshold once, it's much easier for me to see the worthiness in any desire I have, no matter how personal, no matter how insignificant.

This savings goal was worthy. I was certain. And it couldn't be delayed any more.

My husband and I remember the next thing that happened very differently.

My version is that I said, "David, we both say we want this college fund for the kids. I believe I am spending in a manner that will allow us to make that happen. I think you're not. What I know for sure is that I don't want to argue any more. I have done everything I know how to do. I'm out of ideas. So, I think it's best if you take over balancing the finances."

My husband's version is that I threw the checkbook at him and said, "I'm out. This is yours to fix."

This is a hard story for me to tell. I want to tell the truth. But what is the truth? I'm positive I wasn't as polite as the quote above. I'm also positive I didn't throw the checkbook at David.

What I know for sure is that, after that moment of confrontation, David began to balance our bank account. He was completely overwhelmed for a while. He was scared. He was now facing the shame our relationship had given him for decades.

From wishing to willing

When you're ready to move from wishing life were different to being w*illing to change,* you're ready to create a clear boundary. Until then, it's much easier to blame your sweetheart for why your fantasies aren't magically coming true.

You understand that boundaries help reduce conflict.

You know you're entitled to set a boundary.

Now, step three is to be kind as you set a gracious boundary.

Here are three ways we attempt a boundary *without* grace.
- The silent treatment
- Walking out
- Yelling and throwing a fit

These are not boundaries. These are conditions on love. David could have given me the silent treatment: *If you don't let me buy this tent, I won't talk to you.* He didn't do that.

I could have yelled and threw a fit if he spent too much money. (True confession: I did do this and that's part of the reason he felt shame.) This is also not a boundary. This is conditional love.

We all resort to these unresourceful behaviors at times because we want our life to be different, but we don't want to have the responsibility of *making* a change.

This is what David was doing when he ignored the consequences of his actions. He wanted to save for the kids' college fund. He also wanted to buy a tent. These didn't match, so he was arguing with reality.

I wanted to have more say over how we spent our money. However, I didn't let myself feel worthy enough to truly challenge David on the expenditures he made. (I want to be clear here that David ALWAYS felt the money he earned was equally mine. My worthiness, therefore, was an inside job.)

The kids' college fund was the reality check that woke us up. We needed to change or we'd have to suffer the consequences of a reality we didn't want.

This is a common point where people get stuck: The point where an identity will need to shift. Here's some other stuck points I've seen in my coaching practice:

- You want to be a healthy person. You want to eat healthier and/or go to the gym. Your sweetheart says they'll join you, but then brings home a huge gallon of ice cream and says, "Let's have a relaxing movie night." The payoff of ice cream and a snuggly movie is greater than your desire to be a healthy person. Your sweetheart provides the perfect outlet to blame: *How am I supposed to be healthy if you're constantly tempting me with ice cream?*

- You want more sex in your relationship. Your sweetheart agrees in theory, but then is always "tired" when you want to snuggle up. You have an identity script that reads, *If my sweetheart truly loved me, they'd wake up.* You're unable to see that sex in the morning might be a great way to start the day.

- You want to write The Great American Novel. Every time you sit down to write, your sweetheart interrupts you. You have a convenient excuse, *How am I supposed to get anything accomplished in life when I live in a house filled with interruptions?*

Try This Tool: Pinpoint Payoffs

Now examine the payoffs you get from your identity and your sweetheart's identity. (You're tempted to say, "Nothing! It's awful!" but dig in a bit. These are challenging to find.)

Examples:

I get a new tent and get to eat out while also looking like the savior

The Gym Rat gets to blame The Couch Potato for failing to live healthy that day

Nighttime's-the-Right-Time gets to feel like the sexy, if neglected one

The Artist gets to blame The Engineer for not painting that day

Pinpoint your payoff here:

_____
_____

When you can codify these identities and payoffs, it's easier to examine how your coupledom is contributing to the dynamic that's keeping your dream at bay.

It was working for David to ignore the consequences of his spending because I loved rescuing him. This helped me feel *worthy* in the financial department. *If I wasn't earning as much as he was, at least I was better at managing the money.*

I like this example because it shows how a boundary can change even when only one person changes.

On the surface this marital issue looks like David's fault, because he's the spender. But it's a system. As long as I keep protecting David from the consequences of his actions—and appear heroic as I do so—our system of interaction remains the same.

But the minute I said, "I'm done," things began to change.

David was not happy about this change. He didn't take on the financial balancing job with joy in his heart.

You'll hear in a minute why I became unhappy about the change too. I was about to lose the only financial identity I had in our family that made me feel worthy.

In order for me to go from wishing to willing, I needed to feel like my ask was worthy.

In order for David to go from wishing to willing, I needed to stop saving David from the consequences of his actions.

Isn't it interesting how both of these are my boundary to build? I need to feel worthy. *And* I need to stop rescuing David. Every time I saved our financial situation, I was practicing takesies-backsies and sending a mixed signal to David.

This boundary in our relationship shifted because *I shifted*. (And then, thankfully for our relationship, David shifted as well.)

What *shift* do you need to make to have your needs and desires respected in your relationship? How are you perpetuating the system of interaction that you abhor?

Try This Tool: Name Your Identity

Write the topic of your biggest conflict here:

_____

Go to the extreme for a minute and assign an identity to yourself and to your sweetheart when it comes to this conflict.

_____

Examples:

I was Ms Responsibility, David was Mr. Fun

The Gym Rat and The Couch Potato

Nighttime's-the-Right-Time and Too-Tired-to-Love

The Artist and The Engineer

Try This Tool: Map Your Path to a Boundary

Create a map to discover your needed boundary.

See your relationship like it's a map.
You are here. You want to be there.
What is between the two?
This is the boundary you need to build.

Where are you now?
_____
_____

Where do you want to be?
_____
_____

What is between the two?
_____
_____

Loss of identity: a boundary will cause your relationship to change

I was glad David was overwhelmed by the financial job. I felt vindicated.

I wanted him to fail so I could say, "Told you I was right." I know. Really kind of me, right? But you need to know the truth: The beginning of setting your boundary may not be gorgeous and cuddly.

It may be petty and mean.

Just don't allow it to be conditional.

What's the difference between petty, mean, and conditional? Let's go back to our fence definition of a boundary:

- It's fixed and doesn't move.
- It does the job you're asking it to do.
- It's not emotional. It just is.

I was able to love David unconditionally. I'm very proud of this. (Especially so because I had spent so many years not loving him unconditionally.)

Even though I felt petty and mean, what I said to David was, "Sweetheart, you're brilliant. You went to medical school. This is not rocket science. You'll figure this out."

Then I did the bravest thing I've done in our marriage: I left my husband alone. I came to a Full Stop.

By leaving him alone, I sent the message, *I trust you. You'll figure this out.* This gave him the respect that I'd be stealing from him for years. But I wasn't the only one responsible for his shame.

David also had to wrestle with his own shame that he hadn't engaged with the reality of our finances. For the first time in our marriage, I was letting him wrestle with one of his personal challenges. By himself. Full Stop. This, also, was challenging for me. Really, really challenging.

As he took on the job, he made spreadsheets and tally sheets and wrote explanations. All of his sheets looked like things I'd been taking to him for years and he'd been nodding his head, then spending what he felt like spending.

I wanted to say, "Excuse me, I made a spreadsheet that looked just like that. And, if you wanna know the truth, I think mine was better." This is the petty and mean me. I understand why I felt this way. I have compassion for myself.

Remember how I talked about tucking and venting when you come to a Full Stop? Each time David wanted to show me the progress he'd made on our finances, I felt an enormous surge of emotion.

That emotion, however, was mine.

I took myself to the woods to vent that emotion. As I started tossing rocks, I heard myself blame David for spending too much. But as I continued to stomp around in the woods, and let my anger loose, very different words emerged.

Why can't I have what I want for once? Why isn't what I want worthwhile?

Can you hear how my anger is telling me that I don't feel like my desires are worthy? This isn't about David. This is about me claiming my worth.

One of the things I'm most proud of in my life is that I let my anger be expressed: Not so that David would hear it, but so that *I would hear it.* This is why I tout the importance of anger as an informative emotion.

This helped me to see how I had participated in the financial system of my marriage.

When I wanted to be petty and mean to David and tell him that I'd created the same spreadsheet years ago and mine was better, I saw the true blame I felt: *that I hadn't treated myself as worthy decades ago.*

When you practice the Full Stop power of a boundary, the system you've helped to create comes to a grinding halt just like when you take a single gear out of a machine.

When you give control over the WHOLE thing to your sweetheart, your identity will shift. Remember how *I was the responsible one: Ms. Frugality?* Well, I lost that identity.

That. Was. Hard. For. Me.

I got depressed. I floundered.

And.

I remained consistent. I am so proud of how consistent I was. My boundary was a promise of *inaction*. I promised to stay out of it and let him have the money to manage in any way he chose.

He didn't do it my way.

Where I balanced every receipt and every expenditure, he looked through our bank statement and simply said, "Yep, that feels right." He only explored things that confused him or he didn't recognize.

This lack of attention to detail was disconcerting to me. I'd spent hours and hours pouring over minutia. How was he going to keep it together if he took such a global view of the thing?

But the lights stayed on. There was food in the fridge. And he even kept the credit card balance at zero.

Remember how my worthiness came from managing the money and rescuing David from his expenditures? He no longer needed rescuing. He did an incredible job. So where did that put me?

I felt embarrassed that I'd spent so much time in the weeds of receipts. If I was no longer putting things back at the grocery store because I couldn't afford them, where was my power as the woman who managed our money brilliantly?

Gone.

With each of his successes, I felt more and more like an imposter all these years previous. Had I really done such a great thing?

I even asked to have the financial job back and David said, "No. I feel like I'm doing a good job and this is really helping me see when I can spend and when I can't."

He became the guy that suggested we eat something out of the freezer rather than go out for dinner. He patched an old tent rather than buy a new one.

His identity became Mr. Thrifty.

Ms. Frugality was no longer needed to keep our bills paid. I felt lost and adrift. Where was my purpose in our marriage?

I wish I could promise you that setting a boundary will feel like the clouds part and everything in your relationship will suddenly become clear. But then I'd be lying to you. I want to tell you the truth.

It's hard to set a strong boundary, and it will not only feel challenging, but it might actually make you feel worse about yourself, or your place in the relationship. For a time.

But when you stay in your own business, refusing to accept responsibility for what is your sweetheart's, your confidence will strengthen. The love you offer will feel cleaner. You won't feel so confused. This is the soil of intimacy.

Read on to learn about how to pick your moment to build a boundary. Because life is long, and because it takes energy to build a boundary, you want to pick your boundaries with mindfulness.

And, if you're feeling sad about how lonely I felt as a result of losing my identity, just wait until you read Strategy 7 about the love that lives beyond identity.

STRATEGY 6
Pick Your Battles
Because a boundary takes energy and tests your relationship

I want to encourage you to pick your battles carefully. A boundary takes time and energy and consistency to create. It also tests your relationship. Consequently, I recommend you reserve that gigantic deposit of energy for those areas of your life that truly need it.

Your sweetheart might leave crumbs on the counter and you are a clean counter person. I'm going to invite you to clean up the crumbs because they bother you and because your sweetheart probably picks up your shoes or does something else that you don't realize is bothersome.

When you live with your sweetheart and share a front door and a toilet, there will be things that irritate each of you.

But there will come a day when you have a true crisis like losing a job, or you get ill, or someone dear to you dies. I remember the day my brother-in-law had a near fatal accident. We needed money to buy those plane tickets. We needed to be on the same page that this was the right time to pull out a credit card.

Don't waste your boundary-creating energy on crumbs. It's not worth it.

Reserve the energy it takes to build a true boundary for those conflicts that have you gulping tears in the bathroom. The conflicts that actually haunt your relationship.

If you are like most couples, you will experience deep pain in your relationship at some point. Reserve the boundary building for the subjects that create these conflicts.

Decide to clean up the crumbs for yourself. *I want to live happily ever after with this person. They don't clean up crumbs. I will do that. Because I value this relationship. And I want to give my attention to larger issues that will stop me from loving without condition. I want to be able to truly receive the love my sweetheart has to give.* Then stop chewing on the crumbs. Literally.

A boundary says to your sweetheart, "I'm worth investing in. I'm worth sacrificing for." This investing-love goes much deeper than the surface-love when you first met. It's more rewarding than getting to pick your movie or choosing the restaurant when you go out to dinner. This is the love that lasts a lifetime and cultivates a true life-long companionship.

When you waste the *I'm worthy* energy on crumbs, the flavor of your relationship gets petty and transactional. The Big Love I want for you gets swiped right off the counter of your shared lives.

Instead, use the exercise in the "Try this" below to create a timeline of your shared life. Notice the conflicts that separate you and your sweetheart. How can you build boundaries that bond you to face life's biggest moments together, as a united team?

Try This Tool: Create a Timeline of Conflicts

We all have the same fight over and over. On this timeline post the conflicts you and your sweetheart have.

Above the line:
- Silently Clean Bathroom
- Where will we spend the holidays?
- I'm always tripping on your shoes.
- Your mom needs your help again?!

Below the line:
- You're going on a trip again?
- You bought what?!
- We have no money. We need milk.

Your turn:

Here's a list of the types of conflicts you might have. If your conflict isn't on the list, I'd love to hear from you so I can add it to my list.

- **Chores:** All the invisible work that gets done. This includes kid-care, cleaning, cooking etc.
- **Time:** How you spend your time sends a message about what's important to you… and what's not.
- **Money:** What's fair?
- **Sex:** Do you want me? I want you to want me.
- **Extended Relationships:** Where do friends and extended family fit into our relationship?
- **Personal Ambition:** My work matters. Is my work valued in our relationship?
- **Kids:** We have different ideas about how to raise the best human being, or different ideas of what our responsibilities are as parents to our kids.
- **Religion:** Will we go to church? How often? Do we agree or do we pass judgement on each other?
- **Values:** Do we put emphasis on different things in life? Anything from I value a clean kitchen while you value time to relax, to you're a strict Kantian and I'm a free-wheeling Utilitarian.

Try This Tool: Create a Timeline of Conflicts

Use the timeline you created above. Now add categories to your timeline.

CHORES	TIME	CHORES	TIME
Silently Clean Bathroom	Where will we spend the holidays?	I'm always tripping on your shoes.	Your mom needs your help again?!

	TIME	$$$	$$$
	You're going on a trip again?	You bought what?!	We have no money. We need

Notice the types of conflict. Notice the categories where your conflict tends to happen. Notice how two categories can exacerbate each other. In this example, TIME and $ can exacerbate your anger and feelings of resentment.

When your sweetheart spends time away from you, you get lonely because you don't feel like a priority in their life. When your sweetheart racks up credit card debt, you feel used as you write a check to bail them out.

You might consider building a boundary around, "I want to feel important and valued in your life. I want to be respected. So please spend quality time with me before planning your only vacation with friends and racking up bills you can't pay."

Now draw another timeline. This one is about your imagined future. On this timeline place some imaginary stressors.

Try This Tool: Anticipate Potential Stressors

Now imagine stressors that might come in the future.

- Job Loss
- Kiddo needs $ to join club
- Sister-in-law diagnosed
- Parent dies
- Move to a new state
- You're bored at work and want a change

Your Turn:

Stressors are what cause many conflicts, but none of us know precisely what stressors are headed our way.

Notice how stressors can ignite multiple types of conflict. When there's a job loss, that can ignite conflicts over personal ambition as well as money and suddenly your sweetheart thinks you should be taking on more chores at home. All these expectations get tangled together.

Picture how you want to handle life's stressors.

- Who do you want to be as you encounter those stressors?
- What will you need to give yourself so that you will be capable of rising to the challenge of meeting those stressors?
- What boundaries do you need to create today in your relationship to help you become the person you want to be?

Here are some examples:

- **Chores:** I want to be the financial provider for my family. This is a big stressor, so I want to be sure I have a full tank each day I go to work. Having a really tidy home helps me to feel more calm, so I want to create some boundaries around the chores we do.
- **Money:** I value a high standard of living. When I have the freedom to buy things, it allows me to relax, so I want to create a boundary around the way money is saved and spent.

The above priorities will mean you draw very different boundaries than the priorities below:

- **Chores:** I want to put relationships above having the perfect home. So, I want to consciously choose to lower my standards when it comes to what constitutes a clean kitchen.
- **Money:** I value time more than money. I'd rather spend my time with my sweetheart even if it means we don't live in a fancy home or drive a new car.

As you look at this giant timeline, notice how the big categories that cause most conflict will interact, given your unique values. How do your values around these big topics intersect with your sweetheart's values about the same big topics?

Where do you notice potential for conflict? How can you build a boundary that magnifies your love and eliminates the temptation to love conditionally? Can you see how there might be multiple potential conflicts?

That is why it's important to prioritize the boundaries you set. As I mentioned, building a consistent, loving boundary takes energy. I hate to be the one to give you the bad news, but you don't have an unlimited amount of energy, or time for that matter.

This is why it's important to be mindful. To tackle the biggest places of conflict, and **get clear** about your fears as well as your desires. Then make some **clean asks** so you and your sweetheart can come to agree.

Be aware of the **conditional love** that's tempted to creep into these areas of overlapping big topics. **Affirm** your sweetheart **lovingly**, strengthening your commitment to connect in the midst of the difficult as well as the easy.

That's how you **build a boundary** that will sustain and strengthen your love in the decades to come.

What boundaries do you need to build that will foster a true companionship between you and your sweetheart? A companionship so poignant that, even when the circumstances of your life are bitter with turmoil, the hearth of your home is deliciously sweet and nurturing?

Read on to learn about the love that is waiting for you when you learn to come to a Full Stop and build a secure boundary around the big topics in your relationship.

STRATEGY 7

Beyond Identity

Invite the truest love you each want to give and receive

Remember our payoffs for the way our relationship functioned prior to this boundary? I got to feel like the heroine of our finances and David got to buy toys.

This is how we related before we decided to truly grow up and embrace all the complexity that is marriage and intimacy.

Those payoffs really did work for a while. Then they didn't. Have you ever heard people say that they're on their second or third marriage, but it's to the same person? This is the sort of transformation we experienced.

Those identities in our previous marriage died, as did the way that we related to each other.

David became Mr. Responsible. Not only did he earn the bulk of our money, he also managed it so well that we had the privilege of helping both our children launch themselves into the big world without a pile of debt.

So, what happened to my identity? How was I gonna feel worthy now? I'm most excited to tell you this story because I think it's the most compelling reason for you to build the boundary that you need in your relationship.

I'm not gonna lie to you. I struggled. For a long time. My hope in writing this book is that you will struggle less, or maybe you won't struggle at all.

I was more than inelegant. I was petty and small. My hope for you is that you will be able to be both elegant and large-hearted. That hope is real and available to you. And. If you are not able to completely escape your pettiness and smallness, my hope for you is that you will be even more gentle with yourself than I have been with myself.

Because building a boundary that respects yourself and your sweetheart is Big Work. Consequently, you need to give generously to yourself because you are asking so much of yourself.

How was I gentle with myself?

I chose to see myself as worthy. And, when I couldn't see my worthiness, I told myself to trust that my worthiness was there because I believe that all people are worthy. I am a person, ergo, I am worthy.

I'd notice when I felt dreadful: just as I'd resented David's spending when I was in charge of the bank account, now I resented his success. I felt toxically angry. And mean, just like the chained-up dog in our neighbor's yard.

I noticed how this felt neither generous nor like a worthy state of mind.

I treated these feelings like a fear to overcome. I named it to tame it.

Aloud, I'd mention my pettiness to David, "I'm so embarrassed to tell you this, Lovey, but I wish you'd fail." The magic of this confession is that David heard the softness in my voice and I didn't even have to say, *I don't really wish you'd fail.*

What was happening was that I was undoing the shame I'd given to him all those years when I didn't know better. Silently, without words, and filled with that animal-body-intelligence we both were inhabiting, his face would get soft. I could read in his eyes all the forgiveness he had for me and all the forgiveness he was offering to himself.

He'd reach to hug me.

But then I'd feel prickly and resist his hugs or kindness. I couldn't find my spot when it came to the two of us. I didn't feel valuable yet. I didn't feel worthy of those hugs.

I didn't yet know how to receive this unconditional love.

Remember my story about hi and goodbye? Well, one morning as I was kissing David goodbye and I thanked him for going to work (this was typical for us), my thank you shifted a bit. I said, "Dave, thanks for working today so I could be free to write."

The words came out of my mouth and I instantly bit my lip. Tears came into my eyes and I was grateful he was already out the door. I ran to the bathroom and cried. I cried those gulping tears that no one can stop.

What had I just said?

And, worse, what had I just acknowledged? My husband was providing a chance for me to be a writer? Gulp! My husband *provided* that chance for me? Like, he's some sort of *provider*?

That made me sound like some 1950's wife who eats bonbons and watches soap operas. *That's not who I am!* Additionally, it sounds like I'm a "kept" woman. This was against all the values I'd grown up with.

But my husband was keeping the bills paid. And that left me free to write. He was providing that opportunity to me.

I may have put my husband through medical school. And I may have balanced the care of our children, the care of our home and property. I may have cared for all the peripheral relationships in our lives like ailing parents and siblings who needed support. Doctor appointments and cleaning the sinks and baseball team snacks.

But my husband had been our family's primary provider.

The vulnerability of this was a punch in the gut. I hated it. Hated. It.

For months more I wrestled with the sick feeling I had when I realized this. But I'm a good life coach and I gave myself the assignment to acknowledge one tiny provision that David's job provided to me personally. If I wasn't ready to be grateful for those provisions yet, that was OK, but I challenged myself to acknowledge them.

At first the list was transactional.

- He provided the money for the lights that allowed me to see the pages where I wrote.
- He provided the money that bought my colored pencils that helped me doodle ideas.
- He provided the money that paid for my computer.

- And my notebook. And my post-it notes. And my extra fancy mouse that keeps my hand from cramping up.

Inhale. Exhale.

Then the list loosened up. It was no longer transactional.

- His job provided me the freedom to have a job that was our secondary income so I had time to write in the mornings, rather than rush off to see clients in order to pay bills.
- His job provided me the freedom to be the primary parent, which meant I always got to put our kids before my work. This kept my writing feeling privileged and safe.
- His job provided me the freedom to work at my own pace.

Gratitude came rushing into my heart. I didn't have to *practice* gratitude. I couldn't *resist* gratitude.

All those years I'd resented David, now I was the one to feel ashamed. I was ashamed I hadn't realized he had been providing for me for years. I was ashamed I had made him feel guilty about money rather than showering him with gratitude for all that his income provided me.

Mostly, I was ashamed that I'd been so prideful about my work as a writer and justified my value to everyone who'd listen, and now I just felt so privileged. I felt so grateful that I could write and write and write and the bills would still get paid.

Gratitude is like a faucet that turns on your ability to receive love. All the shame that runs through that faucet gets filtered away. Suddenly, you are free.

This is what building a boundary will do for your heart. And for your relationship. You will learn to receive the love—the deepest, purest, wildest love—that has been waiting for you all your life.

When David came home that night, I said very specifically, "Thank you for providing me with such a glorious opportunity to make writing my priority."

Do you know what my husband said? Buckle in. "Oh, Wife," he said, because that's what he calls me. He calls me Wife. "Thank. You."

Thank me? Why are you thanking me? "Because you're always so willing to pause your writing if I want to go hiking. You pause your writing any time I have a big trip I want us to take. Thank you for orienting your life such that you will always pause to be my companion."

Companion? I thought. *I'm his companion? The person he wants to be with?*

The boundary I created to fence out fights about money, eventually, magnified the love I feel in my marriage. I felt worthy because I felt wanted. How lucky am I?

If you are still young in love, this might feel silly to you. Like, of course you're companions. But if you've been married a long time, faced death, and multiple moves, and job changes, and conflicts, you will understand. To be *chosen*—as my husband's go-to-person—after all of that felt like the most abundant love in the world.

This is what is waiting for you when you're willing to create a boundary that opens you and your sweetheart to the depth of a truly shared life. A life that welcomes, rather than resists, responsibility. A life where each of you stay smack dab in the middle of your own business, then come together as whole individuals.

When you are willing to replace shame in your relationship with gratitude, you will feel a kind of worthiness you haven't even dreamt of.

BE with yourself. Treat yourself as worthy, and you'll find others doing it too.

You are resisting a boundary that you can feel, in your gut, your relationship needs. You are resisting that boundary because you can feel it will come at a cost. You'll lose hold of the identity you currently have.

That's terrifying. Who will you be on the other side of that loss?

My hunch is that you will be able to *finally receive* the love you've been resisting.

Receiving love—truly receiving love—is revolutionary. It will change you. It will forever change the way you communicate with your sweetheart.

Try This Tool: Breathe Worthiness into Your Bones

This is a somatic practice. It will help you feel the worthiness you've kept at bay. Imagine the power of feeling worthy and loved simply because you exist.

Light a candle and, as you exhale, keep the candle flame bent over, but don't blow it out.

Do this for **5 breaths.** Then **notice** how your body feels.

Repeat this practice daily, and, when you feel ready, add the following mantra/imagination as you keep the flame bent over:

"I am worthy. I am worthy because I exist. Right now. Right here. I am enough."

Notice how your body feels. There is no pressure to feel a certain way. Your task is simply to notice. Notice your feet on the floor. Notice your gut. Notice your heart in your front body and back body. Notice your neck, throat, and face.

Notice where you feel tightness or resistance. **Bring your breath** to this place. Imagine your breath swirling around this resistance. Let your breath loosen this tight feeling.

Breathe more. Notice more. Repeat the mantra. Breathe again. Notice.

Notice without judgement. Simply notice.

If you would like support with this breathing practice, visit episode 34 of my podcast. You can find that at RebeccaMullenCoaching.com/podcast/ Then search for episode 34: *Your Breath Can Save Your Relationship*

Chapter Review

- **The Invitation to Build a Boundary.** You need a boundary when your sweetheart isn't willing or capable of accepting responsibility for what is theirs. A boundary is kind. A boundary is fixed and doesn't move or waver. A boundary builds a firm line between what you are responsible for and what your sweetheart is responsible for. Finally, a boundary is not emotional, it just *is*.
- **Avoid Takesies Backsies.** Notice all the ways you think you're building a boundary, but then you cross the line of that boundary. Stop taking back the responsibility that belongs to your sweetheart.
- **The Full Stop.** When your sweetheart isn't living up to the terms of your agreement, point to that place, then come to a Full Stop. Don't argue. Don't suggest methods for change. Just stop and give the full weight of the responsibility to your sweetheart.
- **Receiving The Full Stop.** Get curious about the ways you can change. If change isn't possible, grieve your necessary losses.
- **Identities and Payoffs.** It's likely you're violating a boundary because you have an identity that is at risk if you keep that boundary strong. Maybe you get a payoff when you don't hold a boundary. Notice your identities and payoffs to get clear why keeping this boundary consistent is a challenge.
- **Wishing, Willing, and Worthiness.** You go from wishing a boundary would magically appear in your relationship to being willing to do the work to build that boundary when you find—truly find—the worthiness inherent in your desire.
- **Pick your battles.** It takes a lot of mindfulness and energy to create and maintain a consistent boundary. As a result, choose wisely.
- **Beyond Identity.** Having a boundary that says *I'm worthy* sets you up to receive a love you've never before tasted. It's amazing.

You've just taken in a lot of information.

To make real changes, you need time to synthesize.

What will help you turn what you just read into a habit you can practice?

EPILOGUE

Marriage Meeting
How to integrate the 6 Steps into your life.

The Marriage Meeting is the *conscious* space and time where you can talk about the relationship you're creating *unconsciously*.

You've just read a book with six concrete steps to help you communicate better. These steps will do you no good if you don't put them into practice, however.

This epilogue helps you carve out a time and place to regularly practice the six steps and their various strategies.

The more you practice the six steps, the better you'll get at each step, which will make you a better communicator.

At first you might struggle to recognize how fear is holding you captive. Fear feels so real! But the more you practice to name your fears, the tamer they'll become.

Likewise, you'll get more and more clear as you practice honing your desire.

The Marriage Meeting is a dedicated space where you can get practice making a clean ask.

You'd never expect to get better at skateboarding if you didn't practice, right? Same goes for communication. Yet we regularly expect that we'll just fit communication into the cracks of our lives.

Your marriage deserves a higher priority than the leftovers.

In this epilogue...

- **Decide** on a time and place to tend your relationship regularly with a Marriage Meeting
- **Create a container** for the vented emotions and topics you want to bring to the Marriage Meeting
- **Remember why it's important** to invest in yourself before, during, and after a Marriage Meeting
- **Discover two approaches** to the Marriage Meeting: the DUC-Formula or Plan*Do*Review
- **Find** an overview of topics for future Marriage Meetings

Remember how difficult it was to tuck or vent the emotions that arose when you came to a Full Stop to create a boundary in Chapter 6? These emotions are the reason you need a dedicated space and time to have a Marriage Meeting.

We can defer the communication of emotion for a time as long as we know we're guaranteed a safe space to express those emotions. If there's no dedicated space and time for those emotions to be expressed, emotions have a way of exploding! And the timing of their explosion is never convenient.

So put a time on your calendar—Saturday morning over coffee, or Thursday nights after you've put the kids to bed. What matters is the *consistency*.

This feels overly formal for a romantic relationship

I get it. I get a lot of push back about this *official meeting* with the person who shares your home, your bed, and your coffee maker. Many of my clients say the idea sounds good, but the doing feels weird. Fake. Overly formal.

Try This Tool: Schedule Your Marriage Meeting

Decide now the time and place for your Marriage Meeting.

When is a reliable time for you to meet regularly?

_____

Where is the best place free from distractions?

_____

Examples:
- Sunday afternoon while you take a walk together
- Friday night before a date night

My husband's schedule is always changing, consequently a fixed meeting time wasn't possible. We agreed that the first thing we'd do during our Marriage Meeting is put the next meeting on our calendar.

Bonus: Come up with a name you like for your Marriage Meeting

_____

Examples:
- Sweetheart Summit
- The Download
- Dream*Unpack*Celebrate (DUC Time)

It's true. It does feel prescribed at first.

But I want to examine these words: official, formal, and prescribed. The official score of a game is the one that goes into the record books. The formal agreement at an international summit is the one that becomes the treaty. The prescription you take when you're sick is what helps you to get well.

If ever there was a relationship in your life worthy of the record books, I hope your marriage is top of your list. My wish for you is a peace-filled home, one that is worthy of an international treaty. And, finally, if there is a place in your relationship that's sick, wouldn't you want to heal it?

Let's look at a list of other things that feel weird until we get used to them:

- Changing your diet
- Driving a manual transmission
- Learning a new tech app

Here's my challenge: Promise yourselves you'll try three months of Marriage Meetings. This will equal a baker's dozen: 13. By the time you get to the 13th meeting, you will see enough benefit from the Marriage Meeting that it will feel worth any awkward feelings that remain.

The challenge, however, is 13 *consecutive* meetings.

Why is it so important for the first round of meetings to be frequent and consecutive? Because if you wait a month in between each one, you haven't had a chance to *run out of things to talk about* at your Marriage Meeting.

What makes the Marriage Meeting so effective is that is so regular and predictable. Those emotions that clog up your daily interactions—River's fear of intimacy, an unmade bed, or financial disputes—need to be vented regularly.

When you regularly vent or unpack complex emotions, they lose their power. They aren't so scary any more. The power of the Marriage Meeting is to get to the place where you're venting emotions when they're small and germinating rather than when they're pressurized and exploding.

Emotions get easier to handle when you lean in regularly.

Reality Check: I've laid out the ideal for your Marriage Meeting above: to meet weekly.

And.

I've never had a client, nor have I myself, managed to meet weekly on an on-going basis.

It's enough to get close.

Don't let the perfect stop you from pursuing the good. Each time you have a Marriage Meeting, celebrate. You're making space for your relationship.

This I can promise: even if you only meet semi-regularly, this will help you change the way you relate generally. And it's this shift we're looking for most of all.

Reach for weekly, and celebrate even if you only get 50% of the way there.

Want to take a deeper dive into the emotional value of a Marriage Meeting? Listen to episode 27 of my podcast, *Habits for Your Happily Ever After*. In this show, two therapists discuss the psychology of this meeting. They call it *Process Time*.

What if My Sweetheart Doesn't Want this?

How to include your sweetheart in all that you've learned

You just read a whole book about communication. So, now you want to get communicating! You want your sweetheart to practice all the strategies you just read about, right? "Just read this book, and then we'll be better."

I know.

I'm gonna break the bad news to you: Your sweetheart didn't pick up this book. You did. You've decided *you* want to communicate better. But your sweetheart might not see a problem.

Welcome. Welcome to the world of leadership.

I know a gentleman who spent his career as a Navy SEAL. He went on dozens of missions, then later he trained SEALs. Even when he was twice the recruits' age (and his body was full of aches and pains), he put on his 70-pound pack and began running down the beach saying, "Follow me."

Your task, if you want better communication, is to show up to this Marriage Meeting and practice. Practice **overcoming fear** so that your sweetheart can see your vulnerabilities. Practice **getting clear** so your sweetheart can see your desires. Practice making a **clean ask** so that your sweetheart can see you and know exactly what you want. Then continue: **beware conditions**, and **affirm lovingly**.

You're **building a boundary**—slowly, but surely—that says, I want to communicate more effectively.

Invite (with a clean ask) your sweetheart to the Marriage Meeting (even if you don't call it that).

Here are three scripts you can borrow to invite your sweetheart to join you.

Try This Tool: Create a Real Invitation

Script 1: If you suspect your sweetheart will be game for all of this:

"Sweetheart, I just read this book, 6 Steps to Better Marriage Communication, *and I think our relationship could benefit from some of the ideas. Would you be willing to read the book too? Or at least listen to me as I explain the ideas I've learned? I'd love to make it a regular part of our lives. Could we put it on the calendar?"*

Put this in your words:

_____
_____

Script 2: If you're not so sure how your sweetheart will feel about this Marriage Meeting thing:

"Sweetheart, could we pick a time to regularly sit down and talk about the details of life? I feel like life is so fast-paced, and if we just had a regular time to sit down, we'd be able to keep caught up on plans and make sure we're on the same page when it comes to spending, and seeing family, and getting the kids where they need to go. This feels better to me than getting mad at each other when expectations aren't clear."

Put this in your words:

_____
_____

Script 3: If you're pretty sure your sweetheart doesn't want to participate in a Marriage Meeting:

"Sweetheart, I have a couple of things I'd like to chat with you about and I want us each to be in a good head space. Could you sit down with me Saturday morning over coffee?"

Put this in your words:

_____
_____

Then issue the same invitation over and over until it's a habit.

At first, you might be the only one who knows you're having a Marriage Meeting. Or you might feel completely comfortable explaining all the strategies and your sweetheart gets on board right away.

Either way, the thing to do is to start.

If your sweetheart is excited to do all these strategies with you, talk about how you can start slowly enough to make it sustainable.

If, however, your sweetheart thinks books like this are silly, just invite your sweetheart to sit down with you. Don't let it be *A Big Thang*. Just start. Slowly.

My husband and I started with this last option. I kept inviting him to have a Financial Summit because money was the source of most of our conflict. Eventually that Summit expanded. It included calendar discussions. Then it was a place to process hurt feelings.

Trust the process.

Begin. Just begin. Every journey has a first step.

Create an Emotion Container

A safe spot for emotions until they can be fully expressed

Remember in Chapter 6 when I invited you to tuck your emotion in order to build a strong boundary? I invited you to focus on the behavior and come to a Full Stop rather than venting your emotions.

This is hard to do!

And it's why you need a container to hold those huge emotions.

When you give your explosive emotions a container, you promise them, *I'm not ignoring you. I promise to let you out and feel fully expressed.*

And.

You're also not letting your relationship be ruled by your emotions. When you let your emotions explode, your emotions are running the show, rather than letting your emotions inform you of the message they carry.

We'll talk about tending to yourself so you can receive the message of your emotions in the next section, but right now, we just need a container so that your emotions don't get to have free reign in your relationship, exploding any minute just because they're so important.

The truth is your emotions are important. They can't be neglected. And they can't be given center stage either.

So, create a container for your emotions to feel safe, knowing that you will fully feel them, and you'll also let them have full expression.

What does this container look like? It could be a location like the Notes app on your phone, or in a journal where you are free to write in BIG BOLD letters and angry scrawl.

You could also contain your emotions by using a physical expression. When I'm in a session with a client and I feel an emotion rise up inside of me, I imagine myself scooping up that emotion in my hand, then I tuck my hand—and that emotion—into my armpit by folding my arms for a moment.

Choose a place that matches your disposition. If emotions come on fast for you, find a place that's always with you, like a pocket, or tucked

---

Try This Tool: Create a Container for Your Emotions

Decide right now where you will "store" your emotions temporarily so they don't hijack your relationship. Then promise your emotions you will be there SOON to tend them.

I will store my emotions:

_____

I will tend my emotions:

_____

Examples:
- I'll tuck my emotions in my armpit. Then, later, I'll take a shower so I have privacy. The running water will help my emotions flow rather than getting stuck.
- I'll note my emotion on this post-it pad, then later, I'll give myself time to journal about how I'm feeling.

behind your ear. Maybe it helps you to exit the situation and stomp around, cry and scream, or hurl some rocks into the water so they make a huge splash.

If, however, it's difficult for you to find your emotions, choose a place where you can have time to ponder, wonder, and explore, like maybe in the bathroom where you have privacy, or a walk around the block.

The key to the container for your emotions is not to leave them there.

In order for your container to be effective, you need to reach into that container and process those emotions. Give yourself time to truly understand the message those feelings are sending you.

Tend Your Own Emotions
Because emotions need expression

There are many ways to tend to your own emotional health. Many people like to phone a friend because they process out loud. Others, who process their emotions internally, need time to retreat to a quiet space.

My invitation to you is to recognize that each emotion you feel needs your attention in one way or another. When you give your emotions this attention, you're nurturing yourself.

Sadness benefits from tears. Anger likes to be highly physical. Vulnerability wants reassurance.

When you blend the feelings you feel with your body's sensual experience, your emotions regulate rather than getting stuck.

Where do you find time and space to nurture your emotions and give them freedom for bodily expression?
- A regular coffee date with a friend who welcomes your anger, tears, and vulnerability equally.
- While you're driving, or exercising: movement helps to process emotions.
- Any "manual labor" when your hands are busy but your mind is free to roam: knitting, folding laundry, gardening.

- Stillness: if you are a person who finds it difficult to feel any emotion, consider a stillness practice. Just sit. Nothing else. No alcohol, no coffee. Just stillness. You'll notice emotions bubbling up.

I've just written a whole book that basically boils down to tending your emotions, so I can't overstate the importance of creating space to allow that to happen.

If you don't nurture your own emotions, they will pollute your relationship.

Try This Tool: Nurture Your Emotions

Notice behaviors that help you process emotions.

Do you process internally (quietly, with yourself alone), or externally (with the help of a friend, talking things out)?
_____
_____

It's important to give yourself time and space to process emotions. In the space below, write down two reliable methods that help you.
1._____
2._____

Examples:
- I can ask my husband to sit and hug me while I cry. I'll let know I'm just exploring how I feel and I might say things I don't mean as I find my way through the confusion of these emotions.
- I can go outside and stomp around the woods to blow off steam.
- I can retreat to the bathroom and stay there a long time, trimming my nails, showering, or covering my body in lotion.

When you nurture your emotions, you calm down your amygdala that wants to freak out and fight, flee, freeze, or fawn. As you calm down, you can hear the *message* your emotions want to send you about things you desire. The message from your emotions is a guiding light to tell you where you're going.

Now that you've got a container to hold your emotions so they don't explode in the middle of your marriage, and you have a practice for nurturing those emotions, let's look at some options for discussing those emotions at your Marriage Meeting.

The DUC Formula
One option for organizing your Marriage Meeting

Let's talk about two options for orienting the discussion of your Marriage Meeting. The first one—The DUC Formula—is a philosophy. Because the emotions that need expression at your Marriage Meeting tend to arise from your negativity bias, I like to sandwich those emotions between two positives—A Dream, and a Celebration.

The second method—Plan*Do*Review—works well for all the logistical discussions you're likely to have at your Marriage Meeting (see below). Use either or both methods if they provide help.

If you realize you have a better idea, go for it. There's nothing magical about these formulas. The only key element is that you carve out space and time to talk.

Let's talk about The DUC Method first:

- **Dream:** State the dream you have for your marriage.
- **Unpack:** Allow any uncomfortable emotions to be unpacked until they're well seen and understood.
- **Celebrate:** Remind each other of the things you're doing well in your marriage.

I like this name—The Duc(k) Method—because of the power of imprinting. Imprinting is what happens to baby ducks. They hatch out of their shells, then they imprint on whatever they first see: typically, their mama's face.

These baby ducks then learn to follow their mama so they don't get lost. You've seen a little parade of chicks or ducklings and it's adorable, right?

Imagine your DUC Marriage Meeting similarly. You imprint a pattern or habit of conversing kindly onto your relationship as you mindfully process emotions. Then, even in moments of stress, you're more likely to use these imprinted patterns of conversation. This is the dream of the Marriage Meeting.

Let's break down the three phases of conversation.

Create the dream

Draw from Chapter 2, Get Clear. When you know what you want, you can articulate your dream.

When I work with private clients, we spend a little time every session searching for and articulating the dream they have. This helps us know what we're aiming for. Getting clear isn't a one-time-fix. Cultivating a dream is a treasure hunt.

Use each Marriage Meeting to reimagine the dream you had when you said, "I do." You'll do this in a teeny tiny way.

In my early Marriage Meetings, one of the dreams I articulated was, "My greatest wish for our relationship is that we can be on the same team when it comes to spending and saving rather than feeling like adversaries." This dream is what helped me to see the boundary I would eventually build.

My husband always agreed with this dream. He wanted a relationship free of conflict. He wanted to feel free of financial crisis. The dream is where we knew we wanted the same thing. This reminder helped keep us united while we were living that dream differently.

A dream is a way to create a new identity and practice making friends with it before it becomes a reality. A dream lets you borrow from the future.

Have you ever watched Simon Sinek's TED Talk about *The Power of Why*? His talk is an amazing summation. When you know WHY you're doing something, it fuels just about every HOW you will encounter. WHY keeps you motivated.

Dreaming about the relationship you want to create helps you practice WHY it's worth it to have this Marriage Meeting and practice these communication skills.

Try This Tool: Create a Dream for Your Relationship

Imagine a small slice of your relationship. What is your dream for that slice of your relationship?

What relationship slice will you focus on?
_____

What is your dream for that slice of your relationship?
_____
_____

Examples:
- I want to create a safe and reliable system of child care so we each can fly into magnificent and ambitious careers.
- I want to share a kitchen so we both feel well-nourished, and have a time to chat as we chop.
- I want to spend this time unpacking any difficult emotions so that the rest of the week our relationship feels safe and we each feel cherished rather than being surprised by emotional outbursts.

This imagination moment takes 1-2 minutes. Not long. But it creates a shared vision. This grounds you in the realization that, even when you seem to be at odds, actually you both want the same thing.

When you start your Marriage Meeting with a dream, it's like having a target so you know what you're aiming for.

Next use the bulk of your Marriage Meeting to unpack any difficult emotions you've felt during the week as you tried to make that dream a reality.

Unpack tucked or vented emotions

Now that you remember you want the same thing, at least generally speaking, you can talk about the moments in the past week when circumstances didn't line up with this vision.

"When you bought that tent without talking to me about it first, I was angry." At first, you'll feel clumsy and stilted. That's because you're practicing. Have you ever watched someone learn to hula-hoop, or ski, or ride a bike? You fall. You're awkward.

Can you imagine anything that will improve your life more than getting better at relationship communication? Stay with the practice. Even though you feel awkward.

The agreement of this phase of the Marriage Meeting is to listen to your sweetheart. Then to tell your truth. No blaming. No hashing out. If an apology feels natural, you can offer that. If not, simply acknowledge you've heard your sweetheart's truth and thank them for hearing yours.

Don't let this turn into a *Big Thang*. Trust the repetition of this Meeting.

You're simply creating a space where emotion is welcome. Where clarity—for both of you—is more valuable than who is right or wrong.

The essence of this strategy is to let the emotions that you put in your Emotion Container have a safe place to land in the relationship.

You did a great job of tucking or venting those emotions in a moment that triggered you. Then you've nurtured your feelings so you can receive the message of your emotions.

Now the child inside you that still FEELS those emotions needs a place where those emotions can be safely expressed and received.

When you *process* an emotion in the heat of *feeling* that emotion, you often will lose control. That's why you visit the woods. You let yourself lose control as you throw rocks and break sticks. That's why you carve out stillness so *you* see the emotions that *you* feel.

You've let your emotion run wild. You've given your emotional-self space. When you tend to your emotions—and let your emotions be free of the prison of polite behavior—you see yourself. You tend yourself.

Now you know the *message* that emotion was delivering about how you want your life to *change*. It is this message that you take to the Marriage Meeting.

Use the tools in Chapter 3—Ask Cleanly—to unpack your emotions.

This Unpacking might be the bulk of your Marriage Meeting. Some emotions will take longer to process than others.

If your sweetheart starts to use Unpacking as a blame-fest, remember that you can invite your sweetheart to offer you a clean ask using the following prompts:

- What are you most afraid will happen? What's the worst-case scenario?
- What do you most want?

- Can you ask me for exactly, precisely, specifically what you want so I'm clear about what you need?

Try This Tool: Unpack the Previous Week

Unpack your Emotion Container.

*Remember to nurture your feelings first and examine your emotions for the message they offer. Then bring the messages from those emotions to your Marriage Meeting.

As a reminder, the best ways for me to tend my emotions is:
_____

What is the Clean Ask message from those emotions you want to bring to your Marriage Meeting?
_____
_____

Examples:
- When I do the bulk of the child care during the week and then you complain about not getting time to yourself on the weekend, I feel resentful. I want to be appreciated for the exceptional care I offer our kids all week long. Could you stop complaining about taking care of our kids? Or could you use your awareness—that caring for kids is hard—to thank me for the bulk of care that I offer?
- I feel overwhelmed by meals and meal planning and grocery shopping. I want to have days of the week when I'm free to wonder about something other than what's for dinner. Could you take three days of the week to be in charge of feeding us? I'll take the other three, and maybe we could get take out or eat cereal the seventh night.
- I feel self-conscious having this Marriage Meeting. I want you to stop rolling your eyes each time I remind you about our Marriage Meeting. When you roll your eyes, I feel unimportant, like I'm not worth investing time in. Could you show up to this meeting eager to chat with me instead?

Finish this phase by completing the unpacking. Have you ever brought home a suitcase from a trip and it lived in the corner of your bedroom for weeks? When you couldn't find something, you'd dig around in that suitcase looking for it?

When you completely unpack your suitcase, everything gets back into order. It's the same with your Marriage Meeting. Before you finish the unpacking section of your Marriage Meeting, use Step 3—The Clean Ask

—to fully unpack your emotions, by asking cleanly for the behavior you want.

Celebrate

Celebrating helps to counter balance the ever-present negativity bias you have that is your Inner Lizard's go-to. Your Inner Lizard is always asking the question, *What's wrong?* When you celebrate, you give equal if not more weight to *what's going right*.

I've found that people are reluctant to celebrate. They're worried if they see what's going well that they'll lose momentum and will stop striving to improve.

The opposite is more true.

The biggest contributor to momentum I've seen in my coaching practice is a successful accomplishment of the goal or dream my client has. Consequently, I believe it's critically important to find that spot—even if it's microscopic—where things are going well.

Please. Please don't treat this like a Band-Aid where you make an obligatory gesture toward something that's working. Dig deep if you have to. If you truly want the dream you articulated, there is something you're doing (or not doing) to draw that dream toward you.

You will know you've found something authentic when your skin softens and you feel your breath loosen. This is your body receiving the gift of your dream coming true. It's powerful, powerful work to receive.

The essence of The DUC Formula is to use the steps from this book.
- In the Dream portion of your Marriage Meeting, you resist the temptation to **love conditionally**—Chapter 4—and, instead, you regularly revisit the common vision you both have for your relationship. This practice keeps your heart open and tender.
- As you unpack the emotions from the previous week, you **overcome fear**— Chapter 1—and you feel your emotions and let your emotions offer you a message.
- Additionally, you **get clear**—Chapter 2—about what you want.
- Then you **ask cleanly**—Chapter 3—for that desire because you are worthy.

Try This Tool: Celebrate Your Connection

Return to the dream you articulated previously. Then name one thing —even if it's teeny tiny—to help make that dream a reality.

As a reminder, the dream for this one slice of our relationship is:
_____

Name something tiny you're doing to make that dream come true:
_____
_____

Name something tiny your sweetheart is doing to make that dream come true:
_____
_____

Examples:
- When you complain about not having time to yourself, I can feel deep inside you that you recognize how difficult my job is tending our kids all week long. I know it's challenging for you to let yourself accept how much you appreciate my efforts because it's a sacrifice you're not making. Maybe you feel guilty. But I can also feel you beginning to understand the enormity of what I offer to our family. I want you to know I'm glad I get to care for our kids.
- I'm glad we want to eat together. I know it's challenging because we're both tired, but I'm so grateful I have you to share a meal with at the end of a long day. Sharing a meal with you helps me feel grounded. I want to remember that.
- Thank you so much for sitting down with me like this. When we're able to have this predictable time to talk and process the emotions of the week, I feel more calm. It helps me treat you better during the week because I know you've made time to truly hear me and invest in our relationship going forward.

- When you wrap up with a celebration, you **lovingly affirm**— Chapter 5—the ways you're already succeeding at the relationship you crave.
- Finally, this formal Marriage Meeting allows you to restate any **boundaries** you've built—Chapter 6—reminding your sweetheart of behaviors that you will and won't tolerate. Doing this in a predictable space reinforces those moments when you come to a Full Stop and expect your sweetheart to carry what belongs to them.

Now let's talk about Plan*Do*Review so you have a way to keep making improvements on those niggling details of life that can cause so much conflict.

Plan*Do*Review
Another option for organizing your Marriage Meeting

Your life is filled with details. Coordinating your life with another person takes communication. If you don't communicate and set clear expectations, you will likely have an unpleasant emotional outcome. Plan*Do*Review is the method you can use to dial in expectations and cultivate more positive emotions.

PLAN: This is where you anticipate something in the coming week and how you'll handle it:
- A visit from your brother
- Meal planning
- The furnace that needs servicing

DO: This is where you live your life:
- You and your brother go to a baseball game during his visit
- You and your sweetheart take turns making dinner
- A phone call is made to the HVAC Company and you arrange to let them in

REVIEW: This is where you notice how the DOING and the PLANNING overlap. What happened? Did we live according to the plan?
- When your brother didn't want to go to the ballgame, your sweetheart resented not having that time alone at home
- A late night at work meant you missed one of your nights to cook
- The HVAC Company didn't show up

This is life, right? Things don't always go according to the plan. That's why the Marriage Meeting can be so effective: because you're taking time to deal with the emotions and the logistical decisions that happen when life doesn't go according to plan.

Here's an example of how emotional expression can lead to a change in lifestyle:

Week 1: PLAN (Jan 7 Marriage Meeting)

Sarah: "I feel like I do the bulk of the kitchen work. I feel myself getting resentful. Would you be willing to be in charge of taking out the trash?"

Sam: "Sure. No problem."

Week 1: DO (Jan 7-13)

On Tuesday, Sarah takes the trash out because it's overflowing and she's mad at Sam as she does so. On Saturday, Sarah reminds Sam to take out the trash.

Week 1: REVIEW (Jan 7 Marriage Meeting)

There's nothing to review until they have a week of doing.

Week 2: REVIEW (Jan 14 Marriage Meeting)

Sarah, who has lots of emotion about the trash can, uses the Marriage Meeting to unpack her emotions.

Sarah: "You said you'd take out the trash, but the only time you took out the trash, I had to remind you."

Sam: "That's true. I'm sorry. I'll do better next time."

Week 2: PLAN (Jan 14 Marriage Meeting)

Sam: "Here's my plan, I put it on my calendar to take the trash out on Tuesdays and Fridays."

Sarah: "Great. Thanks for being so intentional."

Week 2: DO (Jan 14-20 Living and Doing)

Sarah, who primarily works from home, gets a reprieve when two of her meetings are canceled on Wednesday. She's thrilled because the refrigerator-clean-out has been on her list for a long time. She uses the time to clean out the fridge.

The trash can was empty (Sam was true to his word and took out the trash can on Tuesday), and Sarah had plenty of room for all the moldy foods.

Their teenage daughter took inspiration from her mother's fridge purge and cleaned out her bathroom drawer. As all teenagers are apt to do, when her bathroom trashcan filled to overflowing, this teen just dumped and shoved it into that kitchen trashcan.

Thursday morning, when Sarah makes her coffee and wants to toss out the coffee grounds, she finds a full trash. Instantly, she's angry at Sam. But she is dedicated to the Marriage Meeting concept, and tucks her anger onto her Notes App which is her Emotion Container for keeping track of emotional topics to bring to the Marriage Meeting.

Week 3: REVIEW (Jan 21 Marriage Meeting)

Sarah is proud of herself for waiting until this Marriage Meeting, but her emotions are raw, "Sam! I feel so overwhelmed in the kitchen. You agreed to do the tiniest job of emptying the trash, and yet, on Thursday, when I tried to toss out my coffee grounds, I had to take out the trash before my coffee grounds would fit."

Sam: "Our plan was for me to take out the trash on Tuesdays and Fridays. That's what I did. There was hardly any trash there on Friday, but I took it out anyhow to stay ahead of the game."

This is a crucial moment for Sam and Sarah, right? Can you see how they both feel justified? They both feel like they're right and the other person is being unfair.

This is a moment it's tempting to go to blame and shame.

Here is where the template of the Marriage Meeting can really pay off.

Sarah could say, "Well, it's your job to take out the trash and you obviously can't even handle a simple job like that." Can you feel the conditional love popping in there? Sam is a failure. Not worthy.

Sam could say, "I told you I can't ever measure up. No matter how much I try, you raise the standard. I can never please you." Can you feel the conditional love popping in there? Sarah is demanding and controlling. Not worthy.

But Sam and Sarah are dedicated to using this time of the Marriage Meeting to come together. To increase their intimacy.

So, they both breathe. They both get curious. They both ask themselves, *Is it possible my Sweetheart is right, too?*

They return to their dream: We want to share chores in a way that cultivates a beautiful, peaceful home where our children feel nurtured and safe.

This is where the REVIEW really pays off.

Sam asks, "What happened between Tuesday night when I took the trash out and Thursday morning when you didn't have room for your coffee grounds?"

This curiosity allows Sarah to wonder. And as she wonders, she remembers how much food she tossed away from the fridge. Then she remembers seeing all that toilet paper and dental floss on Thursday morning and how she didn't want to touch it because she just wanted to be able to drink her coffee!

Sarah, who just wants to feel less overwhelmed, realizes this problem could happen again and again.

The power of the REVIEW is that you get a chance to see if your agreements are based in *the reality of how you live.*

Sam is rarely, if ever, in the kitchen during the week. He's the weekend cook. He doesn't even drink coffee, so he just didn't notice the trashcan had filled so quickly.

When you REVIEW with curiosity, based on PLANS you've made, you can adjust.

Week 3: PLAN (Jan 21 Marriage Meeting)

Sam, "I'm happy to take the trash out when I see that it's full, but I don't think that's the best job for me since I'm not in the kitchen much during the week. What else can I do to support all the cooking you do during the week so you feel less overwhelmed?"

This support gives Sarah room to breathe.

They take time to chat about the bigger picture of meals and the kitchen-chaos that ensues all week long. Sarah gets a chance to unpack the feelings of resentment she's had about how big her job is.

Sam doesn't get defensive. He realizes Sarah just needs time and space to voice how difficult life with three kids, two careers, and a dog can be. He listens. He affirms her, "Sarah, you feed us so well. I'm so grateful you find a way to create such great meals when I know you're tired too."

Sarah: "Could you cook one of the nights during the week?" (A Clean Ask, right?)

Sam: "I want to say yes to ease your burden. But I will feel pressure to live up to your high standard of what constitutes a good meal. I'm so tired after work all I'd have energy to do is open a jar of pasta sauce and boil up some noodles. I can't even promise to have energy to chop lettuce. I know you want more than that, and I wish I could give it, but I want to be realistic."

Sarah sits for a moment. It's true. Feeding her family is such a love language for her. Jarred pasta sauce doesn't meet her criteria for success in the nutrition department.

Sam notices that Sarah is reluctant to lower her standards when it comes to good meals. Sam reminds Sarah, "Remember our dream includes peacefulness in the kitchen as well as nutritious food. It feels like a little less pressure to be organic and homemade would nourish you and, thus, our family. Am I wrong?"

Sarah and Sam talk about the big picture of the kitchen and what they want for their family. Occasionally Sarah says, "I just need more help."

Sam replies, "If it were up to me alone, we'd eat from a pot of something we cook on Sunday or get take out. I just can't face cooking during the week."

Try This Tool: Identify The PLAN

The key to PLAN is to identify the niggling details that cause conflict.

What is ONE detail of life where you and your sweetheart need to create a PLAN? Hint: Where do you have conflict?

_____

Ex: Kitchen overwhelm

To create a **Clean Ask,** fill in the following blanks, so you frame your PLAN around a clearly articulated request.

Feeling_____
Desire_____
Clean Ask_____

Ex: I'm overwhelmed and I feel over-worked in the meal prep. I want tangible, predictable help. Could you be in charge of emptying the trash?

Can you feel how they each have a boundary? Sarah doesn't want to compromise on nutrition and Sam knows his limit when it comes to weekday-efforts. Their boundaries are healthy. They each are tending to their core values.

The Marriage Meeting is offering them a chance to negotiate these boundaries.

Finally, Sam says, "How about on most Sundays I cook a big pot of stew or some enchiladas that's easy to repeat on another night of the week? Occasionally, I won't have energy for that. On those weeks I'll be in charge of take out one weekday night?"

For the next few months, meals are one of the topics for their Marriage Meetings. They both agree to take the trash out when they see it's full. Sarah feels support. Sam doesn't feel like the bar just keeps rising.

Try This Tool: REVIEW So You Can PLAN Again

First REVIEW, then make a new PLAN based on the reality of living.

How did this PLAN go? Be super compassionate to both yourself and your sweetheart here. There is often a gap between what we dream for our lives and the reality of daily living. What did you notice?

_____
_____

Now, bring your curiosity rather than your blame: What tiny details need to change so you can try again? Is your dream unrealistic? Is your dream taking into account how complex your life is?

_____
_____

What's the revised PLAN for the coming week?

_____
_____

You can make a PLAN, but then you need time DOING the PLAN to see if it's realistic. Your REVIEW allows you to compare how you live with the ambitions you have for how life should unfold.

When you REVIEW with curiosity no one gets blamed. There's no shame. Just curiosity, support, and a desire to grow more intimately entwined.

After you've made your PLAN, live your life. This is the DOING. Next Marriage Meeting, start with a REVIEW. How did your PLAN go?

Be patient. The magic of Plan*Do*Review typically shows up around three to five times of repetition. This is because we often *want our lives to go differently than the reality of living*. When we're making a PLAN, we're full of energy. When it's time to DO the PLAN, we're tired and unresourceful.

This is good to notice.

Each time you REVIEW, you'll get more realistic about your energy and ability to follow through on the PLAN.

This comparison—between your dreams that are lofty and aspirational, and the reality of life that is filled with bumps—is critical. That's the magic of the REVIEW. It allows you to each see how you're trying your best (or not) and how to shift the PLAN to find the sweet spot between dreams and reality.

Now let's get a list of things that might be important topics for your Marriage Meeting.

Topics for Your Marriage Meeting

Because it helps to know you're not the only one who needs to discuss details

You might not need this list. You might know exactly, precisely, specifically what you want to discuss with your sweetheart. Great!

I've gathered together this list in case it's tough for you to find those topics that cause emotions to flare out of control:

- **Logistics:** chores, repairs, meal planning, and kid duty

- **Calendaring:** vacations, visiting extended family, birthday parties, work travel
- **Finances:** what do we need to buy? What do we need to save for?
- **Communication blunders:** jokes that land with an ouch, things left unsaid
- **Sex:** do our appetites match? Are we making time for sex? Do we have clear signals for initiation?

Here's a list of topics you might want to visit annually or every few years
- **Careers & Ambitions:** Do you each feel supported as you strive to grow professionally?
- **Reinventing yourself:** Are you able to pursue hobbies and leisure that excite you?
- **Bucket lists:** What is on your bucket list? And is this the year to make that happen?

Any of these are great ideas and will improve your overall communication. But remember that, in order to build a healthy boundary, the two most important topics are:
- Imagine and reimagine the dream you have for your relationship
- Celebrate even the tiniest successes you've had as you reach for that dream

I made a concerted effort not to talk to David about money, except when we were at our dedicated Marriage Meeting. We called it The Financial Summit because a fancy name helped us both bring our best selves to the table.

Try This Tool: Keep a List of MM Topics

Life is busy. Sometimes you don't notice what's causing conflict. Keep a list of topics to revisit during your Marriage Meeting.

Take a moment now and add to my list from above. What conversation(s), specifically, would benefit your relationship? Write those here.

1. _____
2. _____
3. _____

The internet is filled with suggestions for your Marriage Meeting and there are tons of great ideas out there.

How do you want to organize your Marriage Meeting? Keep it short? Or agree to meet until everything's out in the open? What's your style? How can you accommodate different needs in your Marriage Meeting?

My Dream for Your Marriage
The reason I wrote this book

When you and your sweetheart first met, there were butterflies. Your sweetheart occupied all your thoughts. This stage of a relationship is called falling in love.

During the falling in love stage, your vulnerabilities are still largely private. Each of you still put on your best face. You want to show up as your best self in order to deserve all the love you're feeling.

Then comes the landing in love stage of your story.

This book will help you land in love with grace and tools that will cultivate your happily ever after. **Fears** that were getting in the way of intimacy begin to fall away as you make friends with them. You **get clearer** about what you want, and you learn to **ask** for it **cleanly**.

You and your sweetheart each practice noticing the **conditions** you each put on love. As you notice those conditions, your heart becomes more forgiving, more open. You get to **affirm** the love you share in a zillion tiny ways.

Each of you gain a deeper understanding of yourselves because there's nothing like a relationship to help you truly examine your own behavior and values. So, you each **build boundaries** that magnify the love between you.

Each of these 6 Steps helps you land into the love where you first fell. You find the gravity in your relationship.

That gravity allows you to *live* in love. When you live in love filled with the potency of these 6 steps, you taste an unparalleled freedom.

Here's an example of that at my house:

Yesterday, while I was making breakfast, I asked if I could talk to David about a large expenditure. We've agreed that any large expense needs to be discussed first. This would be a great topic to bring to a Marriage Meeting, but the truth is we rarely have a formal Meeting anymore.

That's because we did it for so many years that the patterns established during those meetings simply imprinted themselves onto the way we relate.

Without consciously thinking about it, I asked if David was in a headspace to discuss money. There's plenty of times he's answered "no" to that question, as have I. Without the practice of the Marriage Meeting, I don't think either of us would have been able to hear that "no" without freaking out.

David had energy and time, so he sat down at our kitchen island while I cooked. I told him about the big expense I wanted. He nodded. He agreed it felt valuable. While I had his attention, I started to talk about some other things I wanted to spend money on and he began to laugh.

"Why are you laughing?" I asked. My Inner Lizard was on high alert. Was his laugh signaling his disapproval about my spending?

Spending money often signals our values. We spend money on things we value. Was my husband, with his laugh, letting me know he didn't like what I valued? I felt the back of my spine tighten and my breath shallowed.

My husband answered, "Because now you're going to go through a list of teeny tiny things that won't even equal an hour of your pay. And you worry that I'll worry about that."

Now I laughed. I took a huge breath.

His laughter calmed me down. He was right. The money wasn't what worried me. I wanted to buy a few things to nurture the guests that were coming to visit, but the money wasn't the issue. I was feeling insecure about the company.

He sensed that. "Tell me the whole list of things you want to buy," he wanted to know what I was thinking. Not to judge me. He wanted to give me air. To comfort me by listening to my list of ~~gifts~~ nerves.

I was still nervous—about the guests—and didn't realize it was the company making me nervous. It still felt like I was nervous about the money. I felt the agitation of my Inner Lizard's vigilant question, *What's wrong here?!*

David laughed again.

I asked again, "Why are you still laughing?"

His laugh got bigger, and this I don't know how to describe to you. But the laugh that, at first made me wonder if he was laughing AT me, now that bigger laugh reassured me he was laughing WITH me. His laugh was helping me see how ridiculous my fears were.

I stopped being afraid.

Then I was sitting down eating the food I'd prepared, and by now he'd gotten up from the island to get something to eat himself. Now he was at the stove and I was at the island and a whole decade of Marriage Meeting deposits had compounded in my brain and I realized how many times I've laughed when he's been afraid. My skin softened with that realization.

"I laugh when you're afraid and you don't get more nervous with my laughter. Why can't I just let your laughter in like you let mine in?"

It's the next moment that makes me want all of this for your life.

My husband said, "Yes, Wife, but we don't have a history of disparaging laughter when you laugh, whereas we do have that with my laughter."

Tears.

Just a very few.

Historically my husband used his laugh to avoid conflict, or to send me a message of shame.

His words acknowledged a 35-year history in our marriage.

My husband said it so matter-of-fact. Without judgement. Without shame. Just showered in the love we have cultivated together for decades.

We'd dealt with the emotions of his laughter in countless Marriage Meetings. As a result, he became more aware of how he used that laugh. Instead, he leaned into conflict. He spoke plainly about complaints he had rather than shaming me.

It felt like freedom. Love. Forgiveness. All the intimacy I'd longed for. There it was. In my kitchen. On a Tuesday morning.

It was the love of gravity.

You fall in love and you know nothing about all your sweetheart's foibles. Then you land in love and it seems like those foibles are everywhere! Inescapable.

But then you live in love—affirmational, unconditional love—for years and, in addition to being loved for all the wonderful things you do and are, you feel loved in the midst of all those foibles.

This is transformational love.

I want you to feel this love; love that encompasses ALL of who you are: your strengths *and* foibles.

When you spend years making friends with your fears and foibles and you feel compassion from yourself and your sweetheart, you relax. You're able to receive love profoundly.

Chances are pretty high that if you are able to live with your sweetheart for decades, you will have some hurt feelings. Feelings that are so hurt that you have deep wounded places.

My dream for your marriage is that you will also taste the forgiveness of getting past those wounds. When you find your way toward each other after the hurt? It's radically better than the butterfly feeling of falling in love.

You taste the everyday gravity of living in love. Living in love becomes your habit.

A Tuesday-morning-moment is what I want for you. And for your marriage.

When you have your Tuesday-morning-moment, I hope you'll notice and congratulate yourself on how well you've learned to communicate.

Try This Tools

Chapter 1: Overcome Fear
- Identify Your Fear's Disguise(s) — 30
- Imagine Your Fear Embodied — 33
- Befriend to Mend — 35
- Explore the Worst-Case Scenario — 36
- Nurture Your Fear — 40
- Fear's Invitation — 44

Chapter 2: Get Clear
- Identify Your Black Holes — 55
- Stay in Your Own Business — 61
- Overcome Fear Review — 65
- I feel…I want…I don't want… — 69
- Update Your Map — 71
- The Cartographer's Question — 76
- The Pressure Relief Valve — 79
- The Emergency Response Plan — 81
- The Reconnection Plan — 82

Chapter 3: Ask Cleanly
- The Clean Ask Formula — 92
- Identify Your Dirty Ask Strategy — 96
- Design Your Clean Ask — 104
- The Art of Sprouting Love — 114
- Stay Clean by Rewriting History — 121
- Phrases to Help Unearth a Clean Ask — 124

Chapter 4: Beware Conditions
- Just Notice (Gently) — 140
- Remember Differently — 142
- Cherishing and Educating — 146
- Clue into Conditions — 150
- Proud Meditation — 152
- Beauty Meditation — 152
- Identify If/Then Conditions — 154-155
- Cultivate Compassion — 156
- Fear-Clear-Clean Wash — 158-160

Chapter 5: Affirm Lovingly

- Notice Your Hello and Goodbye — 171
- Say "Thank You" More — 173
- Up Your Thank You Game — 174
- Notice Your "Buts" — 176
- How "Buts" Signal Fear — 177
- The But Pause Switcheroo — 178
- Use "But" to Link Up Your "Yes" — 180
- Identify Your Bad-Behavior-Go-To — 183
- Words That Say "I'm Sorry" — 185
- Own Your Bad-Behavior — 187
- Guess at Your Sweetheart's Feelings — 190
- Promise to Do Better — 191
- Demonstrate Belief — 194

Chapter 6: Build Boundaries

- Purposefully Review First 5 Steps — 206
- Take Back Takesies Backsies — 210
- Imagine The Full Stop — 215
- Uncloak Invisible Boundaries — 218
- Grieve Your Necessary Losses — 220
- Pinpoint Payoffs — 228
- Name Your Identity — 229
- Map Your Path to a Boundary — 230
- Create a Timeline of Conflicts — 235-236
- Anticipate Potential Stressors — 237
- Breathe Worthiness into Your Bones — 244

Epilogue

- Schedule Your Marriage Meeting — 249
- Create a Real Invitation: 3 scripts — 252
- Create a Container for Your Emotions — 254
- Nurture Your Emotions — 256
- Create a Dream for Your Relationship — 259
- Unpack the Previous Week — 261
- Celebrate Your Connection — 263
- Identify The PLAN — 268
- REVIEW so You Can PLAN again — 269
- Keep a List of Marriage Meeting Topics — 271

Resources
Links to the sources Rebecca referenced

Chapter 1: Overcome Fear

Anne Lamott is quoting AA when she talks about FEAR = Fear Expressed Allows Relief. Find Anne Lamott on Facebook.

Seth Godin first introduced me to the idea of the Inner Lizard (Lizard Brain). Read on his blog, https://seths.blog/2010/01/quieting-the-lizard-brain/ or watch on YouTube, searching for Seth Godin + Lizard Brain.

Martha Beck's book *Finding Your Own North Star* will give you dozens of helpful strategies to help you overcome fear that is wired into your patterns.

Jerry Lineger's TEDx Talk can be found by searching Jerry Lineker + Changing perspective off the planet.

Chapter 2: Get Clear

Byron Katie's book is called *Loving What Is*. You can also find dozens of free resources at her website TheWork.com.

Have you taken Gretchen Rubin's 4-Tendencies Quiz? Go to GretchenRubin.com/quiz/ to find out of you are an Upholder, an Obliger, a Questioner, or a Rebel.

Chapter 5: Affirm Lovingly

Tina Fey talks about "yes but" in her book, *Bossy Pants*. You can also watch a YouTube clip of this discussion by searching Tina Fey + Improv Lesson.

Chapter 6: Build Boundaries

To understand my reference about "No joy for you," watch *Seinfeld* season 7, episode 6, "The Soup Nazi."

Find John and Julie Gottman's work at The Gottman Institute: gottman.com.

Judith Viorst's book is called *Necessary Losses*.

Watch Simon Sinek's TED Talk, *The Power of Why*, at TED.com.

Check out Crash Course Philosophy on YouTube for entertaining synopses of Kantianism (video #35) and Utilitarianism (video #36), as well as other frameworks to help you understand why you and your sweetheart uphold your values.

Want the latest resources? I will keep updating this book. Go to https://rebeccamullencoaching.com/six-steps-to-better-marriage-communication-book/ to get the latest information.

If you'd like to know more about Rebecca's framework *Partner, Lover, Friend*, mentioned in Chapter 5, check out these resources:

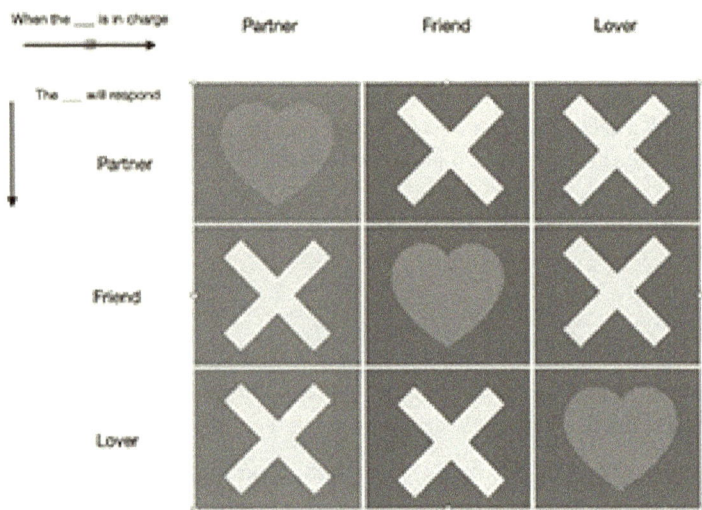

https://rebeccamullencoaching.com/what-happens-when-youre-not-in-sync-with-your-spouse/

https://rebeccamullencoaching.com/episode-5-is-it-hard-to-get-your-partner-to-clean-the-toilet/

https://rebeccamullencoaching.com/episode-6-sharing-secrets-in-your-relationship-is-your-spouse-a-good-friend/

https://rebeccamullencoaching.com/episode-7-this-habit-will-keep-your-sex-life-exciting/

Acknowledgements

Without a story, there's nothing to write. My husband, David, is the reason I have a story in these pages. I want to acknowledge his contribution first. Not every year of our marriage has been "happy" in that happily-ever-after way. But David has been *my person* as I grow and change from youth to adulthood. He is my truest companion. And, undoubtedly, he has helped me learn to communicate more effectively.

My children, Kaitlin and Logan, are responsible for clarifying my happily-ever-after. When they spoke at our 30th anniversary, I heard the story of a happy marriage. They heard kind words exchanged between their parents as they grew up.

My insides didn't always feel kind in those years as they grew. But after I heard the story of the marriage they told, I began to wonder if my communication was doing a better job than I gave myself credit for. When I pondered the idea of writing a book about marriage and communication, they both cheered, "Of course! Who better?" There were many times I borrowed their belief in me as I wrote these words.

OK. I had a solid story. I could share it.

Many people then contributed to help me turn that story into the book you're holding. The first person to thank for that is my brilliant editor, Kaitlin Louise Pettit. She was kind. And demanding. The perfect combination to help a story come out of the shadows and find clarity on the page.

I have many writing friends who also helped. Rosemerry helped me clarify what matters in each two-word phrase. With this clarity, she helped me find my voice. Jill is a fan, and we all need one of those. She encouraged me to tell the Whole Story. Janet and Mark hiked beside me each day as I got this first draft of this book on the page. Then they ate and drank with me in the evenings. The best sort of friends.

The Sages, my writing group, was there when this book was a completely different idea. I'm indebted to them for the many pages they read. The Dollbabies provided more than just a house where we could all write. They gave me that rarest of gift every artist needs: complete love and acceptance (and nourishment, and conversation, and cake during writing breaks).

This book wouldn't be possible without my clients. Their wisdom and vulnerability have given me the rarest of glimpses into why communication matters so absolutely. The best part of my job is the brave people who include me so profoundly in the most personal conversations of their lives.

There are hundreds of people who answered my ever-present question, "Tell me about your relationship." These people—some formally asked, some hanging with me at a party—have contributed to these pages. Thank you for sharing your stories with me.

Then there is Dawn, my Bestie. The best psychotherapist on Planet Earth, and a constant companion to sort out ideas. We talked about my own communication skills, and we talked about communication in the big, wide world of people we know.

Thank you to Katie, my sister, for bringing a visual clarity to the cover and pages inside so that my story looked like the art it felt inside me.

You have all made me better at communicating the love I feel.

About the Author

Rebecca S. Mullen believes love is transformational. End of sentence. No caveats. No disclaimers.

She lives with her husband on the Western Slope of Colorado, in a town so tiny there's only one stop sign. Rebecca walks on the dirt road outside her home where 360 degrees of mountains offer her a daily hug.

She is an artist, writer, and coach. She hosts the podcast *Habits for Your Happily Ever After* and her TEDx Talk invites listeners to create peace at the dinner table with their stories.

She interacts with her students across the globe thanks to the magic of a virtual classroom.

Rebecca believes that when we pay attention to the smallest details of our lives without judgment, welcoming the mud and flowers alike, our greatest potential has room to expand.

You can find her at RebeccaMullenCoaching.com

www.ingramcontent.com/pod-product-compliance
Lightning Source LLC
Chambersburg PA
CBHW031144020426
42333CB00013B/495